Law as a
Gendering
Practice

Law as a Gendering Practice

edited by Dorothy E. Chunn
and Dany Lacombe

OXFORD
UNIVERSITY PRESS

OXFORD

UNIVERSITY PRESS

70 Wynford Drive, Don Mills, Ontario M3C 1J9
www.oupcan.com

Oxford University Press is a department of the University of Oxford.
It furthers the University's objective of excellence in research, scholarship,
and education by publishing worldwide in

Oxford New York

Athens Auckland Bangkok Bogotá Buenos Aires Calcutta
Cape Town Chennai Dar es Salaam Delhi Florence Hong Kong Istanbul
Karachi Kuala Lumpur Madrid Melbourne Mexico City Mumbai
Nairobi Paris São Paulo Singapore Taipei Tokyo Toronto Warsaw

with associated companies in Berlin Ibadan

Published in Canada
by Oxford University Press

First published 2000

Canadian Cataloguing in Publication Data
Main entry under title:
Law as a gendering practice
Includes bibliographical references.
ISBN 0-19-541295-8

1. Women – Legal status, laws, etc. – Canada. 2. Sex discrimination – Law
and legislation – Canada. I. Chunn, Dorothy E. (Dorothy Ellen), 1943– .
II. Lacombe, Dany.

KE4399.L376 2000   349.71'082   C99-932872-7
KF4483.C57L38 2000

Cover Image: Painting by Milly Ristvedt, *Red Red*, 1994.
Cover & Text Design: Tearney McMurtry

1 2 3 4 - 03 02 01 00

This book is printed on permanent (acid-free) paper ∞
Printed in Canada

Contents

Acknowledgements

This book has been a long time in the making and we are indebted to many people for encouragement and assistance along the way. We owe a special thank you to Euan White, Phyllis Wilson, and Laura Macleod, our editors at Oxford University Press, for their support and patience at various stages of the process. We are especially grateful that they never expressed to us any doubts about our ability to deliver a manuscript in the end.

Of course, the book reflects the considerable efforts of others as well. Kudos and bouquets to the contributors for their willingness to invest the energy and time needed to produce original essays that fitted the thematic focus of the book. Two anonymous reviewers provided valuable feedback on the manuscript that also enhanced the final product. Krista Robson and Leslie West, both students at Simon Fraser University, were instrumental in compiling the comprehensive bibliography for the book. And Richard Tallman did a wonderful copy-editing job, ferreting out technical errors and ensuring stylistic consistency throughout the text.

Finally, we want to thank Kegan Doyle and Robert Menzies for not being afraid of feminism and Leo for being his entertaining self.

Contributors

SHANNON BELL is an associate professor in the Department of Political Science at York University. Her work in post-modern theory, feminism, and sexuality (prostitution, pornography, sado-masochism, pedophilia) includes *Reading, Writing and Rewriting the Prostitute Body* (1994), *Whore Carnival* (1995), and (with Crossman, Gotell, and Ross) *Bad Attitudes on Trial* (1997).

MARIE-CLAIRE BELLEAU is an associate professor in the Faculty of Law at Université Laval. She holds a D.E.A. from the Université de Paris II, an LL.M. and an S.J.D. from Harvard University, and is a member of the Québec bar. Her main teaching interests and publications are related to feminist legal theories, the history of French legal thought, and legal theory and comparative law.

KEVIN BONNYCASTLE is a Ph.D. candidate in the School of Criminology at Simon Fraser University.

SUSAN B. BOYD holds the Chair in Feminist Legal Studies at the Faculty of Law, University of British Columbia. Recent publications include *Challenging the Public/Private Divide: Feminism, Law, and Public Policy* (1997) and 'Canadian Feminist Literature on Law: An Annotated Bibliography', *Canadian Journal of Women and the Law* (1999). She is now writing a book on child custody law and women's work.

DEBORAH BROCK teaches sociology at Brock University in St Catharines. She is author of *Making Work, Making Trouble: Prostitution as a Social Problem* (1998) and has worked in support of prostitutes' campaigns for legal and social rights since the mid-1980s.

DOROTHY CHUNN is a professor in the School of Criminology and co-director of the Feminist Institute for Studies on Law and Society at Simon Fraser University. Her publications include *From Punishment to Doing Good: Family Courts and Socialized Justice in Ontario, 1880–1940* (1992). Current research projects focus on the historical regulation of sex, sexuality, and reproduction in the Canadian welfare state and on feminism, law, and social change in Canada since the 1960s.

MARY CONDON is an associate professor at Osgoode Hall Law School. Her current research interests are in the areas of corporate and securities law, retirement income policy, and feminist legal analysis. She is the author of *Making Disclosure: Ideas and Interests in Ontario Securities Regulations*.

JOSEPH COUTURE is an investigative journalist and social activist.

DARA CULHANE received her Ph.D. in 1994 and teaches anthropology at Simon Fraser University. She is the author of two books: *An Error of Judgment: The Politics of Medical Care in an Indian/White Community* (1987) and *The Pleasure of the Crown: Anthropology, Law and First Nations* (1998).

PARIN DOSSA is associate professor of anthropology at Simon Fraser University. Her teaching and research interests include anthropology of diaspora and transmigration, and feminist ethnography with a focus on aging and disability among Muslims in Canada. She is currently doing research on mental health of Muslim women in greater Vancouver.

SHELLEY GAVIGAN is a member of the faculty of Osgoode Hall Law School and the Graduate Program in Women's Studies at York University. She holds graduate degrees in law and criminology and has taught in both disciplines. Following graduation from law school in 1975, she articled in a rural-based community legal clinic and practised as a legal clinic lawyer in Saskatchewan until 1980, when she moved to Toronto to pursue graduate studies. Since joining the Osgoode faculty in 1986, she has been appointed twice as the Academic Director of Parkdale Community Legal Services in Toronto. Her publications include *The Politics of Abortion*, with Jane Jenson and Janine Brodie (1992), and several articles informed by feminist, socio-legal, and historical perspectives on the legal regulation of familial relations, lesbian parenting, abortion, and access to justice.

REBECCA JOHNSON is an assistant professor in the Faculty of Law at the University of New Brunswick, where she teaches constitutional law, criminal law, and feminist advocacy.

DANY LACOMBE is an associate professor in criminology and sociology at Simon Fraser University. Her research interests include the regulation of sexuality, the study of moral panic, and the scapegoating of sexual deviants. She is the author of *Blue Politics: Pornography and the Law in the Age of Feminism* (1994) and *Ideology and Public Policy: The Case Against Pornography* (1988).

RENEE TAYLOR is a member of the N'amgis First Nation of the Kwakwak'wakw. She is the Director of the University of British Columbia, Faculty of Law, First Nations Legal Clinic, Aboriginal representative on the Vancouver and Richmond Health Board, and a member of the British Columbia bar.

Part I

Theorizing Law as a Gendering Practice

Chapter 1

Introduction

Dorothy E. Chunn and Dany Lacombe

In this book, we address the apparent conundrum confronted by contemporary feminists who teach, research, and write about law. Much contemporary literature has framed feminist debates within the parameters of two ostensibly opposed visions of law: the 'modern' instrumentalist view of law as a set of rules that can be remoulded through feminist-inspired legal reforms versus the 'post-modern' social constructionist conception of law as a hegemonic discourse that can be deconstructed and reshaped through the mobilization of feminist counter-discourse(s) (see, e.g., Smart, 1989). This dichotomized depiction of law as either an instrument or a discourse suggests that feminists are ensnared in a theoretical and political strait-jacket and that genuine dialogue and debate among feminist socio-legal scholars are at an impasse. Like all such dichotomies, however, the theoretical division between modern and post-modern approaches is illusory and counter-productive. Neither paradigm is theoretically unified, nor is one paradigm wholly distinct from the other. Consequently, advocates of each position on law tend to create a caricature of the opposing perspective that can be too easily critiqued and dismissed.

Moreover, the seeming feminist fixation on theoretical 'othering' arguably applies more to feminists in the United States and Britain than to Canadian feminists, who historically have developed more inclusive, albeit diverse, ways of theorizing law. In their early review of Canadian feminist legal scholarship, Boyd and Sheehy found theoretical categorization difficult because categories 'proved to be fluid': individual authors often used 'different theoretical frameworks, depending on the issue or the audience at which the piece is directed', and 'themes from more than one "theory"' might be found in the same article (Boyd and Sheehy, 1986: 6–7; see also Bouchard, Boyd, and Sheehy, 1999). We have drawn extensively from feminist work, particularly Canadian feminist legal scholarship, that attempts to theorize both *inter-gender* (i.e., between men and women) and *intra-gender* differences (i.e., among women and among men) (Gordon, 1991) and to avoid theoretical dichotomization. While our primary focus in this book is the analysis of law as a gendering practice (Smart, 1995), we do not dismiss the significant contributions to the theorization of law and gender made by feminist scholars who conceptualize law in more categorical or instrumentalist ways. Our objective in *Law as a Gendering Practice* is to argue for the utility of a social constructionist approach to feminist legal theory that also takes account of social context, structures, and history. Specifically, we want to illustrate how law intersects with other institutions and discourses in the construction of 'woman' and 'womanhood'.

In this Introduction, we briefly trace the historical development of feminist theorizing about law as a gendering practice.[1] We begin with a review of liberal and radical feminisms—two instrumentalist, theoretical perspectives that have characterized much work by feminists in the United States since the 1960s—including the major contributions and limitations of these perspectives. We then examine how the critiques have stimulated a theoretical (re)formation and convergence of liberal and radical feminism, particularly in Canadian feminist analyses of state, law, and gender. Finally, we discuss how socialist, post-structuralist, and post-modern feminisms have contributed to the conceptualization of law as a gendering practice.

Law as an Instrument

Historically, the hegemonic theoretical framework within which to think about the relations between women and men and the relationship between law and women's oppression in Western societies has been based on the 'sameness-difference' dichotomy (Bacchi, 1990). This concern with inter-gender comparisons—are women the same as or different from men?—permeated the writings of many activist women in 'first-wave' Western feminist movements during the late nineteenth and early twentieth centuries, albeit formal theories and theorizing about law and gender are a product of academic feminism during the 'second wave' of the 1960s and 1970s. Liberal and radical feminisms are two of the most influential perspectives on women and law generated by contemporary feminists, particularly in the United States (Jaggar, 1983). Often viewed as polar opposites, what these perspectives share is an instrumentalist, analytical focus on inter- as opposed to intra-gender difference(s) (Gordon, 1991). Where they diverge is in terms of how they explain women's historical oppression and consequently what they advocate as the route to women's liberation or (sex) equality. Thus, liberal and radical feminist theories overlap even though they are premised on very different ideas about the nature of society, law, and the relationship between women and men.

Liberal Feminism and Rule (In)equality

In keeping with liberalism more generally, liberal feminists have assumed that society is based on a social contract among its members and a 'real' distinction between the public and private spheres (Boyd, 1997; Jaggar, 1983: 27–50). A centralized power (i.e., the state) enforces the social contract and acts as a neutral arbiter of disputes and problems, primarily in the public sphere and with the least possible intrusion into the lives of individuals. A major tenet of liberalism, then, is the assumption of sameness among individuals that rests on the (hu)man ability to reason and make rational choices. From a liberal perspective, there are no proven, innate differences between women and men, which means that women and men do not constitute gender classes with intrinsically opposed interests. Therefore, inter-gender relations are not based on *inherently* unequal power relations. Yet women clearly have been and continue to be unequal to men.

This historical inequality of women *vis-à-vis* men is the point of departure for liberal feminists. Significantly, they view women's inequality more as an 'accident' or anomaly of history than a result of male malevolence or conspiracy. Thus, during the late nineteenth and early twentieth centuries, first-wave liberal feminists maintained that it was simply 'bad' (sexist) law and policy that left women in an unequal position relative to men. They believed that women were denied civil and legal rights in both the public and private realms on the basis of unfair assumptions that their biology rendered them less qualified for legal personhood and citizenship than were men. While single women had some legal status, married women were mere extensions of their husbands under the 'unity doctrine' and remained legally invisible until well into the nineteenth century.

By the 1960s, however, most women in Western countries had achieved legal and citizenship status, yet they remained demonstrably unequal to men. Second-wave liberal feminists argued that, although women have the same capabilities as men, few develop their full potential and inequality continues because women are socialized to adopt the 'feminine' sex role of caregivers and housekeepers rather than to strive for economic independence through a career. Moreover, if women do enter the public realm to engage in paid employment, most do not have the same opportunities as men to be successful.

For both first- and second-wave liberal feminists, then, men are the comparison group for women; men's lived experience is the standard to which women should aspire. Therefore, 'mainstreaming'—working to make changes within existing structures and institutions—has been emphasized as the route to equality with men (Adamson et al., 1988: 176–86; see also Jaggar, 1983: 173–206). Law is a primary instrument for establishing the formal (legal) equality that will allow women to be like men: a set of rules that can be transformed incrementally through feminist-inspired reforms. First-wave liberal feminists viewed suffrage as the means whereby women would acquire the political power to end their legal invisibility and to enter the professions, politics, and other activities in the public realm. Second-wave liberal feminists focused their efforts on making all laws gender-neutral and using law to create equal opportunity for women to participate in the (public) world of men.

Overall, liberal feminists believe that women's equality can be achieved without a revolutionary transformation of existing social structures and institutions. In keeping with the liberal notion of ongoing social progress, they assume that eventually the state and the law will become gender neutral arbiters and protect the interests of both men and women in an even-handed way. Once discriminatory (sexist) rules are changed and equal opportunity exists, women's equality will follow.

Radical Feminism and Sex (In)equality

While not a dominant perspective among first-wave feminists, radical feminism has been central in much feminist analysis since the 1960s (Jaggar, 1983: 83–122). At first glance, this theoretical approach seems to be everything liberal feminism is not. Unlike their liberal sisters, for instance, radical feminists assume that society is premised on relations of (male) domination and (female) subordination (MacKinnon, 1982, 1983a). Likewise, they assume that the public/private distinction has been created by men in their own interests; specifically, that the (male) ideology of privacy serves to maintain men's dominance and women's subordination (MacKinnon, 1983b). Therefore, far from being a neutral arbiter of disputes and problems, the state is a blunt instrument used proactively by men against women. Also in contrast to the liberal emphasis on sameness, radical feminist thought is predicated on the implicit assumption that women and men are fundamentally different—two gender classes with irreconcilable interests. Inter-gender relations are based on inherently unequal power relations that translate into sex inequality for women.

Therefore, the sex inequality of women is the starting point for radical feminist analyses. Arguing that women have been subordinate to men in all societies over time, radical feminists point to 'male supremacy', manifested as patriarchy, as the source of this trans-historical oppression. In particular, men's control of women's sexuality and reproduction through violence or the threat of violence is key to the maintenance of patriarchy. Or, as Catharine MacKinnon (1982: 515–16) succinctly puts it:

> The molding, direction, and expression of sexuality organizes society into two sexes—women and men—which division underlies the totality of social relations. . . . As the organized expropriation of the work of some for the benefit of others defines a class—workers—the organized expropriation of the sexuality of some for the use of others defines the sex, woman.

Like the state, then, law and policy are male 'protection rackets' (MacKinnon, 1987: 31), instruments men use directly to maintain relations of male dominance and female subordination. Thus, the sex inequality of women is not merely a historical 'accident' reflected in 'bad' law. Rather, it is the product of male design. Again, in MacKinnon's words (1983a: 644):

I propose that the state is male in the feminist sense. The law sees and treats women the way men see and treat women. The liberal state coercively and authoritatively constitutes the social order in the interest of men as a gender, through its legitimizing norms, relation to society, and substantive policies. It achieves this through embodying and ensuring male control over women's sexuality at every level.

Obviously, if the state, law, and other societal institutions are weapons wielded by men to maintain relations of dominance and subordination, they cannot be the keys to women's liberation. Under the conditions of patriarchy, it is pointless for women to ask men to share power. Legal and other reforms inevitably will be subverted in the interests of men. Therefore, disengagement from existing (male) structures and the creation of woman-centred alternatives are the routes to sex equality for women (Adamson et al., 1988: 176–86; see also Jaggar, 1983: 249–302). In short, radical feminists view separatism—personal and/or political—as a key to achieving women's liberation. They emphasize consciousness-raising strategies through which individual women come to realize that their experiences of sex inequality are not unique and that 'the personal is political'. By exposing the falsity of the public/private distinction, women can pose a direct challenge to patriarchy and begin the process of regaining control over their sexuality and reproduction through separatist initiatives and strategies. For example, new reproductive technologies make it possible for women to live without men, but only if women have access to and control over these technologies.

Contribution and Critique

Clearly, liberal and radical feminists have made noteworthy contributions to the analysis of women's oppression and to the struggle for women's equality/liberation. Their respective theorizing illuminated the gendered nature of the world and challenged the inequality that resulted from the failure to 'take sex into account' (Vickers, 1984). Indeed, by demonstrating the androcentric nature of social and legal institutions that traditionally had been viewed as objective, impartial, etc., feminists achieved a theoretical and practical breakthrough (Reaume, 1996: 266–7). At the same time, both perspectives have been critiqued, and by feminists as well as non-feminists (see, e.g., Jaggar, 1983). Two main problems have been identified, both of which stem from the instrumentalist, dichotomous analytical focus of liberal and radical feminisms. First, abstract concepts such as law and state are reified. That is, 'things' are materialized and transformed into determining and controlling 'actors'; for example, law becomes either the liberator or oppressor of (passive) women. Second, liberal and radical feminisms are characterized by essentialism or the attribution of an innate meaning to concepts, such as law, state, and sex/gender, which unifies the concepts and leads to dichotomization (e.g., male vs female). If we consider women and men to be homogeneous groups, for instance, both intra-gender differences and inter-gender commonalities are erased. In efforts to avoid reification and essentialism, feminists have developed a diversity of theoretical approaches to law that collectively have shifted the analytical focus from law as an instrument to law as a gendering practice.

Law as a Gendering Practice

Theoretical Convergence: Result-Equality and Integrative Feminisms

Notwithstanding their obvious theoretical differences, liberal and radical feminisms have converged in contemporary feminist strategizing and practices around law and policy. The basis for this convergence, which has been particularly striking in the Canadian context, is the modification of each theoretical perspective in light of critique and experience. By the early 1980s, liberal feminists in Canada and elsewhere were beginning to realize that the implementation of gender neutrality and formal equality in law had not produced 'real' (i.e., substantive) equality between women and men (Boyd and Sheehy, 1986; Martin and Mahoney, 1987). For example, reforms to family and rape laws in Canada and other Western countries during the 1970s and 1980s arguably left many women no better off, and others even less able to obtain legal redress, than was the case under the old legislation (Chunn, 1999; Snider, 1994). The limitations of liberal feminist theory became even clearer after the enactment of the Canadian Charter of Rights and Freedoms in 1982, which contained explicit protections of formal equality rights. An early analysis of court decisions related to equality sections of the Charter showed an overwhelming judicial emphasis on the principles of formal equality that disadvantaged women 'while creating an illusion of fairness' (Brodsky and Day, 1989: 38).

During the early 1980s, the theoretical and practical limitations of radical feminism also became evident (Jaggar, 1983). Radical feminists discovered that creating woman-centred alternatives to 'male' institutions and structures, including legal ones, was easier said than done. Notwithstanding their will to do so, they could not stand above or opt out of those institutions and structures. For instance, it became clear to many radical feminists, who were instrumental in establishing rape crisis centres and shelters for women abused by male partners, that they alone could not maintain these organizations indefinitely. At least minimal engagement with the 'male' state and legal institutions was needed, if only to obtain funding and other resources (Adamson et al., 1988).

In Canada, feminist rethinking of the issues related to gender and law was reflected in two theoretical variations on liberal and radical perspectives, known as 'result-equality liberalism' and 'integrative feminism' (Boyd and Sheehy, 1986: 8–13). For liberal feminists, the challenge was to address the issue of substantive inequality between women and men within the theoretical parameters of traditional liberalism. Their early overemphasis on rule equality had to be modified in light of the evidence that treating women in exactly the same way as men through gender-neutral law was detrimental for women. They came to realize that 'equal application of a male-oriented legal system cannot drastically alter women's disadvantaged position' (ibid., 8; see also Mahoney and Martin, 1987; Mossman, 1986). In short, treating unalikes (i.e., women and men) as if they were similarly situated merely reproduced and possibly even exacerbated existing inequalities. Therefore, it was crucial for liberal feminists to think about the *effects* of law as well as the legal rules themselves, to concentrate on achieving equal outcomes or result-equality for women *vis-à-vis* men (Smith et al., 1985).

As liberal feminists adopted a new analytical and political focus on the gendered effects of law, other feminists who embraced the general radical feminist theorization of gender, law, and the state were rethinking the political implications of a separatist analysis. In practice, radical feminists' disengagement from legal institutions and structures often translated into isolation and marginalization, leaving them unable to render support or assistance to women who were victimized by patriarchy (Adamson et al., 1988: 184–6). Ultimately, consciousness-raising is a necessary but not a sufficient basis for transforming patriarchal societies. To effect fundamental change, feminists have to develop strategies with the potential to reshape existing institutions, including law.

In Canada, only a few feminists produced 'pure' radical feminist analyses of law. Most who accepted the radical feminist theorization of patriarchy and male control over women but who 'rejected extreme political positions' have identified themselves as 'integrative feminists' (Boyd and Sheehy, 1986: 9; see also Boyle et al., 1985; Lahey, 1985; Miles, 1982, 1985). They proposed a shift in analytical focus from the traditional radical feminist concern with creating woman-centred alternatives to the institutions of patriarchy to an emphasis on integrating 'feminizing themes' and women's voices/experiences within all social institutions, including law. It was assumed that an integrative approach might be a more productive way of challenging sex inequality than a separatist one.

The theoretical and practical convergence of result-equality and integrative feminisms is reflected in the often collaborative efforts of their respective adherents to achieve legal reforms that synthesize the principles of equality and specificity of women (Boyd and Sheehy, 1986: 9). Or, to put it another way, a synthesizing approach required attention to the principles of formal and substantive equality and therefore to both inter- and intra-gender differences. In the Canadian context, the convergence of result-equality and integrative feminisms is exemplified by the history of the Women's Legal Education and Action Fund (LEAF). Founded by result-equality feminists in 1985 to further women's equality through litigation, LEAF seeks and often achieves intervener status in key cases related to equality sections of the Charter of Rights and Freedoms (Jhappan, 1998; Razack, 1991).

During the later 1980s and the 1990s, collaboration between result-equality and integrative feminists generated some extremely innovative interventions by

LEAF in a number of major cases before the Supreme Court of Canada. Jhappan (1998: 72) suggests that LEAF's 'brilliant innovation' has been the development of a contextualized approach to equality, based on Catharine MacKinnon's dominance/subordination analysis,[2] which posits that women's subordination is not 'natural' but, rather, 'has been socially constructed and legally enforced. The focus is then switched from individual to systemic discrimination.' More importantly, Supreme Court of Canada judgments sometimes have incorporated the analysis of women's subordination and substantive equality presented by LEAF (ibid., 73).

Law, the Creation of Hegemony, and the Process of Uneven Development

While result-equality and integrative feminists worked in and with law to undermine the formalist model of equality, socialist and other feminists influenced by Marxist ideas also were contributing to the reconceptualization of law as a gendering practice (Boyd and Sheehy, 1986; Brophy and Smart, 1985; Gavigan, 1986; McIntyre and O'Brien, 1987; Smart, 1982, 1984, 1986).[3] They challenged the conceptualizations of state, law, and sex/gender that characterize traditional liberal and radical feminist theoretical perspectives. On the one hand, the liberal feminist view of the state as a neutral arbiter and law as an impartial instrument for the redress of (sex) inequality ignores law's historic role in producing and maintaining power differentials in society. On the other hand, the radical feminist view of the state and law as 'male' weapons that eternally reinforce the prison walls of patriarchy paints a picture of a static, homogeneous social world that forecloses possibilities for change or resistance. More tellingly, perhaps, socialist feminists and other historians have demonstrated that neither perspective—law as an abstraction or law as a 'male' tool—can be upheld on empirical grounds (see, e.g., Gordon, 1976, 1988; Walkowitz, 1980). Their analyses have exploded trans-historical and unidimensional conceptualizations of the state, law, and patriarchy and revealed the contradictory nature and impact of these constructs.

An appreciation of the complex and subtle role law sometimes has played in the historical struggles for women's liberation made socialist (and other) feminists wary of reifying law. Far from being fixed and immutable, state, law, and patriarchy are historically and culturally specific constructs embedded in particular social relations, and they assume new forms with different content over time. For example, while social relations in all capitalist societies organize class exploitation and women's dependency, the form/content and therefore the role of law in (re)producing social relations based on gender and class hierarchies are notably different in *laissez-faire*, welfare, and neo-liberal states. Whereas law arguably played an overt and direct part in maintaining women's subordination during the nineteenth century, for much of the twentieth century law has played a more indirect, ideological role, legitimating 'a status quo in which male supremacy is accepted as natural and unchangeable' (Polan, 1982:

297). Therefore, feminist theorizing about law must be based on a historically informed examination of changes in social and legal forms and content.

Drawing on theoretical and historical work in the Marxist tradition (e.g., Gramsci, 1971; Hall et al., 1978; Hay, 1975), socialist feminists increasingly came to view law as a hegemonic process—an apparatus, or ensemble of practices, discourses, experts, and institutions, that actively contributes to the legitimation of a social order (Boyd, 1989a, 1989b; Gavigan, 1986, 1988). Moreover, they assumed that a social order and social relations are not homogeneous or ever totally fixed. Hence, analysing *intra-gender differences* as well as *inter-gender commonalities* is important and change is always possible. Since socialist feminists understood power relations in terms of class exploitation and gender oppression, they were concerned primarily with the analysis of how women may be united by gender and divided by class. Thus, they concluded that neither the liberal feminist analysis of women's inequality in the public sphere nor the radical analysis of the 'personal as political' offered a full explanation of women's position in liberal states. Instead, socialist feminists argued that women's position in such societies is premised not only on their gender subordination in *both* the public and private realms but also on their social class location.

Specifically, socialist feminists concluded that the status of most women in liberal, capitalist societies is derived from the undervalued work they perform inside and outside the family. Therefore, the public/private divide is more ideological than real since most women straddle, and are subordinate in, both spheres; that is, women perform unpaid domestic labour in one and/or underpaid clerical and service jobs in the other (Barrett and McIntosh, 1982). Law is critical to maintaining women's subordination because legislation incorporates certain assumptions—for instance, about men and women and the relations between and among them—that are taken for granted by most of the people who make, administer, or are subject to it (Eichler, 1988; Gavigan, 1988, 1993). Through numerous and often contradictory ideologies affecting law (and other institutions) patriarchal and class relations are shaped and perpetuated in Canada and other liberal states.

Socialist feminists view familial ideology, the hegemonic idea that the 'normal' and highest form of family is a nuclear unit comprised of husband, wife, and children who all have different roles and responsibilities, as key to the construction of women's gender and class positions. The assumption that all women should/will be wives and mothers who depend on a male bread-winner disadvantages both the women who are and the women who cannot or will not be dependants of men. Moreover, familial ideology can intersect with other ideologies—for instance, the ideas that law is gender-neutral and everyone receives equal treatment—in ways that work against a woman who has been a dependent wife and/or mother (Abner et al., 1990; Boyd, 1989a, 1989b). Thus, law may not be a direct instrument of male power, but it nonetheless is implicated in the perpetuation of women's secondary status.

Socialist feminist and other historical studies also have demonstrated that, contrary to what liberal and radical feminists assume, law and legal institutions do not have uniform effects, either good or bad (Gavigan, 1989–90; Gordon, 1986). For instance, the drafters of eighteenth-century constitutional declarations of the rights of 'Man' probably never anticipated, or wanted, the right to self-determination and equality to apply to women, children, racial/ethnic/ sexual minorities, trade unions, or corporations. Most likely, they never intended human rights to encompass issues of gender, ethnicity, and sexual orientation, or the condition of prisoners, the protection of the environment, employment, and the mismanagement of enterprises. Yet, since the eighteenth century, a variety of social actors, including women, have waged unforeseen struggles by engaging with law that was not intended for them. The battles of nineteenth-century feminists—for the right to vote and access to higher education, for example—were significant attempts by women to mobilize principles, such as the right to justice, self-determination, and equality, partly embodied in law to change existing legal arrangements that restricted their identities and needs (Lacombe, 1998).

While admittedly meagre, the historical record on women's and minorities' engagement with law to achieve equality nonetheless includes significant victories and attests to law's contradictions and potential as a *site of struggles or contestation over meanings*. Similarly, in her early work on law, Carol Smart (1995: 144) cautioned against the view of law as a purely coercive male force that creates patriarchy. Instead, she argued for an understanding of law as practices and discourses that in a 'complex and contradictory fashion reproduce the material and ideological conditions under which [patriarchal] relations may survive.' Her examination of law's impact on women in the areas of divorce, child custody, employment, and equal pay revealed a series of successes and setbacks, a process she conceptualized as one of 'uneven development' (ibid., 154). In the field of family law, for example, women in Britain and other Western liberal democracies successfully obtained reforms through the 1970s and early 1980s that reordered existing paternalistic statutes to establish formal legal equality of wives/mothers and husbands/fathers after divorce or separation. Yet the effects of the new legislation were devastating for many women because they were treated as if they were absolutely equal to (middle-class) men upon marital breakdown. In fact, their substantive position was very different from that of men.

Smart's astute observation concerning the uneven development of law forces an analytical distinction between law-as-legislation and law-as-practice. While a focus on law-as-legislation highlights the political gains achieved by feminist campaigns for change, a focus on law-as-practice often reveals the means by which a repressive social order is reproduced. Socialist and other feminists concerned with the uneven effects of law have concentrated primarily on how women in different social classes may experience law and legal institutions/structures very differently. Susan Boyd's analysis in Chapter 9 of the Supreme Court of Canada's judgment in *Gordon v. Goertz* illustrates these contradictions. On the one hand, the decision was a victory for one custodial mother, who was permitted to move with her daughter to Australia, in part because both parents were white professionals and the father could afford the costs of access visits with the child. On the other hand, the Court rejected the gender-based arguments of LEAF and the mother herself that emphasized deference to the custodial parent's decisions, and accepted the arguments of the father and the Children's Lawyer for an indeterminate and individual case approach to the principle of the best interests of the child. Thus, the positive decision for the mother in this specific case may not be replicated in future cases, especially when the parties are less affluent.

As we discuss below, the early work of socialist feminists and feminists such as Smart did not analyse to any great extent how race, ethnicity, and sexual orientation contribute to the uneven effects of law. Viewed retrospectively, however, conceptualizing law in terms of hegemonic process and uneven development generated more reflexive theoretical perspectives that avoided the dichotomization characteristic of theories based on a reified conception of law. In these more complicated formulations, law becomes an ensemble of practices and discourses, or resources, that people can mobilize to reproduce or transform the conditions under which they live. In other words, law becomes a site of struggles. In contrast, as a reified concept, law becomes a homogeneous entity disconnected from people's activities. It exists 'out there' according to its own independent logic, producing predetermined effects. Consequently, law can be only a liberator *or* an oppressor.

Law as a Gendering Practice continues in the tradition of both the result-equality and integrative feminists and the work by Smart and socialist feminists whose efforts to contextualize law in historically specific social relations revealed how it participates in the production and transformation of the social order at any given moment. In her examination of the relationship between the feminisms of Québec and the 'rest of Canada' (ROC), for instance, Belleau (Chapter 2) argues that feminism and feminist legal theorizing and activism must be contextualized in relation to national or cultural identity politics. Using the concept of 'strategic intersectionality', Belleau analyses the intertwined feminist and nationalist/cultural struggles among and between both feminisms. She concludes that thinking about intersections within and between these two emancipatory struggles not only illuminates Québec and ROC distinctiveness but also provides a basis for cross-community dialogues and coalitions around (legal) strategies.

Law as a Gendering Practice also draws on recent social and legal theorizing by post-structuralist and post-modern writers that focuses on issues addressed only implicitly or weakly in earlier feminist literature and research. In the following discussion, we investigate three questions: How is law both a constraining and enabling practice? What is a 'woman' and how is 'womanhood' constructed through law?

Law as Constraining and Enabling Practice

In conceptualizing law as a site of struggles, we reject the liberal view of the (legal) subject as an autonomous, intentional, and free agent as well as the instrumentalist view of the subject as determined by an omnipotent structure such as patriarchy. Instead, we employ a dynamic conception of the social world whereby structures of power and social agents exist in a mutually generative relationship. Our view is based on the assumption that social and legal agents are constituted by a multiplicity of power relations (both discursive and non-discursive) that they concomitantly help to reproduce through their activities and practices. In other words, individuals' subjectivity and activity are constituted through complex and contradictory systems of representations such as gender, race, class, age, sexuality, etc., which they themselves are constantly reproducing.

In her examination of structuration theory, Rosemary Coombe (1989: 90) astutely explains the intimate relationship between structure and agency and the potential for change in every act of (re)production of a structure:

> Every act that contributes to the reproduction of a structure . . . is also an act of production, a novel enterprise which may initiate change by altering structure even as it reproduces it—as, for example, the meanings of words change in and through their use. . . . Every process of action is potentially a production of something new, but at the same time all action arises in continuity with the past that supplies the means of its initiation. Structure thus is not to be conceptualized as a barrier to action but as essentially involved in its inception, even in the most radical processes of social change.

In this model, law clearly cannot be perceived as a homogeneous force that coerces or determines human activity or subjectivity. Rather, law becomes a practice that both constrains and enables agency (ibid.; see also Baber, 1991; Giddens, 1979).

The idea of law as a *practice* that both constrains and enables action also draws on the work of Michel Foucault (1984) and Pierre Bourdieu (1987; see also Bourdieu and Wacquant, 1992). From the former, we take his decentred concept of power, the idea that power is not located in a centralized place or body, such as the state, the law, the economy, or patriarchy, and imposed on people from above. Against this conventional, unidimensional view of power, Foucault argues that power emerges from below, is dispersed through every social relation, and deploys a multiplicity of effects that both control and facilitate agency. Foucault goes on to contrast modern power with sovereign power, an ancient right invested in the King and used to '*take* life or *let* live' (1984: 138). This ancient right of death, mainly used to destroy those who transgressed the King's law, eventually was replaced by a more diverse, diffuse, and dispersed practice that creates obedience primarily by investing and fostering life. 'Now it is over life, through its unfolding,' asserts Foucault, 'that power establishes its dominance' (ibid.). The aim of modern power, then, has become the 'administration of bodies and the calculated management of life' (ibid., 140).

Following Foucault's insights, we believe not only that law is part of the modern strategy of power to foster life but also that law plays a significant role in the process of governing life. The analyses of our contributors illuminate how, in interaction with other powerful institutional practices, law provides the discursive means to give life to specific gendered selves that are subsequently disciplined and regulated through law. For example, in her evaluation of public campaigns against prostitution, Deborah Brock in Chapter 5 shows how, historically, law has incorporated values, rhetorical forms, and symbols of specific social movements to create the prostitute as either fallen woman or victim, or more recently, a public nuisance. While these social and legal constructions support a specific morality separating 'good' from 'bad' women, they also marginalize the prostitute's right to affirm publicly and legally her identity and her right to work free of harassment.

Similarly, other contributors reveal that legal discourse does not exist in a vacuum; rather, legal discourse fosters specific identities through interaction with other institutional discourses. In their analysis of the 1993 'kiddie porn' panic in London, Ontario, that led to the arrest of more than 60 gay men, Shannon Bell and Joseph Couture, in Chapter 3, illustrate clearly how the influence of law in shaping consciousness and activities that contribute to the reproduction of social relations of inequality depends on a variety of arguments and symbols manufactured outside the field of law. They demonstrate how the police, the media, social workers, and the courts actively participate in gendering young male hustlers as victims and gay 'johns' as abusers through a narrative that encompasses ageism, genderism, homophobia, and whorephobia. Mary Condon's examination in Chapter 10 of the importance of corporate law in maintaining gendered identities and opportunities for women in family businesses also reveals the intersection between law and other institutions. She concludes that the gendering of women's role in the family firm through corporate law cannot be understood without a concomitant analysis of the gendering practices of traditional family relations and of the family law that supports those practices.

From Bourdieu (1987), we take the conception of society as a system of relatively autonomous fields. A field is a network of objective relations between positions that are structured hierarchically by the distribution of various kinds of 'capital'—economic, social, cultural, and symbolic. As Bourdieu (in Bourdieu and Wacquant, 1992: 98) explains, a field is analogous to a game:

> We can indeed, with caution, compare a field to a game (jeu) although, unlike the latter, a field is not the product of a deliberate act of creation, and it follows rules or, better, regularities, that are not explicit or codified. Thus we have stakes (enjeux) which are for the most part the product of the competition between players. We have an investment in the game . . .: players are

taken in by the game, they oppose one another, sometimes with ferocity, only to the extent that they concur in their belief (doxa) in the game and its stakes; they grant these a recognition that escapes questioning. Players agree, by the mere fact of playing, and not by way of a 'contract', that the game is worth playing, that it is 'worth the candle', and this collusion is the very basis of their competition. We also have trump cards, that is, master cards whose force varies depending on the game: just as the relative value of cards changes with each game, the hierarchy of the different species of capital (economic, social, cultural and symbolic) varies across the various fields. In other words, there are cards that are valid, efficacious in all fields—these are the fundamental species of capital—but their relative value as trump cards is determined by each field and even by the successive states of the same field.

To think of law as a game in Bourdieu's sense helps us to understand how its rules are structured, reinforced, and at times modified by the players' moves. While law is structured by rules of doctrine and case law that limit the possible moves players can make, those most likely to lose sometimes have succeeded in transforming the meaning of the rules. As Dara Culhane and Renee Taylor suggest in Chapter 7, in 'winning' an individual case the Clinical Program in Aboriginal Law at the University of British Columbia, which provides legal representation and advocacy to Aboriginal people in Vancouver's Downtown Eastside, may achieve only a small victory, but such victories matter. Changing the way that judges and Crown counsel see Aboriginal women, for instance, matters to the women who end up in court and to their families. Experiencing a legal victory also can be extremely meaningful to someone who has never been treated with dignity by authorities.

It is to those strategies of persuasion and negotiation to change the rules of the game in various fields that Bourdieu invites us to attend. The contributors to *Law as a Gendering Practice* have accepted his invitation. Each in her own way investigates how women play the 'game' of law: the moves they make, the stakes they have in the game, the value of specific cards, and the trump cards they or other players use to effect a change of direction or to transform the stakes. Rebecca Johnson's examination in Chapter 11 of a seemingly simple legal question in the *Symes* case—could child-care expenses be fully deductible as business expenses under the Income Tax Act?—reveals fundamental political struggles in diverse fields (family, economy, and feminism) over the meaning and value of motherhood, parenting, child care, and employment of and by mothers of various socio-economic classes. In the legal field, however, these struggles were trumped and displaced by the rhetoric of choice that tilted the judicial outcome in favour of prevailing orders of gender inequality. Shelley Gavigan's analysis in Chapter 6 of recent litigation involving lesbian parents likewise shows how hegemonic understandings of 'family', 'spouse', and 'parent' in law are both challenged and reinforced by the existence of lesbian parents. She concludes that, while these understandings may be 'stirred up' by legal challenges, they are not displaced and, therefore, remain central to the litigation of lesbian parenting cases even though the parties in no way resemble the conventional nuclear family.

Law as a Gendering Practice

This book examines the diverse and contradictory ways that law constrains and enables—i.e., constructs—womanhood. In doing so, we build on a long-standing general critique of feminist theory and practice first voiced by racial minority women in the 1960s who did not see themselves in the '(white) woman of feminist discourse' (see, e.g., Davis, 1981; hooks, 1981, 1984). Translated into the legal realm during the 1980s, this critique has taken the form of challenges to the gender-centric emphasis of liberal/radical feminist theories and to the socialist feminist neglect of race and ethnicity in their anti-essentialist class analyses of law (Collins, 1990; Razack, 1998; Turpel, 1991a; Williams, 1990). More recently, feminists have deconstructed the implicit, and sometimes explicit, assumptions that 'woman' is heterosexual and able-bodied, as well as middle-class and white, that have underpinned much second-wave feminist analysis (Robson, 1992, 1998; Wendell, 1996).

Law as a Gendering Practice takes up these theoretical challenges and seeks to illustrate the many ways in which law constructs womanhood. But, what exactly is a woman? This question may seem absurd for many of us who think we can recognize a woman when we see one. Yet a night out at a drag show, a fetish soirée, or a dyke bar will quickly trouble our most cherished assumptions about the constitutive features of a woman. The ingenious observation of Simone de Beauvoir, almost half a century ago, that 'one is not born a woman, but, rather, becomes one' (1973: 301), paved the way for subsequent feminist claims about the constructed nature of not only gender, but also race, sexual orientation, and even sex. As Carol Smart (1995: 192) so succinctly put it: 'Woman is no longer self-evident.' The moment we think we have accounted for all her characteristics—she has a colour, a sexuality, a body, a gender, a class, an age, an ethnicity, and so on—she starts eluding us, for there always will be another woman whose difference(s) we have not been able to consider in our definition.

Once confronted with a new difference, however, it is not just a matter of adding it to the collection of familiar traits we use to define woman. As soon as we include a difference in our list, it will have an impact on all the other characteristics on the list. For instance, as Parin Dossa shows in Chapter 8, disability interacts with gender and race to transform radically a woman's subjectivity. When Shayida, a woman with the trinity of constructs—gender, race, and class—uses her disability to seek permanent status in Canada on compassionate grounds, she suddenly finds herself in the web of the medico-legal complex and in the process acquires an identity at odds with her self-definition. Who is she? Who has she become once confronted with law? And how does she negotiate her newly produced self?

A woman's identity, then, is fluid and dynamic, never fixed and stable. Woman is always in a process of becoming. Her identity corresponds to the different subject positions she acquires as she finds herself in a variety of social relations. We do act differently in different contexts depending on the power relations involved, the possibilities to manoeuvre, the expectations we or others have of the situation, and so on. Our ability to act and express ourselves—our agency—does not come naturally. On the contrary, it is shaped by historically specific forces that constrain and enable our interpretations of any situation. For example, we know that we are not exactly the same women when we teach in front of a classroom full of students, when we spend holidays with our aging parents, and when we strip in front of our sex-mates. We *become* different women for each occasion as we draw on and negotiate between historically specific representations or scripts to give meaning to whomever we are in each situation.

But are there limits to becoming a woman? Does our sex more or less determine our gender? Judith Butler (1990) cleverly undermines the connection between sex and gender when she epitomizes the act of becoming a gender in the case of drag. The drag queen might have a penis—the axiomatic sign of maleness—but when 'she' performs the feminine gender 'she' surpasses most women at it. By outdoing women at the ultimate game of femininity, the drag queen troubles the naturalness of the connection between sex and gender: one's sex has nothing to do with one's gender. In other words, Butler challenges the idea that sex is a biological given or a precultural entity onto which gender, a social construct, is anchored. She proposes instead that sex, or the sexed body, only comes into being once it is stamped by gender. Kevin Bonnycastle, in Chapter 4, takes up Butler's anti-essentialist arguments about sex and gender in her analysis of Bill C-49, the feminist-inspired amendments to Canada's sexual assault laws enacted in 1992. She concludes that, despite feminist input, Bill C-49 incorporated assumptions about prefigured gendered subjects and, specifically, 'the rapist' and 'the rape victim' as pre-existing entities, which codified existing gender stereotypes and power relations. Bonnycastle suggests that, if feminists want to challenge the status quo, they need to think about sexual assault/rape as a gendering strategy and to develop 'textual strategies' that will destabilize dominant cultural scripts about sexual assault.

In light of the above discussion, it becomes clearer why the question—What is a woman?—is so difficult, if not impossible, to answer. If we accept that woman is not reducible to a biological category or an essence, then there are cultural strategies involved in her process of *devenir*. Law is one of those strategies. For a long time now, feminists have shown how institutions such as the family, media, advertising, popular culture, religion, medicine, education, and language shape gender in often rigid oppositions between women and men or among women along differences of class and race. Understanding the role of law in the construction of gender is all the more important today because law is so pervasive, having penetrated almost every minute corner of our lives.

Our objective in *Law as a Gendering Practice*, then, is to reveal how law intersects with other institutions and discourses in the construction of woman, 'a task', in Smart's words, 'which is never fully completed and is always open to modification' (1995: 228). In the spirit of feminists who have struggled to eliminate essentialism and reification from their theorizing about law, the authors of the empirical investigations that follow all attempt to conceive law as a hegemonic process—a strategy involving a multiplicity of agents who, drawing on a variety of knowledge(s), experiences, and resources, struggle to institutionalize their specific goals. Yet, because those goals are diverse, contradictory, and open for interpretation, once they are written in law they can be mobilized to undermine, support, or refashion whatever institutional arrangements exist at a particular time.

Notes

1. Our intention here is to illustrate the theoretical origins and development of a 'law as a gendering practice' approach rather than to present a comprehensive discussion of the extensive feminist legal literature in Canada or elsewhere. Therefore, while we use the work of individual authors to illustrate particular arguments or positions, we also acknowledge the diversity among feminist legal scholars who may share the same general theoretical perspective.

2. MacKinnon has been very involved with LEAF, despite her belief that equality is incompatible with patriarchy, because she views 'legal activism as a necessary evil' (Jhappan, 1998: 65).

3. We concur with one of our anonymous reviewers who suggested that in Canada, socialist feminisms also have contributed to the transformation of liberal/radical feminisms and this influence 'accounts for the pronounced emphasis on materialist analysis in substantive equality and integrative feminisms.'

Chapter 2

L'intersectionalité

Feminisms in a Divided World
(Québec-Canada)

Marie-Claire Belleau

Emancipatory struggles, such as feminism and national or cultural identity politics, produce exhilaration and anxiety. If national or cultural identity politics (nat/cult) and feminism form complex struggles when viewed separately, their intersection in the cultural, political, and socio-economic settings of Québec and the rest of Canada (ROC) (Stychin, 1997: 4) creates seemingly infinite complexities. In this chapter, I advance the notion of 'strategic intersectionality' as a way of describing some of the consequences of the intricate interactions between feminism and nat/cult in Québec and the ROC. Playing the intricate, if dangerous, game of strategic intersectionality can empower us to imagine innovative tactics and create new coalitions both within and between the communities of Québec and ROC feminists.

This chapter reconceptualizes the relationship between the feminisms of Québec and the ROC around two main theses. The first focuses on a rejection of differences that portray one feminism as more or less developed than the other. I seek to replace common clichés about 'distinct feminisms' with strategic intersectionality (Crenshaw, 1989, 1991) to explain differences as emerging out of separate political contexts and struggles. I thus hope to promote dialogue based on better understanding of the Québec and ROC situations. The second thesis relates two fundamental consequences of the heritage of conquest to the ways nat/cult and feminism intertwine in Québec. I argue, first, that the feminist and nat/cult intersections in Québec provide an indispensable perspective from which to work on one of the central tenets of feminist critique: the private/public split. In addition, Québec's singular position in Canada reinforces the legislation/adjudication divide in ways that have proven harmful to women. In short, legal feminist struggle in Québec requires a simultaneous analysis of the province's position within Canada.

These theses work against the common understanding of the differences between feminism in Québec and in the ROC. Indeed, at times, we French-

Canadian women argue that feminism in Québec essentially differs from the feminism prevalent in the ROC. Proponents of Québec culture often position themselves at the intersection of two worlds: Québec people are too North American to be European and too European to be North American. Québec feminists at times point to this cultural difference to explain the distinct manifestations of feminism in law in the two main Canadian legal systems. I, too, take for granted differences between feminisms in Québec and in the ROC. I argue that differences among the two groups are unavoidable because of the divergent political positions that feminists occupy in their respective settings. Québec women thus engage in nat/cult struggles in ways distinct from the ways feminists are implicated in such struggles in the ROC. However, I advocate neither eternalizing such differences (essentialism) nor erasing them (universalism), but rather see these differences as inscribed in specific cultural practices, political settings, and institutional frameworks. From this perspective, I celebrate differences between feminists in Québec and in the ROC as expressing the strategic deployment of differences in differently situated feminist struggles; yet I also call for new kinds of coalitions based on these differences.

If both feminism and nat/cult are sensitive subjects, the combination of the two generates even more delicate issues requiring, at the outset, two cautionary comments: the first relates to the use of the term 'nat/cult', while the second concerns issues about Québec and ROC identities.

First, I will use 'nat/cult' throughout this chapter to refer to the necessary critique of Québec's position in Canada for feminist purposes. I will abstain from taking a position in the nationalist/federalist political debate because this critique should concern all feminists: Francophones, Anglophones, Allophones and immigrants, Québec nationalists, and federalists. At this moment, structures of both federalism and Québec nationalism engender detrimental consequences for women. The harmful effects of Québec's position in Canada for women will not necessarily be eradicated either by sovereignty or by remaining in Canada. Neither political outcome, for example, will eliminate the problematic private/public dichotomy reinforced by the civil law/common law split in Québec's legal system. For these reasons, when I describe an intersectional move made by a Québec feminist, I do not mean that she is or is not a Québec nationalist but rather that she displays a manoeuvre that emerges, in part, out of a critique of Québec's position in Canada. Finally, I use the term 'nat/cult' because not all those concerned by Québec's cultural issues identify with nationalist politics. Similarly, I do not make any assessment about the political positions of ROC feminists about Québec or Canada.

Second, some readers may already feel uncomfortable by the way I seem to have generalized Québec and ROC identities, thus casting doubt on my simultaneous anti-essentialist and anti-universalist appeal. Yet, I aspire to address issues relating to Québec and ROC identity without denying their historical and contemporary complexities. Québec people rarely admit, let alone confront, their difficult and contradictory position as both colonizers and colonized. Indeed, Québec people occupy a site of complex relations as both conquerors of the First Nations and as a people conquered by the English. Québec people also seldom face their problematic relations to the many French-Canadian communities outside of Québec, which form important and diverse, but always endangered, culturally specific Francophone populations. In addition, Québec participates in an intricate web of metropole/provincial relationships to France, related to the history of colonization and to a continued set of shared origins, history, language, and legal system linking them across the Atlantic for centuries. The Anglophone, Allophone, and immigrant communities also constitute vital parts of Québec's anatomy. Thus, the place of Québec people both as a minority within a majority—that of the ROC—yet as a majority in its territory complicates its predicament even further. As I shall show, this singular Québec positionality carries important gender implications as well as repercussions relating to relations with its own minority groups.

Similarly, some readers may justly object to any generalizations about the 'rest of Canada'. The ROC combines a mosaic of wide regional and cultural differences that also give rise to their own sets of complex webs of identities and nat/cult encounters. Like Québec, the ROC combines intricate sets of relations between minorities and majorities over numerous identity struggles as well as issues related to its own colonial encounters. Feminist issues in one English-Canadian province may resemble those in another region, yet have little in common with the experience of women from other parts of Canada, because of strong differences and similarities concerning linguistic, socio-economic, religious, and nat/cult questions. Indeed, some of these regions and provinces share more striking commonalities with Québec than with other parts of English Canada. In addition, some ROC feminists neglect acknowledging the way their own ethnic and linguistic dominant position inflects their feminism, making their practices more or less adapted to their own needs or those of others.

In this chapter, I consider mainly Québec's identity. However, the complexities of the sense of belonging (*appartenance*), either to Québec or to the ROC, demonstrate that any description of identity encloses an unavoidable partiality that cannot be assimilated with essentialism. Indeed, the differences *within* Québec's identity as well as the differences *in relation to* the ROC's identity can only be explained on a relational level—i.e., by the effect of reciprocal links of dependence and influence between identity elements that coexist in their specific strategic contexts. For example, a complete description of Québec identity requires a relational analysis of the Francophone majority identity with the 'belongingnesses' of First Nations, Anglophones, Allophones, and immigrants both within Québec and in the ROC, as well as of Francophone communities outside of Québec. Thus, I propose an inevitably truncated version of Québec identity, primarily in relation to the ROC. To summarize, I use the terms 'Québec' and 'ROC' throughout this chapter as shorthand to designate the complex set of identities that each of these sites encompasses. I thus propose reconceptualizing Québec and ROC identities towards imagining new stratagems and building new coalitions.

Consequently, I use the concept of 'strategic intersectionality' to analyse the correlation between feminism and nat/cult in the Québec context but mostly in relation to the ROC. I examine the strategic relations between these two emancipatory struggles. Strategic intersectionality attempts to substitute analysis of differences based on essences for those based on political and cultural contexts, thereby creating the possibility for deeper comprehension and political alliances between feminists. Strategic intersectionality opens up an infinite number of partnerships between sites of cultural practices, both dominant and marginal.

In the first section below I describe what I mean by strategic intersectionality. Next, the potential of strategic thinking for Québec and ROC feminists around the theme of 'distinct feminisms' is illustrated. In the final section I analyse the impact of the intersection between feminism and nat/cult in relation to two traditional dichotomies: private/public and legislation/adjudication.

Strategic Intersectionality

Often, considerations of emancipatory identity struggles, viewed in isolation, dissimulate the demands of other protests. For example, feminist requests at times stay hidden under other types of nat/cult aspirations and vice versa (Crenshaw, 1989, 1991).

The concept of intersectionality implies complex analysis and understandings of the simultaneous engagement in more than one emancipatory battle, without subordinating one to the other. The intersectional study of these distinct but intertwined struggles demands a contextual examination of how nat/cult and feminism interact with one another. The cultural, political, and socio-economic context in which these struggles are inscribed enriches our understanding of the diverse meanings, consequences, and different manifestations that result from the crossroads of identity battles.

In advocating the concept of intersectionality, I argue against both essentialism and universalism. I reject claims that attempt to make Québec's feminism, Québec's nat/cult, or Québec's civil law as necessarily, objectively, and abstractly distinct from the ROC's feminism, nat/cult or federalism, or common law. Yet, I also reject assimilationist attempts that silence cultural distinctions and aim at an undifferentiated sense of 'universal' belonging. For example, merely adding the experiences of Québec women to a ROC research project may constitute an essentialist move when conducted abstractly and without examining Québec's political and cultural context. Similarly, generalizing French-Canadian experiences to all Canadian women without an effort to comprehend English-Canadian identities in their complex settings would be unduly universalist. I do not mean to suggest that the Québec or ROC contexts by themselves provide determinateness to otherwise indeterminate concepts;

rather, they enrich our understanding of the various possible meanings of those concepts in particular struggles.

Strategic intersectionality thus consists in imagining new strategies that require consideration of dimensions of experiences invisible to those who view feminism and nat/cult in isolation from each other, failing to capture intersecting patterns of gender and national subordination in both Québec and the ROC. As we shall see, imagining such new strategies presupposes stating hidden differences or similarities, deconstructing myths, revealing processes of projection and dissociation, building new kinds of coalitions. These measures may apply inside one site of struggle (for example, between different feminist approaches and thus within feminism) or between sites (for example, between feminism and nat/cult). They serve to support innovative practices, to foster original strategies, and to create shifting and productive alliances.

My particular interest consists in highlighting the specific context of Québec feminists—whichever nationalist, federalist, or other political position they adopt—who unavoidably participate simultaneously in both nat/cult and feminist emancipatory struggles. Ultimately, I aim to restart a dialogue between Québec and ROC feminists. I want to foster conversations premised on tactical thinking rather than on essentialist or universalist desires of recognition and demands.

Distinct Feminisms

Each component of the 'distinct feminisms' theme brings to the fore the intersection between feminism and nat/cult. Often, feminists situated at the crossroad of these emancipatory struggles manoeuvre to avoid subsuming one to the other. Indeed, their nat/cult endeavours may remain hidden by the boundaries of gender struggles and vice versa. Thus, their emancipatory strategies can only be fully envisioned by looking at the crossing of these roads. To illustrate my thesis, I will make occasional reference to two recent issues of a Francophone and of an Anglophone law review devoted to legal feminism: 'L'influence du féminisme sur le droit au Québec' published in the 1995 *Cahiers de droit* and the 'Special Issue: Women and the Law' in the 1992 *Alberta Law Review*.[1]

Québec's Marginal Feminism

Québec feminists acknowledge and lament the scarcity of feminist critique and scholars in the province's law schools. In *Cahiers de droit*, the dedication to Marlène Cano by Michelle Boivin poignantly highlights this scarcity. Boivin deplores the 'circle—alas so narrow—of French-Canadian feminist jurists', which lost one of its precious members in September 1994 (Boivin, 1995a: 4). Marlène Cano, a young feminist professor of civil law at Ottawa University, died of breast cancer at the age of 38.

The editor, Louise Langevin, makes a similar point in her preface to the special issue of *Cahiers de droit*. She explicitly invokes the absence of French texts on legal feminism and the rarity of courses in law school curriculums, as well as the dearth of feminist arguments before the Québec courts. She condemns the apathy towards feminism in Québec law and sets the issue's objective as that of 'reflecting, in French, on this question' (Langevin, 1995a: 4–5). Her description of the Québec situation seems to build on an implicit comparison with the English-Canadian situation. She implicitly suggests a projection of the enviable status that feminist professors and feminist scholarship enjoy in the ROC and in the Anglo-Saxon world in general. The feminism issue of *Cahiers de droit* thus simultaneously deploys nat/cult and feminist strategies in an intersectional advocacy of legal feminism in Québec. For example, the provocative title, 'L'influence du féminisme sur le droit au Québec', boldly presents the issue as a manifesto. Yet, the lament about the absence of feminism in Québec law schools somewhat undercuts the title's bold statement of the influence of feminism (Boivin, 1995a; Langevin, 1995a; Stoddart). Thus, the title communicates the *désir* for the greater influence of feminism on the Québec legal system rather than the reality of such an impact. In addition, three authors (Boivin, 1995b: 29; Bouchard: 141, citing Boivin, 1992; Langevin, 1995b: 101 n.8) defined what they meant by the term 'feminism', attempting to fix the boundaries of legal feminism presumably for the purpose of determining and establishing a distinctive field within Québec's legal system. The title of the special issue, the declarations of Boivin and Langevin, and the definitions of feminism underline *one* intersectional strategy that aims at the admission, recognition, and acceptance of feminist theory in Québec's legal community. As we shall see, directing a feminist critique squarely at those elements of Québec law that are solely within the province's competence also participates in this strategy. The intersectionality of this strategy resides in the authors' placing feminist and nat/cult identities in Québec's legal domain.

Another strategy to gain broader recognition but also to foster mutual understanding and support between Québec and ROC feminists in legal academia would involve a common commitment with English-Canadian feminist communities. Such a strategy to promote a better mutual understanding between Québec and ROC feminists would consist in reconsidering some of the descriptions of the positions occupied by feminists in both legal communities. For example, Québec feminists often project an image of a well-recognized and accepted ROC feminism in English-Canadian law schools. These projections have been beneficial to Québec feminists. They provide us with hope and encouragement. These projections are also deployed, in part, to convince colleagues of the fundamental importance and interest of feminism as an unavoidable movement of legal thought—to provoke a sense of urgency among Québec jurists, a sense that if they do not recognize feminism, they will lag behind in cutting-edge legal thought.

However, the deployment of such projections also carries risks. Indeed, these Québec projections minimize the severe backlashes that have assailed women professors in English Canada. In her *Alberta Law Review* article, 'Violence Against Women in Law Schools', Teresa Scassa looks at the threats of violence and acts of discrimination, as well as the resulting 'silencing', that women students and professors endure in ROC law schools. One could, therefore, envisage renewed efforts to provide support to feminists isolated in their environments on both sides of the divide—acknowledging the different though related vulnerabilities of Québec and ROC feminists.

Obviously, generations of Québec and ROC feminists have acted and fought along these lines. I do not pretend to be advancing these ideas for the first time. But these attempts need to be reinvested with tactical objectives and political activist stamina. Strategic thinking presupposes celebrating the strengths but also criticizing the weaknesses of the feminist movements in law in specific institutional and disciplinary contexts.

Feminism and Identity Politics

At times, many Québec feminists, including myself, attempt to explain and to justify the marginality of feminism in Québec law schools through a 'cultural' argument based on a purported essential division between two Canadian cultures—a division often generalized to differences between 'Latin' and 'Anglo' historical origins and contemporary cultures. Such attempts to explain the indifference, antagonism, and even patent rejection of outspoken feminism in Québec law schools often involve the deployment of at least three claims. First, we reject the dubious assumption that all Québec feminist jurists suffer from a severe case of 'false consciousness'. Indeed, the fact that feminism in Québec's legal community may have a different expression than that of Anglo-feminism should not lead to the conclusion that Québec feminism does not exist. The supposition that all Québec women are the helpless victims of patriarchy and gender oppression verges on the absurd. Second, we refuse to explain the split between Québec and ROC feminisms as merely an excuse invoked by Québec feminists and non-feminists to avoid facing the 'real' issues raised by Anglo-feminism. Third, we project a combative, aggressive, and even belligerent Anglo-feminist tradition that serves as a 'straw woman' in relation to the distinct Québec feminism. This last argument hinges on a highly problematic—even if strategic—projection of Anglo-feminism, as discussed previously.

Thus, some feminists argue that the aggressive and confrontational approach of Anglo-feminism does not suit Québec society. Such authors contend that since the 1970s, Québec women have exercised a 'power of influence' as opposed to a 'power of confrontation' (Stoddart: 16). The nat/cult struggle thus intersects with feminist demands, in part, by specifically asserting the existence of a distinct feminism: Québec feminism has, and should have, a different face. Québec women succeed in achieving the same advances in the battles against patriarchal oppression by more subtle but as effective moves as their English-Canadian counterparts. Indeed, these contentions have a strong measure of truth in Québec. For example, there are as many women law professors and judges proportionately in Québec as in the ROC legal communities (Dumont, 1993; Association du Barreau Canadien, 1993). Indeed, for the past 20 years, enrolment in Québec law faculties included 20 per cent more women law students than did law schools in the ROC.

Understandably, the argument for a distinct feminism stems, in part, from the need for a common front to preserve nat/cult specificity. Fragmentation due to internal divisions and struggles would threaten the nat/cult project. It should be noted that the anti-confrontational argument is not specific to feminism's role in Québec's political history. Rather, this contention often arises in nat/cult movements around the world, when feminists challenge the subordinate role of women in such struggles. Like other nationalist movements, Québec's nat/cult suffers from a general subordination of most grassroots progressive political struggles to the state-building project.

Many feminists rightly argue that Québec women have been heavily involved in the nat/cult project since its inception (Stoddart; de Sève, 1992). However, the projection and dismissal of a perhaps mythic confrontational Anglo feminist tradition risks missing important emancipatory strategies. In addition, an anti-confrontational approach risks underestimating the potentially non-optimal tactics of women's subtle—even if persuasive—manner in Québec. Strategic thinking implies staying clear of reductionist projections of feminist false consciousness and aggressiveness, as well as of the united front of nat/cult.

Multiple Belonging: Feminism and the Cultural Context

Québec feminists occasionally support the distinct feminism thesis by pointing to Québec's divergent historical and cultural origins as well as our multiple sources of intellectual influences. Feminists acknowledge the impact of American feminist scholarship on Québec's feminism. However, some Québec feminists believe that French and European influences play an even greater role on the development of feminist ideas in Québec (Stoddart). Québec lies at the crossroads of North American and French ideas on the intellectual maps of the world. Yet, despite the undoubted influence of French writers, Québec feminist scholars are much more influenced by American than by French theorists.

A convenient, if anecdotal, survey may be conducted by comparing the feminist authorities cited in *Cahiers de droit* and the *Alberta Law Review*. Of course, authors only cite a limited number of the readings, conversations, and cultural events that make an impact on their writings. Nonetheless, this comparison may provide some insight.

Judging from the footnotes, the authors of the *Alberta Law Review* articles are much more influenced by their southern neighbours, American feminist theorists, than are their Francophone counterparts. For example, Sheila Noonan proposes an excellent critique of the essentialism of Robin West, an American jurist. In doing so, Noonan specifically mentions her debt towards

American 'critical race theory' (Noonan: 737 n.78). Other *Alberta Law Review* contributors also cite American feminists profusely, though not always to the same extent as Noonan. The second most cited feminist authorities are English-Canadian (Kobly; MacDonald; Munro). In many articles, writings from other Anglophone countries—especially England (Hodgson; Bunting; Munro)—supplement the American predominance. However, there are exceptions to the American focus: Hodgson cites no American scholarship and Ross et al. refer only to English-Canadian sources. French and French-Canadian feminist writings are cited only rarely in the *Alberta Law Review* articles. Thus, the perception of an Anglophone feminist community extending beyond national boundaries emerges vividly from reading the special issue of the *Alberta Law Review*.

If ROC feminists seem engaged in an Anglophone-dominated discussion, the French-Canadian authors, true to their multiple sense of identity, draw their ideas from both American and European feminist sources. Indeed, Québec feminists refer to a wide range of American intellectual sources and thus participate, in French, in the Anglo debates. For example, like their ROC counterparts, the Québec authors cite, and seem influenced by, Catharine MacKinnon far more than any other single author (Stoddart; Boivin, 1995b; Langevin, 1995b; Bouchard; Noonan; Martin; Scassa; Munro; MacDonald). However, only Louise Langevin, in *Cahiers de droit*, seems to borrow her sources for reflection principally from Americans (Langevin, 1995b). Either by training or by habit, or because of their multiple sense of belonging, the other authors in the *Cahiers de droit* special issue cite a wide variety of ROC, European, and American sources, and they also cite one another. The article they most often cite is Boivin's excellent and comprehensive 'Féminisme en capsule' (Boivin, 1992) (Stoddart; Des Rosiers; Langevin, 1995b; Bouchard).

Thus, the sources cited by the contributors to *Cahiers de droit* seem to contradict the claim of a distinct feminism specifically influenced by French feminist scholarship. Only Michelle Boivin (1995b) refers to Simone de Beauvoir's classic *Le deuxième sexe* and to Odile Dhavernas's well-known *Droits des femmes, pouvoirs des hommes*. This observation comes as no surprise given the dearth of French feminist legal scholarship. The issue is not so much that Québec feminists should or should not quote classic feminist texts, but rather that the French intellectual influence on legal feminism is less predominant than often thought. The myth of overwhelming French intellectual influence on Québec's legal feminism does not hold. Nevertheless, the intellectual influences of the Québec feminists are diverse, even if not mainly French.

Interestingly, none of the *Cahiers de droit* authors cite Hélène Cixous, Luce Irigaray, and Julia Kristeva, the so-called 'New French Feminists' whose writings have had a tremendous influence on the legal feminist Anglo-Saxon world (Frug, 1992; Williams, 1991; Cornell, 1991, 1993; Bottomley, 1996). Paradoxically, Québec feminists sometimes seek inspiration from Anglophone authors who have themselves been decisively influenced by 'fancy French' theory, particularly feminist theory—the French influence thus comes back to us mediated by its Anglophone reception (Des Rosiers, citing Frug).

Even a cursory analysis of the footnotes thus casts a different light on the intellectual influences on Québec and ROC legal feminisms than would have been predicted by the distinct feminism thesis. One may draw several alternative conclusions from this observation to be explored from intersectional perspectives: (1) Québec and ROC feminists read similar American scholarship differently; (2) Québec and ROC feminists participate differently—or similarly— in the Anglophone debates; (3) the variety of intellectual sources from which Québec feminists draw their ideas contributes—or not—to the emergence of a distinct feminism. In any event, I would like to draw Québec and ROC feminists deeper towards strategic intersectional thinking, linking these different intellectual influences to the availability and usefulness of strategies in different contexts. If distinct feminisms exist, what strategies are facilitated or impeded due to the difference in intellectual influences? Ultimately, I believe that Québec and ROC feminists could devise strategies to widen their intellectual range through mutual 'contamination'.

Subordination and Dissociation

Finally, many feminists argue that the radical feminist analysis of women's subordination does not correspond to Québec's culture and history. According to this argument, Québec men, more than—or at least as much as—women, have suffered from the historical disadvantages related to the 'male' English conquest. The effects of conquest, the argument continues, have produced a hierarchy between the conquerors and the conquered that is deeply internalized by Québec men. The serious wounds inflicted on men by conquest would thus have significantly affected the patriarchal hierarchy between men and women in Québec society. This argument is also often raised in nat/cult struggles around the world and expresses some profound truths. In Québec, the argument opposes the Anglo-Saxon conception of women's exclusion and inferiority in patriarchal societies to the classic nat/cult ideal of partnership between men and women to overcome the effects of conquest. Implicitly, this appeal evokes the nat/cult gender identity myths of the Québec matriarch and her somewhat meek consort, contemporarily designated as *'l'homme rose'*. Simultaneously, it conjures the stereotypes of the 'Latin' relations between men and women defined in terms of seductiveness, sexiness, and desire, a set of attitudes that do not fit the combative cadres of Anglo-feminist battlefields.

As mentioned above, Québec feminists make the strategic claim of a distinct feminism through their projection of a confrontational Anglo-feminist identity. They dissociate themselves from this Anglo image using nat/cult rhetoric and a complex sense of belonging to the Latin cultural family. Québec women embrace Latin stereotypes of femininity partly out of a still vivid, if diminishing, allegiance to a distant French past, partly out of a desire to assert their distinctiveness in North America. At the same time, they reject the blatant sexism associated with French and other Latin cultures. In addition, the hold of the 'French past' decreases as the proportion of Québec women without any historical or 'ethnic' ties to France increases; moreover, this French past never had any positive meaning for First Nations women. Thus, the same projection and dissociation mechanisms that operate towards Anglo-feminism also operate in relation to French and other Latin cultures. The North American influence makes Québec women critical of the blatant sexism prevalent in these 'sister' cultures. By dissociating themselves from both Anglo-feminism and Latin femininity, Québec women and feminists attempt to construct a sense of their own intersectional identity.

I stress that I celebrate and embrace these strategic efforts of projection, dissociation, and distinction, which succeed in creating a sense of feminist identity fitted to the Québec context. However, these efforts should be viewed for what they are: strategies.

Focusing separately on traditional gender or national boundaries risks either subordinating feminist struggles to nat/cult battles or nat/cult claims to feminist demands. Subordination occurs because the borders of one struggle hide or render invisible demands made in the name of the other struggle. For example, nat/cult claims may be ignored by transnational feminist analysis. Conversely, nat/cult struggles have often 'postponed' feminist demands to the post-liberation period rather than fully integrating them in the emancipatory process—a postponement that may last forever.[2] Failing to account for the impact of double allegiances on Québec and ROC feminists also limits the potential of constructive dialogues and coalitions. However, strategic thinking does not imply that a consensus on goals will necessarily be reached. Distinct strategies are unavoidable, as are political and ideological disagreements about which tactics to adopt in different settings. Yet, such conflicts may lead to imagining and deploying even more creative and original intersectional strategies because of the struggles and coalitions they will compel.

Heritage of Conquest: The Private/Public and the Adjudication/Legislation Dichotomies

Québec's position in Canada has implications for two issues of fundamental importance to legal feminists: the private/public and the adjudication/legislation dichotomies. The reinforcement of these dichotomies by Québec's position in Canada places crucial obstacles in the path of struggles on behalf of women. Thus, feminist struggle in Québec can only fully advance through problematizing the province's position in the federal system.

This intersection between feminism and nat/cult requires a critical evaluation of the conventional view of the relations between civil law and common law.[3] Québec jurists—both feminist and non-feminist—regard Québec feminists' 'different' perspective as stemming, in part, from the specificity of Québec's civil law. Traditionally, civil law jurists dismissed all political critiques, such as feminist, anti-racist, or class critiques, due to their implicit belief in the civil law system's greater 'objective' and 'neutral' 'scientific method'. However, the French civil law tradition possesses significant critical trends that have dealt severe blows to these outmoded beliefs (Belleau, 1995, 1997) and important parts of contemporary Québec legal academia reject these remnants of 'classical legal thought'. Yet, when it comes to dealing with feminism and other critiques, these old ghosts often re-emerge from the closet to scare off perceived threats to the civil law tradition and specificity. Legal feminism's association with common law, like its association with Anglo-feminism, serves to dismiss it as too 'political' to fit Québec's civil law system.

Québec's constitutional position in the current federal system perpetuates the classic dualisms of the private/public and legislative/adjudication dichotomies. The federal system limits Québec's civil law to the private and legislative parts of the divides. The constitutional division of power thus reinforces two of the dichotomies most problematized by legal feminist scholarship. These reinforcements show the necessity of facing the feminism and nat/cult intersection in the Québec context.

Private/Public Dichotomy

In the 1995 special issue of *Cahiers de droit*, the themes of the articles chosen by the French-Canadian authors show their marked interest for financial issues (Bouchard; Lippel and Bienvenu; Cipriani), torts (Bouchard; Des Rosiers; Langevin, 1995b), feminist theory (Boivin, 1995b; Néron), and history (Stoddart; Parent and Postolec). Surprisingly, four of the nine *Cahiers de droit* articles deal with evaluation methods of prejudice, financial compensation, and procedural remedies (Langevin, 1995b; Bouchard; Lippel and Bienvenu; Cipriani). In contrast, the themes in the special issue of the *Alberta Law Review* are strikingly diverse. The authors deal with questions of violence (Scassa; MacDonald; Kobly), feminist theory (Noonan; Bunting; Munro), equal pay (Hodgson), and the place of women in the legal profession (Martin; Brockman; Ross et al.), among other themes.

The interests of the *Cahiers de droit* authors may be explained in part by their strategic aim of dealing with issues of Québec law and thus of civil law,[4] as I have suggested above. In the Canadian constitutional context, the provincial governments hold exclusive powers over private law, whereas the federal government's jurisdiction relates to public law domains such as criminal law and constitutional law. Thus, private law rules devised by Québec's Civil Code and other provincial legislation and public law rules coming under federal common law or legislation form Québec's partly hybrid and partly bifurcated legal system. The strategic decision made by the French-Canadian authors to focus their inquiry on Québec private law is laudable. The shortage of legal feminist writings in French in Québec needs to be addressed urgently. Concentrating in large part on Québec's civil and private law issues constitutes the most assured way of putting feminist theory on the Québec agenda and of gaining recognition in Québec academia and legal practice. Indeed, the mere publication of a feminist manifesto in a mainstream Québec law review amounts to a remarkable exploit. The *Cahiers de droit* feminist issue constitutes a historical event in the Québec legal community and a shrewd intersectional strategy. '*Chapeau!*'

However, in making the decision to deal specifically with Québec legal issues, the journal may have inadvertently reinforced the public/private distinction, long a target of feminist criticism (Olsen, 1983). The decision to avoid dealing with public law issues makes public law appear irrelevant to Québec's legal system. A different set of intersectional considerations may lead us to adopt a different strategy in the next phase of Québec legal feminism due to the problems caused by the private/public split. From a nat/cult perspective, the private/public split reinforces the conquered position of the civil law system in Canada by sanctioning the removal of public law from provincial competence. By focusing on private law issues, Québec's civil law system retains its specificity, but also keeps its subordinated status in relation to ROC law. From a feminist perspective, the private/public split makes it difficult to challenge the ways that split can render women's issues invisible.

While the *Cahiers de droit* special issue should thus be praised as a successful feminist début on the Québec legal scene, one could imagine *other* intersectional strategies for the next phase of Québec feminism. This alternative intersectional intervention would begin the emancipatory process from a feminist strategy aimed at questioning the very distinction between provincial and federal competences in order to widen Québec's conception of law. The strategic extension of Québec law by an appropriation of federal law for feminist purposes would aim at exploding the constitutional division between private and public law around issues of particular interest to women's lives. For example, one such strategy would involve dealing simultaneously with the complex and multiple consequences of violence against women in both public and private law. In so doing, this approach would participate in both feminist and nat/cult struggles by widening the traditional legal boundaries of Québec through the inclusion of federal law for emancipatory ends touching the integral experience of women's lives. This alternative strategy would challenge the private/public organization of Québec's legal system, a challenge only possible in Québec by deploying feminist and nat/cult critiques at the same time. A Québec feminist critique of the private/public dichotomy would thus necessarily present a viewpoint distinct from ROC feminism because of the institutional and political settings in which they operate. This intersectional strategy would participate in a radical redefinition of the place of public law in Québec, a long-standing nat/cult concern, through the reappropriation of public law issues for women.

The strategy deployed in the *Cahiers de droit* feminist issue's focus on private law consisted in isolating the unique character of Québec's law to incorporate a feminist analysis tailored to the Québec context. The alternative strategy supposes an expansion of feminism to critique the isolation produced by the specificity of Québec law, a questioning aimed at avoiding the fragmentation of women's experiences by the legal system. The choice between these alternative measures depends on a situational analysis and on the priorities set by participants involved in the front lines of both battles.

To summarize: Québec's position in the provincial and federal constitutional arrangement as well as in the civil law and common law divide makes it difficult for Québec women to deploy the crucial feminist critique of the private/public dichotomy. Moreover, the subordinate situation of Québec actually prevents the Québec government and institutions from intervening in ways that require a transcendence of this dichotomy. Finally, respecting these dualisms reinforces the segregation of Québec feminist jurists by preventing them from engaging with their ROC counterparts. Intersectional analysis thus reveals the double isolation imposed by the separate spheres (private/public) and the legal systems' specificities (civil law/common law); it also opens up possibilities for alternative manoeuvres and coalitions.

Legislation/Adjudication Dichotomy

Many jurists in the history of French and North American legal thought (Gény, 1919; Belleau, 1993, 1995; Horwitz, 1992; Kennedy, 1997) have harshly criticized the classic dichotomy between adjudication and legislation as legitimating and justifying unacknowledged ideological preferences. An intersectional analysis of the Canadian constitutional context shows how its reinforcement of the dualism separating judge-made-law from laws adopted by the legislature is detrimental for women.

Looking once again at the two law reviews on feminism provides useful insights for an assessment of the impact of the adjudication/legislation dichotomy on feminist critique in the Québec and ROC contexts. Remarkably, seven out of the nine *Cahiers de droit* articles deal with case law analysis.[5] One would have expected analysis of '*la doctrine*' (scholarly commentary) given the civil law tradition and article topics. Many of the authors study Québec courts' decisions (Des Rosiers; Langevin, 1995b; Bouchard; Lippel and Bienvenu; Cipriani). They describe the limitations on women's rights imposed by judges and they denounce judicial conservatism. In each case, the author suggests avenues for legislative or social reforms or alternative judicial interpretations. Contrary to the Francophones, the English-Canadian authors in the *Alberta Law Review* borrow an amalgam of approaches, mixing theoretical and empirical case law with legislative analysis. They rarely propose legal reforms.[6] How should one explain this contrast?

The authors of the *Cahiers de droit* articles identify conservative judicial interpretation in the Québec courts as one source of limitation on women's rights. This question is crucial for understanding the difference between feminist strategies in Québec and in the ROC. If many feminists have rightly pointed to the legislative and institutional gains of Québec women, the authors in the *Cahiers de droit* denounce the conservatism and positivism of the judicial body in the interpretation of these gains. Provincial courts actively participate in putting up barriers that frustrate women's advances in the legal milieu. Federally appointed Québec judges have counteracted the progressive legislative interventions of Québec governments since the 1970s. The *Cahiers de droit* authors' critique of these institutional obstacles to feminist law reform thus emerges from an intersectional analysis—a critique of federal restrictions on Québec legal institutions as they affect women.

Québec courts' obstruction of the legislative relief intended by the compensatory allowance at dissolution of marriage constitutes a most eloquent example of judicial conservatism. In 1981, the Québec legislature enacted a provision to counteract the negative effects of the common Québec practice of the separation of matrimonial property. Under this regime, at dissolution of marriage, the spouse whose name did not appear on the title of the family property—most often the woman—found herself with no property. The *prestation compensatoire* was adopted to compensate the spouse by taking into consideration her contribution to the marriage. The Québec courts invoked a number of formal rules, including freedom of contract doctrine, to defeat the compensatory objectives of the legislation. In her *Cahiers de droit* article, Lucille Cipriani decries the stratagems of the courts. Both the Québec legislature (Loi modifiant le Code civil du Québec) and the Supreme Court of Canada (*Lacroix v. Valois*) intervened to reverse the restrictive Québec rulings.

From this perspective, the feminist question in Québec law does not emerge in terms of legislative reform because the legislation seems relatively satisfactory. At least five of the nine *Cahiers de droit* articles point to the conservatism and positivism of the Québec judicial body as the most important problem facing women's rights. This observation once again links the feminist struggle to the nat/cult program, by raising the constitutional issue of the separation of powers between federal and provincial governments and the federal power over judicial appointments.

The *Cahiers de droit* articles thus denounce the sad fate either of progressive legislation enacted in favour of women or of existing legislation, such as torts law, which held emancipatory potential for women but that judges refused to adapt to women's needs. By criticizing Québec judicial decisions, the authors reject the civil law stereotypes that traditionally privilege legislation and scholarly commentary as superior sources of law over case law. The Québec authors thus implicitly challenge the legislation/adjudication dichotomy to advance their feminist agenda. Furthermore, this Québec feminist critique of case law participates in a tradition of 'legal realism' familiar to the North American Anglo world and also part of the history of civil law—although much less known (Belleau, 1995, 1997). Moreover, like these 'realists', the Québec feminists' case law analyses, as illustrated in *Cahiers de droit*, criticize the biased and ideological underpinnings of adjudication. Again, Québec's feminists, through their intersectional strategy, enter the debates by shaking

Québec's legal academia and community. Thus, while the feminist authors of *Cahiers de droit* opted to remain within the confines of the private/public dichotomy in an effort to target the specifically Québec legal debate, the same authors deployed quite a different intersectional strategy in challenging the legislation/adjudication divide.

One could imagine still other strategies aimed at promoting feminist victories and at identifying failures in Canadian courts and legislatures. How are feminist arguments presented and received in the legislatures and courts of the country? Did different strategies succeed or fail in the Québec, the ROC, and federal legal institutional contexts? How were such strategies presented? Why did they fail or succeed? Michelle Boivin's essay daringly takes on this challenge by unravelling the victories and achievements of feminism through an analysis of Supreme Court of Canada decisions. Telling stories in French of feminist triumphs at the Canadian level actively participates in the intersectional strategy of gaining recognition in Québec's legal academia and of making feminist theory an unavoidable presence. Moreover, telling stories of victories engenders much needed feelings of hope and enthusiasm, which will prove essential to further emancipatory struggles.

In short, the situation of Québec legal feminists must be tied to a critique of the private/public and legislation/adjudication dichotomies and understood within the context of Québec's legal and institutional position within Canada— a position that is an artefact of conquest. Notwithstanding significant—and possibly incommensurable—political disagreements that divide Canada, emphasizing strategic intersectionality may encourage specific contextual understandings generating dialogues and alliances both within each setting and between Québec and ROC feminists.

Conclusion

Writing this chapter in English constitutes one more example of strategic intersectionality, entailing many risks. On the one hand, my efforts may be appropriated by those seeking arguments against feminism—either within Québec or in the ROC—and/or national or cultural identity politics. On the other hand, my feminist and nat/cult colleagues from all parts of Canada may feel disturbed by my desire to focus on strategic approaches. I have attempted to position myself delicately in the intersection between my own feminist and nat/cult loyalties. In conclusion, I draw on a conceptual framework useful to situate the position I wish to take in the debates about the interactions between feminism and nat/cult. I seek to play the role of the Double Critic, a juxtaposition of two opposed positions: the Apologist and the Informant.[7]

At one end of the spectrum, the Apologist feels compelled to justify and legitimate her ideological position to outsiders. For example, the feminist or nat/cult Apologist portrays feminism or nat/cult in the best light possible without revealing the conflicts among feminists or nat/cult proponents. She silences the 'bad' sides of her feminist or nat/cult selves and projects a straightforward, unambivalent description of feminist or nat/cult struggles and debates. Her lack of self-criticism makes her particularly vulnerable to denunciations, which she refuses to address in order to avoid weakening the position of the common front by denying the often already gaping fissures within her movement(s). In the present context, I may come across as the Apologist in many specific and intertwined ways. First, I may come across as an Apologist of ROC feminism because my own training in feminist analysis of law came from the Anglo-Saxon traditions. Second, I may come across as an Apologist for the ROC because I am a Canadian. Third, I may come across as an Apologist for Québec and for a distinct Québec feminist position because I believe in the distinctiveness of Québec's culture.

At the other end of the spectrum, the Informant, although committed to 'the cause' of the end of nat/cult or women's subordination, openly displays the wounds of deep internal feminist or nat/cult disputes and denounces the pitfalls of feminisms or nat/cult not only to those within the ranks but also to outsiders. Her attempt to present a sophisticated and complex portrayal of feminism or nat/cult with all their contradictions and oppositions leaves her frustrated and conflicted about her identity. Thus, in addition to being the eternal sceptic, she constantly questions her own sense of belonging. Insiders accuse her of providing valuable ammunition to the enemies of 'her camp'— which, indeed, she does. They view her as a traitor to her 'people' in her obtuse refusal to *laver son linge sale en famille* (keep the battles and the dirty secrets within the family). Here again, I may come across as the Informant in conflicting ways: (1) Informant in relation to Québec's claim for distinction in the feminist arena, being myself an insider of the legal academic circles in Québec; (2) Informant in relation to Anglo-feminism because of my sense of belonging to that tradition but also my uneasiness about it; or (3) Informant in relation to Québec's nat/cult positions because of my ambivalence towards them. The Double Critic, in the fashion of a conjurer, attempts to play the conflicting roles of Apologist and Informant simultaneously. This double posture does not consist in the propagandist's playing the Informant in the insider's network and reverting to the Apologist when confronted with the unsympathetic outsider or outright anti-feminist or anti-nationalist. Rather, the Double Critic attempts to draw a more nuanced and complicated version of the full picture while remaining committed to her identification with the nat/cult and feminist communities. The Double Critic performs on a tight rope with no safety net, always tempted by the allure of seeking refuge in just one of the two positions—or by the position of the propagandist.

In this chapter, I have attempted to take on the delicate and perilous role of the Double Critic towards the intersectional relations between feminist and nat/cult struggles in the Canadian context. My efforts were made in the spirit of opening up the intersections within and between these emancipatory struggles to create alternative sites for dialogues and coalitions around strategies.

Isolating feminist and nat/cult practices relegates Québec and ROC feminists to positions that resist such a cross-community engagement. Thinking about the intersections between feminism and nat/cult provides insight not only into the construction of Québec and ROC distinctiveness, but also a way to critique the essentialism and universalism that lead to our mutual isolation. Focusing on strategic intersectionality fosters renewed and shifting stratagems and alliances between feminists in Québec and the ROC, whose struggles will remain distinct and yet intertwined for a long time to come.

Notes

I would like to thank especially Nathaniel Berman but also Brenda Cossman, Diane Lamoureux, Louise Langevin, Teresa Scassa, and my research assistant, Johanne Carrier.

1. *Cahiers de droit* united the writings not only of Québec feminists writing in Quebec, but also of Québec women writing in Ontario (Des Rosiers) and of French Canadians outside of Québec (Boivin, Bouchard). Volume 30 of the *Alberta Law Review* combines the writings of English Canadians who teach or practise in all of the Canadian regions. The collection includes no texts from Québec. Except for Boivin and Langevin, both of whom wrote short introductory articles in *Cahiers de droit* as well as scholarly essays for the same issue, the years of publication for contributors to these two journals are not included in the parenthetical text references.

2. However, sometimes, the same phenomenon operates in a reverse way. Women are given more rights and power during the nat/cult emancipatory struggle, which they are denied after liberation.

3. Traditionally, the civil law and common law are held as fundamentally distinct systems of law that give rise to fundamentally different legal reasoning processes. The civil law is based on the codification of law enacted by legislatures; the common law, in contrast, is founded on the judgments and decisions of courts. However, the increased influence of case law in civil law countries and the corresponding augmentation of legislation in common law jurisdictions have led to the progressive coming together of these two legal families.

4. Interview with Louise Langevin.

5. In *Cahiers de droit*, the dominant approach, by far, is case law analysis. Seven of the nine essays adopt an analysis of judicial rulings (Boivin, 1995b; Des Rosiers; Langevin, 1995b; Bouchard; Lippel and Bienvenu; Cipriani;

Parent and Postolec). Only Lippel and Bienvenu's article focuses on legislative analysis. Lippel and Bienvenu, and in part Cipriani, emphasize empirical data.

6. The 10 *Alberta Law Review* articles offer much more varied and mixed types of analysis than those in *Cahiers de droit*. Munro, MacDonald, Hodgson, and Kobly offer a case law analysis, with the last two also focusing on an assessment of legislation. Five authors undertake a more theoretical approach (Noonan; Martin; Scassa; Bunting; Ross et al.). Finally, the articles of both Brockman and Ross et al. base their analysis on empirical findings.

7. The concepts of Apologist, Informant, and Double Critic have been conveyed to me by Lama Abu-Odeh in many contexts. They have been the subject of many fascinating discussions in the course of the last years but more recently at the 'Fin de NAIL' conference at Harvard Law School in May 1997. My own contribution to this analytical framework is to have argued in favour of deploying this conceptual tool not only in the context of territorial sites, such as Québec or the ROC, but to extend it to conceptual sites such as nat/cult issues or feminisms.

Part II

Constructing the (Hetero)Sexual Subject of Legal Discourse

Chapter 3

Justice and Law
Passion, Power, Prejudice, and So-called Pedophilia

Shannon Bell and Joseph Couture

This is an analysis of the tale of the 'child' pornography panic that gripped London, Ontario, in 1993. The axes of analysis are moral panic, gender, age, sexual orientation, and prostitution. The approach is deconstruction. The essay takes very seriously Jacques Derrida's contentious claim that 'Deconstruction is justice' (Derrida, 1992: 15). One of the main reasons that deconstruction is justice is that it opens space for others whose story/narrative is lost in the discourse of law. 'Deconstruction is on watch for the exclusion, the victims, the injustice produced by the law' (ibid., 86). The London courts, with the help of the psy professions (particularly the social workers and therapists at the London Family Court Clinic), the police, and the media, gendered the young male hustlers as victims and their gay male clients as abusers in a hegemonic narrative of justice. This narrative, we contend, is premised on homophobia, ageism, and whorephobia. The justice of deconstruction involves 'a preferential option for the disadvantaged, the differends, the losers, leftover, the little bits and fragments' (ibid.). Deconstruction as justice is an activity of 'making one's way along an *aporia*, along an almost impassable road, where the ground may at any moment shift' (ibid., 4). The child porn panic is such an *aporia*. The texts we read include court transcripts,[1] interviews, newspaper articles, and radio and film documentaries.

'Stories get told and read in different ways in different contexts. The consuming of a tale centres upon the different *social worlds* and *interpretive communities* who can hear the story in certain ways and hence not others' (Plummer, 1995: 22). When a story can be told, how it is told, who does the telling, and when it can be heard are all political matters. There are some sexual stories whose time has not yet come to be told; consequently, they are only narrated by dominant social authorities. Pedophilia is one of these stories. Ken Plummer observes that even the post-modern literature and theories on marginality, the other, and silenced voices do not open space to the voices of pedophiles (ibid., 119). In the moments, such as London, Ontario, where the story slips through into the public realm it is in the context of a moral panic so expansive that the category 'pedophile' is extended to include sex between adults and youth 15, 16, and 17 years old. The very category *hebephilia* has been erased. 'It means love for a *hebos* . . . by which was understood a young man who had passed the age of puberty' (Brandt, 1963: 414); this is the love of many of the men for the male teenagers in London.

This telling is an attempt to read the story of two groups of sexual others, groups othered by both hegemonic heterosexuality and acceptable homosexuality: johns and hustlers. The submerged story of these two groups can be read in the margins of the official court transcripts. The gaps in the submerged story are supplemented by Joseph Couture's interviews with the hustlers and his investigative reporting.[2] The format will be to outline the event, locate and theorize it in the context of moral panic, examine the play of four categories that were thrown into crisis—gender, age, sexual orientation, and prostitution—and then provide a deconstructive reading of four key trial transcripts.

The Event

The porn panic began when the London police came into the possession of two bags containing 40 videotapes found by a teenage boy fishing in the Thames River north of London, a southwestern Ontario city of 360,000. 'Official court documents say that a number of the tapes were Hollywood movies, some were legal commercial gay pornography, and some were homemade sex tapes of mostly teenage males and . . . one boy who was eleven years old' (Couture, 1995b: 16). Morality squad officers viewed the tapes, and one of the officers recognized one of the boys; as a result, a massive police investigation into a 'ring' of 'child pornographers' began.

The investigation was empowered by Canada's new controversial child pornography law (s. 163. 1 C.C.C.), which criminalizes any material that shows people who are under 18 or appear to be under 18 in sexual situations. The law, which came into effect on 1 August 1993, imposes a harsh maximum penalty of five years in prison for people found in possession of or distributing what is broadly defined as child pornography. Production of child pornography—visual, written, and auditory representations of anyone under 18 or appearing to be under 18—has a 10-year maximum penalty. The law provided the context for the police to orchestrate a national crusade against child pornography.

On 8 November 1993 Gary Gramlick and Edward Jewell, two middle-aged London men, were arrested on child pornography charges. On the same day, London Police Chief Julian Fantino held a press conference in London and announced that the London police had broken the largest child porn ring in Canada. He told the reporters that police had seized a large quantity of homemade pornographic tapes involving a number of boys, some of them small children. He announced that the London police force had launched Operation Scoop, a major investigation into organized child porn in the London area. The *London Free Press* began the media part of the campaign by naming the video-tape find by the police as an investigation into 'one of the largest kiddie porn rings in Canada' (Herbert, 1993: 1). The story was picked up by the Canadian Press, other newspapers, and radio and television stations. To the end, most of the media contextualized the investigation and charges as the 'London kiddie porn ring'.

With the arrest of Buryl Wilson six months later, on 28 May 1994, we heard that 'more than 800 videotapes have now been seized in this child-pornography ring' (CBC, 1995: 25); only later and less flamboyantly was it indicated that the tapes were 'mostly Hollywood movies, *National Geographic* specials and programs taped off television' (ibid.). In fact, 'none of the 800 tapes has been charged. What has been charged in the haul . . . is one eight-millimetre film, some albums of snapshots, and some gay magazines of the sort you can buy in bookstores' (ibid., 25–6). The fact that the seized videotapes were not chargeable as child porn or any type of porn did not in the least affect their currency in the child porn panic: the London Chief of Police gave a press conference on 29 May, surrounded by the hundreds of seized tapes. This image of the Chief of Police surrounded by what was represented as child porn got provincial funding for Project Guardian, the province-wide joint-forces Child Pornography Task Force. 'What touched off "Project Guardian" . . . was not pornography but rather a public-relations image, a picture of a mountain of tapes' (ibid., 26).

Moral Panic

'London, Ontario [was] in the grip of what sociologists call a moral panic. It was generated by the police, with the help of therapists and social workers, and it's been fuelled by the media, particularly the *London Free Press* (the only newspaper in town) and London's leading radio station' (ibid., 17). This was picked up and reported by media throughout Ontario.

Sex, morality, and paranoia coalesce in moral panics. Fears attach to some sexual activity or population; these fears are channelled into political action and social change. The standard targets are pornographic materials, prostitutes, and erotic deviants. The London moral sex panic focused on pornographic materials (the so-called Child Porn Law) and targets erotic deviants: gay men, prostitutes/hustlers under 18, hebephiles. The hysteria mounts the closer the sexual activity gets to or can be portrayed as getting to children. Perhaps that is why 'seventeen year olds at the height of their sexual powers are called children' (ibid., 38) in the London porn panic.

What are the features that mark an event a moral panic? According to Erich Goode and Nachman Ben-Yehuda, five social segments play into constructing a moral panic: (1) the press, (2) the public, (3) agents of social control, i.e., law enforcement officials, lawmakers, (4) politicians and legislators, and (5) action groups (Goode and Ben-Yehuda, 1994: 24). In the London child porn panic the key agents who constructed the moral panic were the police and the media, with strong support from social workers and Crown attorneys.

The media, in a moral panic, focus exaggerated attention on the event, engaging in the distortion of facts and the stereotyping of the 'perpetrators'. London's leading radio station made the following constructions in its news broadcasts and talk shows:

> . . . child pornography ring . . . the perpetrators of this child-pornography ring . . . to help ferret out child pornography in this province . . . enormous reality of the most recent development in this child-pornography ring . . . the London police in this child-porn investigation . . . the latest developments in this incredible child-pornography ring . . . (CBC, 1995: 1)

'In the first year, *The London Free Press* [ran] over a hundred stories on what they continue[d] to call "the child-pornography ring", most of them written by [one] police reporter' (ibid.). Although the press continued to give the impression that the police were breaking a child pornography ring, only one person was charged with making child pornography and only a handful of the 60 men arrested were charged with possession of child pornography, and none of the pornography was made for commercial purposes. The child pornography ring turned out to be a group of teenage boys who introduced one another to men. Very few of the men even knew each other. The most common charge was (s. 212(4)) obtaining sexual services of a person under 18 for consideration. This charge involved primarily gay men who were alleged to have had sex for money or gifts with teenage hustlers. Of the 60 men arrested, 58 have been gay or bisexual men accused of homosexual acts with boys, the majority of whom were 15–18 years old.

The Homophile Association of London, Ontario (HALO), a London area gay group, the only group to challenge the London police and media, in its report, 'On Guard: A Critique of Project Guardian', claimed that police operations were an organized attack on the gay community. HALO called for three corrections to the reporting of the police investigation: (1) 'the investigation and arrests are not primarily concerned with pornography, (2) the majority of the men charged as a result of Project Guardian did not know each other and therefore could not be part of a ring which "passed around boys", (3) the boys involved are not primarily pre-teens' (HALO, 1996: 21).

London media simultaneously fed into and constructed a not so unconscious link between gay sex and pedophilia and prostitution, a linkage premised on dominant understandings of gender, sexual orientation, and prostitution. Goode and Ben-Yehuda (1994: 26) contend that for a moral panic to take off '[t]here must be some latent potential on the part of the public to react to a given issue to begin with, some raw material out of which a media campaign can be built.' This latent potential was the raw material of genderism (an essentialist conception of appropriate gender behaviour), ageism, homophobia, and whorephobia.

In terms of law enforcement, Goode and Ben-Yehuda note that in a moral panic '[t]ies between and among local police forces are established and strengthened, and those between the local and national levels of law enforcement are activated'. This certainly was the case when Operation Scoop became province-wide Project Guardian. Goode and Ben-Yehuda also note that '[e]fforts are made by officers to broaden the scope of law enforcement and increase its intensity; punitive and over zealous actions already taken are justified on the basis of the enormity of the threat the society faces' (ibid., 27). The London police pushed the event to crisis proportions with three images repeatedly presented in police press conferences and reported by the media.

The first image was the suggestion of organized underground crime in the often repeated phrase, 'the child pornography ring'. Police Chief Julian Fantino justified the repetition of the phrase in a CBC *Ideas* interview with Gerald Hannon, proclaiming '[w]hether we call it child pornography, sexual exploitation, or whether we get technical and quote a criminal code section, what's the difference?' Hannon responded, 'I think there is a fear with the suggestion of "ring", that there was an organization . . . at [a] level far beyond what I understand to be really only two men who knew each other.' Fantino conceded that there was no ring of men 'but a whole lot of boys who . . . networked amongst themselves.' Speaking for the police, Chief Fantino concluded, 'we can . . . put whatever definition we want on it' (CBC, 1995: 35).

The second image was the pictorial representation of Fantino surrounded by 800 videotapes, the implication being that these tapes represented the biggest haul in child porn in North America; this representation was repeated a number of times in electronic and print media. The image revealed the supposed enormity of the problem of child porn in London and quickly led to provincial government funding and an expansion of police investigative powers to cover all of Ontario.

The main method of the investigation, which began with police identifying the youths involved in the Gramlick and Jewell videos, consisted of repeatedly questioning the youth regarding their involvement with additional men, which is how most of the men came to be charged with prostitution, sexual touching, and anal sex with someone under 18. The police extended this practice under Project Guardian to a blitz of the gay community, with a total of nearly 2,000 interviews. Couture points out '[a]lmost everyone knew someone who had been questioned by the police' (Couture, 1995b: 22). The investigation turned into what could be termed a witch-hunt, with the mere suggestion that someone might be involved in child pornography being enough for police to procure a search warrant. Ex-friends and ex-lovers were turning each other into the police (ibid.). The police, according to three hustlers interviewed on the *Ideas* series, 'The Trials of London', appear to have initiated and deployed sanctions and rewards for the youths' testimony against clients. Three youths (D.A., S.B., and M.N.) repeatedly interviewed by the police disclosed the following on national radio:

D.A.: They called me down . . . probably about seven times . . . and asked me about mostly the same people.

S.B.: I don't remember myself saying things weeks later because they—it's almost as if they've worked their way somehow of getting you to say something which you weren't planning . . . to say, and then later on you don't remember what you said because it wasn't important to you, and then they use that against you. You know, well, 'You said this. You know you could get charged if you hold back information.'

Journalist Joseph Couture: Did they tell you that you could be charged if you didn't give them the information that they wanted?

S.B.: Yeah.

D.A.: . . . they didn't say that to me. They just said: You know it will help *you* out a lot more, the more information you give the less you're going to get in trouble, you know, and all this shit.

S.B.: They said I could be charged.

Joseph Couture: Did they say with what?

S.B. I think it was prostitution.

CBC *Ideas* producer Max Allen: But nobody in London has been charged with prostitution, since it's not illegal. Selling sex, *per se*, is not a crime. It's only a crime to *buy* sex from somebody who's under 18.

(M.N., who is now 19, is involved in cases against at least six different men.)

M.N.: They said I could be charged with prostitution, but I never knew there was no law about that. (CBC, 1995: 29)

The third image that fuelled the moral panic and heightened police investigation was the mental image of 'victims as young as eight', whose existence was evoked in a number of news reports. On 8 February 1994 the *London Free Press* ran a report headlined 'Seven-year-old Latest, Youngest Victim in Case'. The report claimed that the seven-year-old and a friend were playing in the Thames River when they were approached by Alan Seymour, who was alleged to have waded into the water, fondled, spanked, and given the boy $5. Seymour was charged with one count of sexual assault. A week later, on 16 February, the *Free Press* ran a second story. It reported police statements that the same two boys, both nine, were the latest victims. According to the police report, between 1 September and 3 November 1993 the two boys were dragged into an apartment and sexually assaulted by Johnathon MacEachern, who was charged with two counts of forcible confinement and two counts of sexual assault.[3] The boys and their families stated on the CBC *Ideas* series that the events never took place. The following is what one of the boys said about his interrogation by the police.

Joseph Couture: So what happened when you sat down in the room?

Boy: They just asked me questions. They asked me if I remembered anything, and what happened. I said I couldn't remember anything, and it didn't happen to me.

Joseph Couture: So you're saying no one ever assaulted you sexually.

Boy: Right. . . .

Joseph Couture: Did you ever tell anybody that nothing happened?

Boy: Yeah. I told the police that nothing happened, and it's the truth. (CBC, 1995: 41–2)

All the charges relating to these two alleged incidents were withdrawn. The *London Free Press* reported the charges but it never reported that the charges were dropped, leaving the public with the understanding that there were eight-year-old victims of child porn. MacEachern remains a pedophile predator in the eyes of the public. It is Canadian policy to publish accusations. London's Project Guardian issued press releases about their charges, and the London media publicized them: names, addresses, and often occupations (ibid., 46).

Politicians and legislators, in a moral panic situation, take 'immediate and considerable interest in disturbances in their own constituencies' (Goode and Ben-Yehuda, 1994: 28). This is evidenced in the Ontario Solicitor-General's agreement to finance the intensified province-wide Project Guardian. Goode and Ben-Yehuda claim that '[m]oral panics generate appeals, campaigns, and finally, "fully fledged action groups" which arise to cope with the newly-existing threat' (ibid.). In the case of the London moral panic no action group arose to support the project; rather, support came from the traditional authorities: the police, the media, an extensive social workers' network, and the public by their complicity with the reported story. The only action group to challenge the London police and media was HALO, which named the child porn ring a fictional creation of the police, the media, and the social welfare/abuse industries (HALO, 1996: 5–25). In addition to the efforts of HALO leaders Richard Hudler and Clarence Crossman, the most effective challenge in the media came from four individuals in journalism, broadcasting, and filmmaking: Joseph Couture, Gerald Hannon, Max Allen, and John Greyson. Couture and Hannon are freelance journalists, Allen a producer of the CBC *Ideas* series, and Greyson an independent filmmaker.

Categories in Crisis: Gender, Age, Sexual Orientation, Prostitution

The London sexual moral panic was filtered through four categories: gender, age, sexual orientation, and prostitution. Gender is a slippery category full of expectations, codes of behaviour, and rules of interaction. In many ways it is similar to Derrida's concept of justice. Derrida understands justice as that which 'exceeds calculation, rules', as infinite, *à la* Levinas, 'that owed to the other, before any contract'. This gets narrowed in justice as law to that which is calculable, 'a system of regulated and coded prescriptions' (Derrida, 1992: 27, 22, 25). Law intersects with the practice/power of hegemonic heterosexuality to produce knowledge about gender. Core determinants in social gender identity are the others one is bodily engaged with (sexual orientation) and the sexual acts involved in this engagement. Gayle Rubin uses two metaphorical representations, the erotic pyramid and the charmed circle, to depict the stratification of gender and sexual practices according to a hierarchical system of moral value that structures modern Western society.

> Marital, reproductive heterosexuals are alone at the top of the erotic pyramid . . . below are unmarried monogamous heterosexuals in couples, followed by most other heterosexuals. Solitary sex floats ambiguously. . . . Stable, long-term lesbian and gay male couples are verging on respectability, but bar dykes and promiscuous gay men are hovering just above the groups at the very bottom of the pyramid. The most despised sexual castes currently include transsexuals, transvestites, fetishists, sadomasochists, sex workers . . . and the lowest of all, those whose eroticism transgresses generational boundaries. (Rubin, 1984: 279)

The sexual value system dichotomizes sex into good and bad, normal and abnormal, natural and unnatural. 'Good', 'normal', 'natural' sexuality falls inside the charmed circle; other sexuality is at the outer limits of this circle, and outside the limit is intergenerational sex. Combine intergenerational sex with commercial sex and homosexuality and what occurs is in the realm of moral excess, the fuel of 'erotic hysteria' (ibid., 271) and moral panic.

Rubin compares the dominant sexual morality, the heterophallic morality of the law, to ethnocentrism: 'This kind of sexual morality has more in common with ideologies of racism than with true ethics. It grants virtue to the dominant groups, and relegates vice to the underprivileged.' A sexual ethics based on justice, the obligation one owes to the other, should assess particular sexual acts by 'the way partners treat one another, the level of mutual consideration, the presence or absence of coercion, and the quantity and quality of the pleasure they provide' (ibid., 283).

But gender, sexual orientation, and age get in the way, making it difficult to recognize that a 16-year-old male prostitute and a 50-year-old male client, engaging in commercial sex, who treat one another with respect, dignity, and friendship are just as ethical as a monogamous same-aged heterosexual couple, or a lesbian couple, who treat one another with respect, dignity, and friendship.

If the body is a 'boundary, a surface whose permeability is politically regulated, a signifying practice within a cultural field of gender hierarchy and compulsory heterosexuality', and it is the 'acts of gender [that] create the idea of gender, and without those acts, there would be no gender at all' (Butler, 1990: 139, 140), then one could read the moral hysteria around acts of same-sex prostitution between men and teenage youths as not just the fear for the corruption of children, but as a fear for the corruption of gender. 'Good, normal, natural' gender acts for young men do not involve allowing older men to perform fellatio on them for money or pleasure and do not involve young men performing fellatio on older men for money or pleasure.

Although age appeared as the dominant category in the police and media reports, gender always accompanied this representation. Moral outrage overtly focused on age, but fear solidified around gender and what 'normal' sexual acts are expected to accompany gender.

Child, like gender, is a contested category, a term whose meaning shifts according to context, a category-in-crisis. It is a lived category that since the passage of the child pornography law has been reified to refer to anyone under the age of 18. In a parallel case, occurring at the same time and involving a 22-year-old man and two 14-year-old boys who made two sexually explicit videos just months before the child porn law came into effect, the Judge, Bovard J., contended: '[Child] is one of those terms that everyone thinks they know the meaning of, but no one can define clearly for all circumstances. Its definition varies in different legal and non-legal contexts' (*R. v. McGowan*, 1995: 9). The currency invested in the term and category of 'child' in this case and in the cases of the London men is great: 'category-in-crisis, men-in-jail' (Bell, 1997: 226).

Bovard J. argues that prior to the 1 August 1993 child pornography law there was no general definition of child in the Criminal Code. In the judge's words:

> It is difficult to determine whether at 14 years old the two persons in the video are among the persons that would fall into the category of children as the term is used in *Butler*. It is somewhat artificial to state an age at which a young person stops being a child. Persons develop at different rates. One person can demonstrate the characteristics we associate with a child at the age of seventeen, sixteen, or fifteen. On the other hand, some persons at those ages have developed more rapidly, and do not demonstrate those characteristics. So at what age is a person no longer a child? (*R. v. McGowan*, 1995: 10)

Bovard J. shatters the presumption at the heart of the child porn law: that society can know when childhood ends and adulthood begins, that this moment is the same for everyone, and it is precisely at age 18. With the new child porn law the answer to Bovard's question 'at what age is a person no longer a child?' loses its ambiguity. It is 18 for everyone.

Bovard J. recalls the *Oxford English Dictionary* definition of child as 'a young person of either sex below the age of puberty. One who is considered to have the characteristic manners or attainments of a child' (ibid.). The judge notes that Section 153(2) of the Criminal Code 'defines "young person" as a person 14 years of age and more, but under 18 years' (ibid., 12). He cites the Young Offenders Act, in which '"child" is defined as a "person who is, or in the absence of evidence to the contrary, appears to be under the age of 12 years"' (ibid., 13). These sections have little relevance to the men in London because, although the age of consent is 14 and all the youths on the witness stand, when cross-examined, acknowledged that they consented to sex with the men, the age of consent 'for consideration for sexual services' [s. 212(4) C.C.C.], i.e., prostitution, is 18. 'Consideration' includes almost any exchange of material goods: money, food, clothing, a place to stay, computer games, cigarettes, alcohol, drugs; 'as if money [and all its derivatives] made an otherwise tolerable act so intolerable that prison must be part of the answer' (Bell, 1997: 216).

The bulk of the charges in London's so-called child pornography ring are for using the sexual services of teenage prostitutes. It is legal for an adult to have sex with someone 14 or over, providing the teenager is not given anything that can be construed as payment. Two laws deal with sexual contact with a person under 18: s. 151 C.C.C. (sexual interference) and s. 152 C.C.C. (sexual touching). Before 1989 it was legal to pay someone 16 or over for sexual services. After 1989 the age was raised to 18. This change sat unenforced, more or less, until the passage of the child porn law in 1993. 'At that point the consent laws began to be enforced, almost like an ex-post-facto law, to clients of male hustlers' (Bell, 1997: 217).

How can one discern whether the law was applied in a gender-biased manner to hustlers and clients? First, we can determine if there were any instances where female prostitutes and male clients were treated differently; second, we can examine the response of the London police to female teenagers in the same situation as the male teenagers.

There are two instances in London where female prostitutes and male clients have been treated differently by the London police apparatus, and there have been no media reports of the charging of clients of female teenage prostitutes in London, even though teenage female prostitutes have as strong a presence in London as teenage hustlers, perhaps stronger.

In November 1994, at precisely the time of the burgeoning moral panic, the London police raided the Exec-U-Stress massage parlour. Ten 'girls' between the ages of 14 and 17 were working there. Massages were conducted topless or nude and included 'sexual services for consideration'. Although the owner was charged with a number of sexual offences involving 'girls' under 18 and with keeping a common bawdy house, 'none of the heterosexual clients were ever charged for their involvement with female "children"' (Couture, 1995b: 20). A list of customers was seized during a police search of the premises, but the police maintained that they were unable to charge the customers because the girls would not co-operate (ibid.). However, as reported by three hustlers on the CBC *Ideas* series, 'The Trials of London', the boys also did not want to co-operate until the police introduced the threat of punishment (prostitution charges) and the reward of the provincial victims' compensation fund with maximum compensation set at $25,000.

The second instance in which a gendered double standard is discernible is the case of Officer Gateman, of the London police. The incident involves a 17-

year-old female escort who alleged forced anal and vaginal intercourse with Gateman and a male friend. The HALO report, 'On Guard: A Critique of Project Guardian', states: 'This appeared to be an opportunity to lay charges similar to those laid against men charged in the Project Guardian Investigation: sex for consideration with someone under 18, anal intercourse with someone under 18, anal intercourse with more than two people present, and sexual assault' (HALO, 1996: 16). However, '[t]he 17-year-old . . . was told by the crown attorney's office that no criminal charges would be laid . . . because [she] was working as an escort, [so] a jury would not believe [her]' (Herbert, 1994: 2). Gateman was initially subject only to an internal police investigation, which resulted in his demotion. Charges were eventually laid after the woman persuaded a Justice of the Peace to lay criminal charges.

What is at question is why a 17-year-old female escort would be less believable in court than a 17-year-old hustler. The answer is not clear: is it the assumption that females lie about sexual assault and, thus, the assailant is presumed innocent until proven otherwise? This is particularly mystifying given that most of the teenage boys were claiming consensual sex, yet their partners were charged. It is even more incomprehensible when one considers that male prostitution is arguably less exploitative then female prostitution:

> [M]ale prostitution, or hustling, is different from female prostitution.
>
> The differences are as follows: unlike prostitution involving women, generally speaking there are no pimps [this is not to suggest that the majority of female prostitution involves pimps] in the realm of homosexual hustling (and those engaged in it are more independent, less under threat); sexual acts between males—this is true of homosexuality generally, and also applies to hustling—tend to be more reciprocal or equal than those between men and women (I'm especially thinking about acts of anal intercourse, and their symbolic as well as actual effects) and thus some of the disparities of power in the encounter are more likely to be evened out; the question of desire in homosexual prostitution encounters is more complex than our stereotype of unreciprocal desire in heterosexual prostitution; finally (and this is more of a generalization based on my observations than an established fact), relationships between customers and young men in homosexual prostitution strike me as more 'sociable' . . . than relationships in heterosexual prostitution. (Persky, 1995: 206)

This seems to be corroborated by one of the young men in his cross-examination in the preliminary inquiry in *R. v. Chappell* (1994: 47):

> Defence Attorney: Selling sexual services for money you knew was against the law?
> Youth: Yes, for women.
> Defence Attorney: Not for men as far as you were concerned?

Youth: I didn't know you'd classify it for men. I thought it would . . . just call it being gay.

Rubin (1984), supporting Persky's characterization of the difference between hustling and female prostitution, suggests that 'heterosexual exchanges have more potential to reflect and reproduce the gender inequalities of the social structure.' Rubin stresses that the sex industry reflects the sexism of the society as a whole (Bell, 1994, 1995). This being the case, it would seem that if a justice system were concerned about righting the wrongs of social gender inequalities, there would be more, or at least the same, concern for teenage female prostitutes, especially if one of them had filed a charge of sexual assault.

In a London Family Court Clinic study of 126 cases of sexual abuse to determine what happens once these cases reach the court, the finding was that '[w]hen a boy was the victim, there was always a conviction' (CBC, 1995: 14). The Family Court Clinic reported, 'We were alarmed to discover that the victimization of male victims attracted much longer sentences compared with the abuse of female victims. . . . the sentences were on average twice as long when boys were involved. . . . This is not because the abuse of boys is a more widespread or more serious problem; just the reverse is the case.' Maureen Reid, a London Family Court Clinic social worker, hypothesizes: 'our society is saying that there's somehow an acceptance of females as victims, and that somehow it's more of an affront to hurt our male children' (ibid.). Our hypothesis would be different: we think the increased penalty for the 'victimization' of boys is mainly related to the crime being seen as causing the likely breakdown of rigid male gender identity for the boys and potentially affecting sexual orientation.

Max Allen points out in the *Ideas* series that 'London's victims are all boys . . . not one of Project Guardian's cases has involved girls. And it's not because there aren't girls in the sex business in London.' He presents documentation from people living near the heterosexual stroll that girls younger than 15 were working on a regular basis, 'yet during the busiest hours . . . between ten and midnight, there was never a policeman in sight' (ibid., 37). What has taken place in the London porn panic is a gendered application of s. 212(4) of the Criminal Code and of justice. A reading of London court transcripts corroborates this gendered application of justice.

London Court Transcripts: A Deconstructive Reading

The following is a deconstructive reading of four key court transcripts—*R. v. Gramlick* (trial), *R. v. Waite* (preliminary inquiry), *R. v. Storey* (preliminary inquiry), and *R. v. MacEachern* (proceedings on application). Deconstruction, as a way of reading texts, focuses on the inconsistencies of a text, its ambiguities, gaps, and silences. There are two basic strategies of deconstruction: (1) the inversion of hierarchies; (2) the liberation of the text from the author. The inversion of hierarchies involves a pivot of what is present, i.e., presented in the text, to get to what is absent, a trace of something other that will undo the dominant argument. The point is not to establish a new hierarchy, but to destabilize the old and see what happens when it is reversed. The liberation of the text from the author means that a text is no longer approached as a representation of the author's intent. The emphasis, in deconstruction, has shifted from authorial intent to the position of the reader approaching the text.

A deconstructive reading provides a means for critiquing existing legal doctrines by showing that they are not Truth, they are not Objective, but come from particular positions in the world. In the four court cases under scrutiny the particular position is the dominant position of heterosexuality, which encompasses ageism, genderism, homophobia, and whorephobia. What we are curious in pursuing is the *other* story, that of hustlers and the johns, from their position, a position buried in the official reading of the court cases.

It was the charging of Gary Gramlick that touched off the child porn panic in London. Gramlick's convictions include making child pornography (s. 163.1), making obscene material (s. 163[1][a]), possession of child pornography (s. 163.1[4]), and five counts of counselling a person under 14 to sexual touching (s. 152). Some interesting facts are to be found in the Gramlick case. Of the 261 tapes (found in the river and in Gramlick's apartment), 57 contained identifiable and chargeable incidents, 33 of which were associated with the accused (*R. v. Gramlick*, 1994: 112). The original massive discovery of pornography is thus narrowed to 33 tapes. All the tapes have the date of the filming superimposed on the screen. Is time a fetish for Gramlick, making one wonder about time and boys—'Do you have some time?'—or is it simply the technology of his video camera? The ruse is that it makes it very easy for the police and court to determine the exact age of the boys at the time of the taping and to determine which tapes were produced after 1 August 1993, when the child porn law came into effect. The tapes were made with the boys' and teenagers' knowledge. Gramlick could be heard in the background in some of the tapes giving instruction as to activities. He never participated. The content of each of the numbered films was briefly narrated in court by the counsel for the Crown. Typical narrations can be found in videos T–40 and T–77.

Tape T–40: 6 June 1992, 9:55 p.m.
N. [13 years old] was seen to remove his clothing and begin to masturbate in front of the television while a cartoon was playing. There were then different camera angles with closeups of the boy's genitalia, until the end of the footage, when the film captured the complainant dressing. (*R. v. Gramlick*, 1994: 119)

Tape T–77: 13 July 1992, 4:02 p.m.
Both N. and G. [who is sixteen and two months] are on the couch clothed with exposed penises, masturbating. G. then comes to the couch and pulls down

N's pants and performs fellatio, and then G. removes his clothing, and that is followed by N. fellating G. N. then later lies on top of G. and has anal intercourse with him. (Ibid., 121)

How to read the tapes? Is it shocking to see or read of those not normally seen in sexual situations engaging in activities that for many are on the margins of 'good' adult sex? The police described their viewing 'as one of the most unpleasant tasks . . . looking at this garbage' (Herbert, 1993: A1). Max Allen, on the CBC *Ideas* series, described the videotapes as 'show[ing] in-your-face teenage sex' (CBC, 1995: 20). It seems that for the boys it was 'normal' activity that they engaged in for fun and money—$30–$50. The reader learns that 'there was not violence or threats, but the victims were always rewarded with money and gifts' (*R. v. Gramlick*, 1994: 113). The sex was consensual, except that the participants under 14 cannot legally give consent; those over 14 can consent to the sex but not to the filming or the money. The age range of the 12 youths involved in the post 1 August 1993 filming was 11 to 18 years old. Three were under age 14; nine were between 14 and 18.

Gramlick was reported to have informed his lawyer that he wanted to protect the boys from having to testify (ibid., 163). Neither Gramlick nor the boys testified in this case; excerpts from some of the boys' victim impact statements are read by both the prosecution and the defence attorneys. The reader learns that Gramlick 'would take some of the victims . . . on deliveries with him, having befriended them' (ibid., 115). The reader also learns that Gramlick met some of the parents and loaned money to the mother of one boy (ibid., 116). The Crown prosecutor repeatedly painted a picture of the boys as coming from economically disadvantaged families, broken homes, being mentally challenged. What is the need of this characterization if it is a crime to produce representations of youth under 18? Would it be any less of a crime to produce representations of wealthy youth with high IQs and two parents? There is an effort to portray Gramlick in the same light: as someone who was raped on two occasions, the first time when he was 11 (ibid., 155), as someone who also came from a broken home, who was hospitalized for nerves after his mother died, and who has been on social assistance ever since (ibid., 162). What is the relevance of this information? Would his crime be any less or more if he had not been raped, if he came from a two-parent family, if he did not suffer severe depression after the death of his mother, if, rather than being on social assistance, he was earning $150,000 as a corporate executive? Both the Crown prosecutor and Gramlick's lawyer are painting a similar picture. Could it be to set the man and the boys as outsiders, outside the charmed circle of normal society both in their daily life and in their sexual activities, and thus 'not-I', not a threat to the stability of the dominant gender construction?

Gramlick, it appears, is concerned for the boys, that they will not have to suffer the embarrassment of testifying in court. We also learn from the transcript that '[t]here wasn't filming every time. There were a lot of young men who were fed by him and who stayed overnight . . . when they had no place to go' (ibid., 164). What do the boys have to say about Gramlick and their interaction with him? The following are excerpts from three victim impact statements:

D.B.

[A] depressed and withdrawn adolescent with limited social and verbal skills. . . . He is estranged from his family. He comes from an impoverished financial situation, which in the conclusion of the author set the stage for his vulnerability to the offers of money for sexual favours. . . . he made several hundreds of dollars on occasion, through perhaps other sources as well. . . . the author of the report sees a dependency on these men, an outlet for social contact, which he didn't otherwise have. Perhaps a sad comment. 'A part of him he says felt valued by Mr. G., because he was wanted for something'. He goes on to say, 'he has flashbacks, upset, depression', and sadly again, he cannot categorically say he wouldn't involve himself with Gramlick again. Fond memories of going to an amusement park as compensation. The conclusion . . . a damaged adolescent, traumatized sexually. Craving relationships he developed from an emotional point of view. Long term treatment forecasted in the form of psychiatric counselling.

D.K.

Court: What seems to be different in Mr. K's victim impact report is his use and dependency on drugs before and during any of the sexual encounters.

Prosecutor: [A]ccording to him in the victim impact, he had that problem perhaps in any event, but the funds provided the source to sustain that substance abuse problem . . . one gets the impression . . . that perhaps he used them prior to some of these events, and he has low average skills . . . he . . . appears as the most street wise of the group, but if one looks at . . . the last full paragraph, 'on the occasions when cracks appeared in his self-protective veneer, he seemed anxious, fearful, insecure and confused' and . . . that's proven empirically by some . . . specific psychological testing he was put through. The family was economically disadvantaged and again sadly 'felt a certain pride as he started to offer small supplements to the family income'.

A.M.

[T]he youngest of the victims . . . brought [Gramlick] home to meet his mother, who apparently . . . said, 'he seemed all right, nice and everything.' . . . Clinical findings for him, diminutive, fair haired eleven year old. Four foot seven inches in height and seventy-three pounds. Somewhat unable, it would appear from the report, to deal with the victimization and appears to not want to talk too much about it. A. maintains he believed the sexual activities . . . were normal because so many people, both children and adults seemed to be quite openly involved. . . . sadly, A. does not appear to feel that he's been victimized but rather describes his dealings with Mr. Gramlick as a business transaction. . . . the conclusions, this boy will require intensive therapy for a whole range of problems, and the conclusion that he was systematically socialized to view sex as a commodity, which afforded him the illusion of power. (Ibid., 172–5)

The victim impact statements of the teenagers were not written by them, but narrated to therapists and other professionals. The research co-ordinator at the London Family Court Clinic explains: 'victim impact statements . . . are written by clinicians who have a lot of experience in . . . child victimization' (CBC, 1995: 22). There is 'the victim's version of the story' and 'what we think it means' (ibid., 22). What escapes through the confines of clinical interpretation, the normalized gloss of the psy professions, is the boys' ambivalence about their relationship with Gramlick. D.B. is upset and depressed, yet has fond memories of an outing with Gramlick to an amusement park; he would not say that he would not involve himself with Gramlick again. The conclusion for the therapist is a damaged adolescent who requires long-term treatment because he does not realize his full victimization. Yet, if we listen to what the youth is actually saying he does not consider himself victimized by Gramlick.

There is an absence in the court version of D.K.'s victim impact statement, which is present in the full version of the victim impact statement: 'D. considers Mr. Gramlick to be a friend with whom he sustained a relationship, based on Mr. Gramlick's concerns for his well-being' (London Family Court Clinic, 1994: 2). In the case of the youngest, the court report of the victim impact statement makes it clear that he does not feel he is a victim, but he sees his interaction with Gramlick as a business transaction. From Judge Livingstone's Reasons for Sentence, one learns that A.M. described Gramlick as 'a nice normal old man' (*R. v. Gramlick*, 1994: 200). It seems that it is difficult for the court system—the London Family Court Clinic therapists and social workers, the police, the lawyers—actually to listen to the youths' experience without recoding it in the dominant knowledge field's assumptions about gender and age behaviour and sexual orientation.

The Waite case contains perhaps the most bizarre human interaction. Norman Waite, an elementary school principal in London, pleaded guilty to 11 counts of paying for the sexual services of males under 18, three counts of sexual touching (males under 14), and one count of sexual assault. What stands out in this case are the incongruities. On the one hand, we read of Waite driving the youths to the locations where they purchased drugs, providing them with the alcohol they requested, taking them to McDonald's, letting one youth drive his car, taking one out for his birthday, buying the youths the jackets and track suits they requested, paying them for oral and anal sex. On the other hand, we read of him anally raping at least two youths when they had drunkenly passed out, one at least twice. The same youth consensually engaged in anal intercourse with Waite when conscious. In his testimony the youth, who was 15 at the time of the occurrences, states, 'I was peeved about him touching me, having anal intercourse while I was sleeping' (*R. v. Waite*, 1994: 17). Then the youth reports that the next time he saw Waite was on his buddy's birthday, when he and two other youths were at Waite's for 'sort of like . . . D.'s birthday party' (ibid. 18).

It could be argued, and this is the dominant construction, that the youths were not aware of their victimization and kept returning for the alcohol, gifts, and money. Yet when the youth felt abused by having non-consensual anal intercourse, he informed Waite. The youth himself makes a distinction between forced anal intercourse and anal intercourse that he agrees to. We learn from the youth that he 'had been at . . . Waite's house about 200 times for sexual services. . . . Fifty times anal with him' (ibid., 26). In the Waite case one could read the youths as being both exploited and not exploited—the exploitation that takes place is outside the categories of gender, age, and same-sex sexual activities (although it is these categories that positioned the presence of the youths for the exploitation to take place). It is exploitation of the body: the person to whom it was done could be female and 35 years old, it could be a heterosexual act, and it would be exploitation of the body. The question, then, becomes, is it seen as being more grave when the age is 15, the gender male, and the sexual orientation involved in the act is same-sex?

The *R. v. Storey* case provides a striking difference to the Waite case. Storey was charged with three counts of sexual assault for touching the lap of a 14- to 15-year-old, the leg of a 17-year-old, and the genitals of a 17-year-old. The first youth testified that Storey stopped when 'I punched or pushed him' (*R. v. Storey*, 1994: 11). The second told the court 'he reached over a couple of times and touched me . . . I just pushed him away and tell him no, but then he'd stop' [ibid., 15). The third also stated that 'I said don't. . . . it seemed to be effective' (ibid., 31). One could derive from this case that Storey, although misguided in his attempts at initiating a sexual encounter, listened to and respected the wishes of the youths. When they said no, he stopped.

There is something very odd at the close of the Storey preliminary inquiry transcripts: the Crown counsel, after the cross-examination, re-examines the third youth with one question: 'Is there anyone in the courtroom right now that you've spoken to about this matter, media or otherwise?' The youth responds, 'No, other than the officer' (ibid., 40). If one goes outside the text of the preliminary inquiry one learns that the youths spoke to the media and that the police in fact pressured two of the youths to testify against Storey. One teenager signed a statutory declaration that was forwarded to *Xtra* and the CBC *Ideas* program: it was printed in *Xtra* and part of the statement was read on the *Ideas* series. In it the youth states:

No sexual assault took place between myself and Mr. Derrick Storey. There was never any sexual contact between myself and Derrick Storey. I did not discuss Derrick Storey with the police or lodge a complaint of sexual assault with the police. I make this declaration of my own free and independent will. (Couture, 1994: 21)

Joseph Couture, who was at the Storey hearing, reports:

An hour before giving testimony at Storey's Oct. 4 preliminary hearing the teen again repeated his story. 'I'm going to tell the truth. I don't know what the police are talking about.'

He was then taken into an interview room by a police officer. The teen later appeared in court and testified that he had been sexually assaulted by the defendant. (Ibid.)

Couture notes that a second of the three witnesses told him 'nothing ever happened' (ibid.). He, too, emerged from the police interview room to testify against Storey. What is absent in the Storey inquiry is what went on in the police interview room.

R. v. MacEachern is a curious case on two accounts. First, MacEachern was charged with the phantom forcible confinement and sexual touching of the two eight-year-old boys; this charge was dropped. Second, he was charged with having mutually consensual anal intercourse with his boyfriend; the boyfriend 'victim' lived with MacEachern between the ages of 14 and 17; MacEachern was 25 to 28 during these years. From the court transcript we learn that:

. . . the 14 year old C. moved in with the accused. . . . During that year the accused and the 14 year old were having a sexual relationship, which involved masturbation and fellatio. The victim, C., turned 15 years of age. . . . [a]nd . . . the relationship between the victim and accused progressed to acts of anal intercourse. . . . They were both involved in the anal intercourse, on each other. . . . [T]he victim moved out . . . and eventually lodged his complaints with the department . . . . (*R. v. MacEachern*, 1994: 4–6)

The reader is momentarily left wondering if C. filed the complaints after some dispute. But then it is learned that the 'victim' moved back in with the accused a month and a day later. The question becomes, why would the 17-year-old lodge a complaint against his 28-year-old partner? More precisely, if he did lodge a complaint, what form did this complaint take, did the police get him to lodge a complaint, and if so, how? Later in the transcript we learn that C. is also charged with offences 'involving—having sex with [sic] young boy' (ibid., 12). Again, going outside the court transcript, one finds the answer in a verbatim transcript of the police interview with C. that was read on the CBC *Ideas* series.

Constable S: This is not about any charges against you. . . . I am asking about the guy you're living with. . . . What about intercourse?

A: Mm, him? No, no.

Q: You're telling me that he never did—never had anal intercourse with you?

A: No.

Q: Why—why does he—why does he lead me to believe that you guys have?

A: I don't know. Ask him. . . .

Q: I'd like to get the truth from you about that, and I've got to ask you, has he had intercourse with you? Simple question.

A: Yeah, probably.

Q: And how many times would that have happened over the two years?

A: I don't know.

Q: Like, once?

A: I don't count. . . .

Q: Well, is it more than ten or more than a hundred?

A: More than a hundred? No. I don't know. Say ten then. . . .

Q: I don't believe you had a choice in the matter.

A: I could have said no if I wanted to.

Q: Yeah, but he's twenty-eight.

A: Yeah, So?

Q: And you're a kid of what? Fifteen? Sixteen? Seventeen? Don't you think it is weird for him to be having sex with a person of your age?

A: Mm-hm.

Q: That's what I'm getting at . . . he's used you for these acts. . . . Did you ever feel used by him?

A: Sometimes, I guess. (CBC, 1995: 23)

C. moves from a position of claiming that no anal intercourse occurred, to choosing the least number of times the police constable gives him when he is told that his lover has said they have had anal intercourse. He goes from stating that he could have said no, to stating that he might have felt used, sometimes, maybe. When questioned about the 'weirdness' of the age difference, the youth merely replies 'Mm-hm.'

Conclusion

What one learns from the trial transcripts, with the aid of the few published counter-narratives of the youths, the investigative journalism of Joseph Couture, and the CBC *Ideas* series 'The Trials of London', is that the moral panic was a creation of the police and the media; that the hustlers were not listened to but cajoled by the police and social workers into making certain kinds of statements. We see that the youths' view of the acts and of the men involved is complex, dependent upon how the youth were treated in the encounters. Justice in these cases has little if any space for the stories of the others, the hustlers and johns; it is the justice of law, and law is the terrain of the dominant. The application of the law to young males selling sexual services is shown to be different from its application to young women selling sexual services: the young male hustlers are gendered as victims. What is crucial in this gendering is homophobia, which is then articulated with ageism and whorephobia.

Notes

1. The transcription of Ontario Provincial Court trial documents was made possible by a York University Faculty of Arts Research Grant, which is gratefully acknowledged.

2. The reading of the story of the others in the official court transcripts is made possible by the investigative research and reporting of journalist Joseph Couture. His work has been produced by Max Allen in a four-part CBC radio *Ideas* documentary, 'The Trials of London', in a CBC *Newsworld* television documentary, 'After the Bath', by filmmaker John Greyson, and in many articles in *Xtra*, Toronto's gay newspaper, as well as in a feature for the American magazine *The Guide: Gay Entertainment, Politics and Sex*. The *Globe and Mail* published the results of Couture's investigative reporting in a feature, 'The Kiddie-Porn Ring That Wasn't', by Gerald Hannon on 11 March 1995, fourteen months after the beginning of the porn scare in southern Ontario. Couture fractured the dominant narrative; the analysis in this paper is generated by that fracture. The paper is written by Shannon Bell; the primary research was done by Joseph Couture.

3. Seymour and MacEachern were reported in the media as separate occurrences. However, court documents indicate that the seven-year-old boy in the Seymour case and one of the nine-year-olds in the MacEachern case are the same person (Couture, 1995a: 14). In the MacEachern court document they become eight-year-olds (*R. v. MacEachern*, 1994: 9).

Chapter 4

Rape Uncodified
Reconsidering Bill C–49 Amendments to Canadian Sexual Assault Laws

Kevin Bonnycastle

Introduction

On 23 June 1992, Canada's Parliament passed an Act amending sexual assault laws. Bill C–49—as it was then called—marks 'an historical breakthrough in terms of women acting as framers, rather than objects, of the criminal law' (Boyle, 1994: 5). More important, perhaps, Bill C–49 was a collaborative undertaking by very different, often antagonistic, Canadian women's groups. Recognizing that such wide-scale coalition-building across diversity was unprecedented, Sheila McIntyre (1994: 293) published an insider's account chronicling this 'historical' process. She hopes that 'the story of the coalition will provoke new thinking about old debates concerning whether and how women and other historically disempowered groups should pursue egalitarian social change through law.'

In this chapter, I take up McIntyre's challenge to rethink the 'old' feminist debate about whether or not law invokes ultimately 'a power that will work against [women] rather than for them' (Smart, 1989: 138). Conventionally, feminists remain divided, either as advocates for social justice through law reforms or as sceptics wary of working within existing socio-legal frameworks for transformative change. The latter group is stymied into monitoring law for antagonisms and contradictions signalling potential for radical change. The former group endures serial exasperation when feminist-inspired law reforms are 'deradicalized' and incorporated into existing legal discourse, or else mobilized to serve politics antithetical to feminism. Notwithstanding the widely documented negative or unanticipated consequences of feminist legal reform initiatives, I argue that struggles over legal language can help harness 'the power of law' for feminist concerns. Returning to what McIntyre has written, my dispute is not with *whether* feminists should engage law—although this viewpoint must be defended, not simply asserted. Rather, I am concerned with *how* feminists engage law. The 1992 feminist-drafted Bill C–49 amendments to Canada's sexual assault provisions provide a concrete vehicle for addressing this broader question of theory and practice.

I begin and end with Bill C–49. En route, however, I borrow from a collage of literatures, moving far beyond the specific legislation, to examine the productive qualities of language rarely foregrounded in feminist legal struggles. I conclude that, by accepting dominant imagery about 'the rapist' and 'the rape victim' as its point of departure, Bill C–49, despite substantial feminist input, reinforces 'constructed normality' about gender stereotypes and gender power relations. Equally troubling for a social movement under attack for neglecting the lived realities of disempowered women, Bill C–49 does not address growing criticisms that existing legal narratives limit women of colour from telling their stories about rape (see, for example, Toni Morrison's 1992 anthology). I begin, however, by outlining why the process underlying Bill C–49, if not the product, signifies a feminist victory. Then I respond generally to a recurring theme within much feminist socio-legal work: namely, that law, in the final instance, maintains the status quo.

The Enactment of Bill C–49: A Pyrrhic Victory for Feminists?

What might a feminist legal victory look like? McIntyre and other women applaud Bill C–49 because diverse women's groups united to draft legislative amendments to Canadian sexual assault laws; five of their proposals appeared in the tabled bill (McIntyre, 1994: 306). Historically disempowered groups, including Black women, immigrant women, disabled women, sex trade workers, First Nations women, lesbians, and others, were included in, rather than erased by, government consultations (ibid., 309).

Three key feminist-driven amendments emerged. First, laws relating to sexual assault now define 'consent' or lack thereof and provide five concrete instances negating consent. Second, a new clause narrows the defence of 'mistaken belief' (in consent) by placing an onus on the accused to take *reasonable steps, to ascertain that the complainant was consenting*. Third, statutory language replaces judge-made principles (as outlined in *Seaboyer*, 1991) for determining whether or not evidence on past sexual history is admissible. In theory, these new legislative passages regulate rape trial judges' discretionary powers to admit a complainant's sexual history (Mohr and Roberts, 1994: 10–11).

As Dawn Currie and Marlee Kline point out, the challenge for any movement purportedly representing all women is 'to build the coalitions between privileged and marginalized women' (1991: 18). This has proved a formidable task. Seemingly, in the 1990s, the women's movement embraces the discourse of race, class, sexuality, geopolitics, (dis)ability, and others as modalities in which gender is lived. Yet many women of colour insist that 'white women [still] don't get it' (Agnew, 1996: 49). What they 'don't get' is that these dimensions of women's lives are not 'mutually exclusive' fields of domination, but intersecting matrices of domination operating indivisibly (Crenshaw, 1994: 94). It follows that strategies, practices, and politics that prioritize one form of oppression, at the expense of others, do not resonate with all women's lives.

In retrospect, 'doing good' has even generated new forms of violence against women (Crenshaw, 1991), casting 'white feminism' among the most tenacious oppressors of women of colour. In misguided attempts to reverse this track record some Canadian feminists, says Radha Jhappan, now offer white feminism's dismal history with race as a 'politically correct' excuse for avoiding, not confronting, race and/or culture issues incomprehensible to white women (1996: 46). In turn, she charges all feminists retreating into the comfort zone of white women's lives with 'e-racing' women (ibid., 47, 15). Clearly, if white feminists want to confound this pattern, they must cede to those women marginalized politically, economically, and culturally some of the former's authority to direct feminist agendas, to define 'the truth' about women's oppression(s), and to monopolize discourse about women's needs (see Agnew, 1996; Currie and Kline 1991; Jhappan, 1996). The problem now is how to share power in fact, not just in theory (Kline, 1989). For McIntyre, the Bill C–49 coalition signifies one such exercise in feminist praxis. Notwithstanding covert attempts to turn women's groups against one another, she reports that the experience of 'power-sharing' across genuine diversity was 'literally indescribable' (McIntyre, 1994: 296, 309).

Arguably, these temporary alliances (not mergers) equal success stories for the women's movement—particularly next to earlier feminist lobbying to amend Canadian rape laws. Prior to the 1983 amendments, Maria Los (1990: 163) recounts that diverse women's organizations submitted reform proposals to the government. But these were all overshadowed by the National Association of Women and the Law, whose proposal was drafted outside the debate and dialogue, which distinguished the 1991–2 consultations. The resulting three-tiered, gender-neutral offence of 'sexual assault', replacing the older gender-specific offence of 'rape', is contentious still (see Fudge, 1989).

Compared with this earlier law reform campaign, McIntyre's account suggests that the recent changes, bode well for feminist engagement with law. In other words, the dynamics of collective mobilizing, which multiply political sites and political subject-positions for women, are productive *per se* (see Lacombe, 1994). But, aside from this success, can amended sexual assault laws help the constituency that feminists purport to serve, in this case, women assaulted sexually? Can evidentiary and procedural refining, aimed at increased reporting, charging, and conviction rates, reduce this form of violence?

Laureen Snider says no. Addressing violence against women, she captures feminism's *raison d'être* when she writes that empowering or improving women's lives 'must be the prime, if not the only criterion for evaluating the success or failure of law reform' (Snider, 1994: 85). Despite improved responses from different moments in the criminal justice process, Snider reminds readers that its emphasis on punishment merely widens the net for men, targeting poor men and racialized men. Yet, heterosexed violence against women continues unabated. In her opinion, these symbolic victories reproduce class and race inequities (ibid., 86–7).

Snider's review challenges two feminist socio-legal strategies, exemplified in the 1983 rape law reforms. The first is the tacit assumption that women can be empowered by affirming and voicing a victim status (Los, 1990: 164). For Snider (1994: 103), only 'ideological, economic, and political' empowerment will prevent gender(ed) injuries. Second, Snider regrets that feminist lobbying to 'get tough' on men perpetrators (Los, 1990: 167) linked feminism to a law-and-order discourse. In hindsight, then, feminist optimism that criminal law reforms could protect women and children from sexual assault was misplaced.

Snider agrees that some laws have empowered some women politically, legally, and economically. Nonetheless, for her, criminal law and criminal justice are not flexible enough to respond to women's needs and concerns because both were designed to censure and punish, not empower (Snider, 1994: 82). Throughout her analysis, she emphasizes the 'educative and symbolic' or 'repressive and coercive' functions of law (ibid., 80). Not surprisingly, Snider is troubled when 'violence against women' rhetoric is appropriated by the state to justify extending punitive control networks.

Snider's pessimism about criminal law as a means of empowering women has a long history in feminist socio-legal scholarship. In the area of sexual assault, Susan Edwards's classic study, *Female Sexuality and the Law* (1981), is often used to show how ideological constructions of women and women's sexuality—borne out of extra-legal medical, psychiatric, psychological, gynecological, and everyday discourses—permeate legal decision-making. The problem is that many of these assumptions are assimilated by statute law and, more problematically, case law, where the pathologized imagery of female sexuality can remain unassailable for years (Edwards, 1981: 51–2). Much like Bill C–49, the 1976 British Sexual Offences Act restricted defence counsel's options to discredit witnesses by interrogating rape victims' sexual histories. But Edwards concludes that, even denied access to plaintiffs' sexual histories, 'constructed normality' about women's sexuality—derived from psychoanalytic literatures documenting rape fantasies, female masochism, or false allegation hypotheses—infiltrates and influences judicial decisions (ibid., 101, 114, 157–9).

To support their claims that (criminal) law reforms have not produced real changes in women's lives, both Snider and Edwards present empirical evidence from official and unofficial criminal justice system data. Using these measures, both women argue compellingly that criminal law generates negligible or iatrogenic (rather than liberating) consequences for women. From this perspective, Snider might say that merely 'acting as framers of [criminal] law' cannot count as an unqualified good without testing the new amendment's effects on women's lives. Arguably, Bill C–49 merely streamlines the probability that, all else being equal, more men can be convicted and punished for sexual assault, without remedying those material, economic, and political inequalities structuring some women's susceptibility to sexual assault and, perhaps, some men's susceptibility to assaulting them.

Bracing Snider's prognosis, the implication drawn easily from Edwards's study is that sexist ideologies 'that have little foundation in reality' are *fixtures* of rape trials (Edwards, 1981: 171). And after examining the 1983 Canadian rape law amendments, Maria Los's conclusions are similarly dismal. In other words, feminists cannot use law to 're-appropriat[e] the definition and meaning of rape' or sexual violence (Los, 1990: 169) because 'the state is guided by men's ideologies and interests' (Radford, 1987, cited ibid., 170).

I agree with Snider that 'the most urgent need[s]' are structural changes in both women's lives and communities to which violent men return (Snider, 1994: 89). Also, Los notes correctly that focusing on law reform individualizes sexual assault and occludes the wider social and political relations in which rape occurs. Both Snider's and Edwards's conclusions stem from quantitative data. Towards this end, Snider examines criminal justice statistics, civil injunctions, and increased program funding. When she fails to find tangible evidence of direct causality between criminal law reform and women's empowerment she dismisses criminal law as a site to challenge 'dominant ideologies about women'. Although this struggle is key to Snider's praxis (ibid., 99), she is adamant that it cannot be waged successfully on the terrain of criminal law.

The conclusions of Snider, Edwards, and Los invoke variants of 'mirror' metaphors, wherein dominant legal ideologies reflect oppressive capitalist and patriarchal power relations. The corollary of this is that women cannot resist hegemonic gender representations. In other words, until social relations are transformed, judicial ideologies are impervious to feminist politics.

An underlying angst that law is masculine emerges explicitly in Catharine MacKinnon's famous assertion that 'the law sees and treats women the way men see and treat women' (1983a: 644). Undoubtedly, law *is* male in the sense that it has emerged over time from 'conversations' among men (Connell, 1995: 73) and reflects one-sided interpretations from privileged men's positions within relations of power. Nevertheless, the point I want most to make is that feminists who refuse to be left with MacKinnonesque representations of heterosexed women as always victims and heterosexed men as always victimizers must avoid essentializing law, including criminal law, as a mechanism that represses and reproduces relations of androcentric, Eurocentric, and heterosexed domination.

Alan Hunt's proposition that 'law is constitutive' represents one attempt to theorize the transformative potential in law. Hunt, among others, argues that we must avoid a 'unidirectional' mode of causality—which is labelled positivistic in non-feminist work. In other words, we must be open to possibilities that law also shapes social relations: we must insist on reversing the process (Hunt,

1993: 226). Hunt presses the point that legal and social relations are mutually constitutive. This suggests that legal language, for example, what we can and cannot say about sexual assault, and emergent legal subjects—all of which and whom are circumscribed by the Criminal Code—are not simple reflections of existing social relations, but also infiltrate those extra-legal sites.

Contra Susan Edwards, whose 'arrows' all point in one direction—from patriarchal social relations to law—legal discourse can also traverse other institutional and discursive fields and be incorporated into extra-legal narratives. From Hunt's perspective, we can assume neither that law incorporates other discourses, such as psychiatric or psychoanalytic ideologies (of 'women's nature'), nor the converse. These are always 'empirical questions' (ibid., 118) that, rather than ahistorical or theoretical givens, are sensitive to history and context. Without adopting such language, Hunt invokes the indeterminacy of all legal struggles.

He borrows Niklas Luhmann's concept of 'structural coupling' to think about the relationships among autonomous institutional sites. Using courts and police as examples, Hunt illustrates how relations of mutual dependence, linking law and other disciplinary sites, can be positive, negative, or mixtures of both. Structural coupling signifies that apparently permanent linkages between and among institutional sites are 'inherently unstable' and vulnerable to uncoupling and recoupling to other sites (ibid., 296, 297).

Granted, Luhmann's use of such mechanistic imagery immediately sounds the alarms of post-structural vigilantes. Nonetheless, Hunt uses Luhmann's work to open up possibilities for resistance that many feminist analyses tend to close down. He targets two sites. First, law (content and form) is a production site for ideologies, not simply a bearer of ideologies produced elsewhere. Hunt thereby recentres ideology as an accomplishment of discernible social relations. This suggests that feminists should regard law, including criminal law, as sites of ideological struggles, wherein redefinitions and reinterpretations of legal categories can always be contested. More originally, by using the concept of structural coupling, the tenuous links between institutional or discursive sites can be conceptualized as terrains of struggle, for example, the link between psychiatry and law, or social sciences and law, to name but two.

Of course, Hunt's legal analysis must be tempered by much feminist work demonstrating that dominant legal ideology has been resilient, historically, to feminist challenges. At the same time, however, work such as Susan Boyd's in Canadian family law reveals that legal discourse is not monolithic, but fragmented by competing ideologies of motherhood, modern fatherhood, and liberal equality, none of which exercises hegemony (Boyd, 1991). In sum, then, Hunt's work provides a theoretical opening for us whereby engaging the law—including criminal law—does not pre-exist as 'always already futile' for women. But what disruptive strategies might be generated by engaging sexual assault laws—beyond those symbolic and punitive effects identified aptly by Laureen Snider?

Rival Feminist Narratives:
The Truth about Rape as Contested Terrain

Among the earliest feminist tenets, shaken somewhat by post-modern scholar-ship, is the indissoluble link between theory and political practice. In other words, feminist engagement with substantive rape law reform derives from feminist theorizing about the historical conditions generating different forms of violence against women. While the 'truth' about 'rape' has always been contested, traditional feminist analyses draw primarily from (variants of) two theoretical approaches. In turn, these drive feminist legal strategies. The first targets relations of patriarchy. The second examines the intersection of capital-ist and patriarchal social relations.

Very briefly, Susan Brownmiller's provocative *Against Our Will: Men, Women and Rape* (1975) theorizes rape and men's violence against women as necessary elements of patriarchal domination. Calling rapists the 'shock troops' of male privilege, she writes: 'Rape became not only a male preroga-tive, but man's basic weapon of force against women, the principal agent of his will and her fear' (1975: 14). Depicting all men as 'potential rapists', Brownmiller inverts the 'myth of male protection' of women and children. She argues instead that all men participate, directly or indirectly, in women's regulation through intimidation. To illustrate this point, she cites non-violent men's reluctance to sanction other men for exercising male privilege—whether informally by denouncing misogynist conversations, or formally by arresting, prosecuting, or convicting men accused of sexual offences. Brownmiller-inspired analyses reduce law and state to functional sites for reproducing male power, intervening only reluctantly to punish men who step beyond the 'normal' parameters of (white) male privilege.

A second narrative is informed by Clark and Lewis's *Rape: The Price of Coercive Sexuality* (1977). According to their thesis, contemporary rape law is a trajectory of historical legal relations that once prosecuted rape as a property offence (Clark and Lewis, 1991: 294–5). Borne out of this ideological legacy, 'law' compensates only those women affiliated with the protection of father-care or husband-ownership. In this account, women flouting the dominant, white, middle-class constructed normality of (heterosexed) marriage, morality, and motherhood have 'little sexual value', placing them beyond the pale of legal redress (ibid., 296).

Clark and Lewis re-centre gendered divisions of labour in capitalist and patriarchal social relations. From this viewpoint, rape is underpinned by mutually reinforcing material and discursive relations. More specifically, rape is one inevitable expression of two intersecting historical conditions: women's economic marginalization within both private and public divisions of labour, and coincident cultural narratives making it possible to contemplate female sexuality as a commodity or physical violence, including rape, as expressions of masculine power (ibid., 297). In contrast to Brownmiller's premise, however, rape is more an effect, than the original locus, of women's subordination.

Clearly, both accounts overlap. In the former, however, sexual assault is more instrumental and purposive, representing an ahistorical strategy preceding capitalist economic forms. This account is functional and, implicitly or explicitly, biologically determined. 'When men discovered they could rape', Brownmiller writes, 'they proceeded to do it' (1975: 14). In short, sexual violence resecures male dominance and female subordination.

The second narrative is more attuned to masculinity as a social construction. Nonetheless, it consistently evokes non-fragmented images of masculinity as a unitary (and foregone) product of patriarchal and capitalist socialization. This second account pushes 'class', and to some extent 'race', to the forefront of understanding how rape is policed and punished. But both modes of oppression recede as explanations when it comes to investigating the social meanings and motivations for rape.

Both narratives conjure up a sexual violence continuum wherein all women experience all men's potential to abuse power, on a scale ranging ordinally from staring and whistling to violent death (Segal, 1990: 240-1). For Lynne Segal, traditional feminist explanations of male violence are too 'general' and 'pervasive', failing to distinguish between men who rape and men who do not, as well as different rates of rape (ibid., 243-5). Such analyses not only foreclose men's ability to change, says Segal, but miss the possibility that the disproportionately high rates of sexual assault in Western societies signal a crack in the armour of male control. Along this line Segal asks: 'might not rape be the deformed behavior of men accompanying the destabilization of gender relations, and the consequent contradictions and insecurities of male gender identities . . . in modern America?' (ibid., 240).

Clear as well (in hindsight), both feminist accounts only partially address the rape experiences of women of colour. By ignoring how gendered and racialized systems of power relations converge to generate qualitatively different rape narratives for non-dominant women, many women are rendered unrapeable (see Crenshaw, 1991, 1992). For black women, Crenshaw argues, the prototypical white rape victim, anticipated by law and reflected in white feminist theorizing about gendered (or economic) power relations, yields 'standard[s] of victimhood' precluding black women by fiat (1992: 423). As Wahneema Lubiano (1993: 340-1) explains further, 'the black lady' is either an 'oxymoron' or an 'aberration' that threatens male dominance and, by implication, stability in Afro-American families. Hence, black rape victims remain unrepresentable in rape trials (Crenshaw, 1992: 406).

Rethinking Rape; Rethinking Rape Reform

A burgeoning 'masculinities literature' theorizes that Western patriarchal capitalist cultures produce a hegemonic, idealized masculine form expressed, in our historical present, through the domination of women and the distancing of men from femaleness. James Messerschmidt (1993: 82) writes that '[i]n contemporary Western industrialized societies, hegemonic masculinity is defined through work in the paid-labor market, the subordination of women, heterosexism, and the driven and uncontrollable sexuality of men.' To explain why some men choose sexual violence, masculinities literature focuses on structurally reproduced marginalization, proposing that some men denied access to masculine status through economic or educational success may resort to physically and sexually dominating behaviours to effect their masculine identity (Segal, 1990: 246–7, 256). In other words, rape becomes one modality for 'doing gender' (West and Zimmerman, 1987).

Few feminists extend gender analyses to investigate the category of 'man' as contested terrain or to distinguish between masculine dominance and hegemonic masculinity (see Segal, 1990). This misses one of the key insights of masculinities literature: namely, hegemonic masculinity controls and censures not only femininity, but alternative masculinities as well (Connell, 1995). In fact, both dominant feminist accounts outlined above explain rape/sexual assault using conceptual frameworks that prefigure men as sexual predators and women as victims of that sexuality. Extended to rape law reform, and all strategies to disrupt male domination, this conceptual currency becomes troubling. The problem is not with feminists engaging rape through law reform, but feminist theories of rape undergirding reform initiatives.

Along this line, Segal (1990: 269) suggests that feminists retheorize violence and masculinity as relatively autonomous, rather than linked eternally, and investigate empirically both men's and women's relationship to violence. In addition, feminists must extend their analyses of 'the structures which generate the discourses and practices of phallocentrism and male power' (ibid., 93) to investigate the psychic links between gender subjectivity and sexual violence (ibid., x).

Towards this end, I now consider two questions. First, how does gender(ing) 'work'? To do this, I draw on Judith Butler's work, rather than the 'masculinities' genre. My preference stems from Butler's framing of the relationship between gender and time. Although Connell and Messerschmidt foreground the historicity of gender, Butler extends the temporal quality of gender(ing) to 'psychic identification'. For Butler, the materialization of gender is never fixed firmly but is always in the process of rematerialization. It follows that the interval between each 'repetitive performance of identity' is filled with disruptive and destabilizing possibilities (Butler, 1993a: 317). In this way, Butler 'preserves gender practices as a site of critical agency' (1993b: x) without losing sight of material constraints on 'doing gender'.

Second, I investigate two related questions. What is the relationship between language (or texts) and subjectivity? And, how does gender work through legal text, such as sexual assault laws? Two insights are critical. The first is the Foucaultian understanding that all subject identities are the products, rather than origins, of language. Second, the corollary of this first insight is that we can only (re)iterate and destabilize those 'scripts' and subject positions generated within existing power relations. Both these points are accomplishments of language (speaking) and text (writing). I propose that rape, reconceptualized, demands new law reform strategies. And I believe these can be derived from insights borrowed from scholars writing currently within post-structural frameworks. My proviso is that this work be grounded materially in existing social relations.

Inspired by Foucault's *History of Sexuality*, yet pressing beyond his acceptance of the body as the irreducible point of departure, Judith Butler (1990: 7) invites us to think that sex, by which she means sexed bodies, might be as socially constructed as gender. She abandons the ritual feminist distinction between sex and gender as biological and social, respectively. For her, this means that if naturally sexed bodies are not pre-discursive, then they cannot be the 'passive medium' upon which culture inscribes gender (ibid., 8). It follows for Butler that if gender cannot simply be referred back to a natural sexed body, one's identity as a male or female cannot be an expression of an essential or unchanging inner self. Rather, identity is an effect of repeated gender 'performativity' that reconstitutes an illusion of stable, gendered, and sexed bodies (Butler, 1993b: 314).

Following her lead, categories of identity never pre-exist the discourse or 'performativity' materializing individuals as subjects. Butler (1994: 33) never implies that we can voluntarily subvert and resignify sex/gender. But she creates a way to think about sex/gender as inherently unstable and subject to change, instead of invariable end products of socialization. In 'Imitation and Gender Subordination', Butler's specific object of inquiry is heterosexuality, but her analysis applies to all apparently stable identities. She writes '[t]hat heterosexuality is always in the act of elaborating itself is evidence that it is perpetually at risk, that is, that it "knows" its own possibility of becoming undone' (Butler, 1993a: 314).

Extrapolating from Butler's argument, hegemonic masculinity is also a precarious identity 'permanently at risk' and compelled to repeat itself to maintain an illusion of stable, coherent, masculinized subjects. Following Butler's evocative lead suggests that we can regard sexual assault or rape as one strategy culturally available to men for gendering women (see Marcus, 1992: 391), which simultaneously reconstitutes hegemonic masculinity. Rather than sexual assault/rape as the effect or result of socialization into hegemonic masculinity, or a technique of masculine dominance, as suggested by the two feminist analyses discussed previously, rape is constitutive of hegemonic masculinity. In the former, rape and male violence reflect or reinforce feelings of masculine identities located somewhere within the subject. But in the latter, rape *generates* masculine subjects and identities as its effect—an effect that Butler (1993b) insists is revisable.

Continuing with her scepticism of all pre-political identities, Butler (1990: 2) rejects the ontological assumption that a priori subjects exist who, in turn, can become subjects before the law. But, since the law operates only through centred stable subjects, these must be fashioned as discursive 'fictions' in trial proceedings (ibid., 3). In unison with Butler's analysis, Dragan Milovanovic (1991: 92) has also noted that juridical subjects are created by their insertion into 'preconstituted discursive subject positions'. Thus, by extension, both 'the raped woman' and 'the rapist' always already exist in dominant legal discourse. And although Butler is investigating the materialization of sexed bodies, in subsequent work she acknowledges a confluence of discourses as not only sexed but racialized (1993a: 17–18). The implication is that the black rapist and the white rapist or the black raped woman and the white raped woman of legal discourse are prefigured differently. In other words, racist narratives, coupled to legal institutional sites and practices, create qualitatively different subject positions across racial and ethnic boundaries (see Collins, 1990; Lubiano, 1993). These identities in turn are reproduced and affirmed in legal institutions and everyday legal practices. Thus, to what extent do legal practices form gendered identities that perpetuate and police dominant forms of masculinity and femininity?

For instance, Chris Weedon draws our attention to the subject positions offered to women through language. She points out that legal texts presume rape narratives wherein sexual violence and rape are 'natural extension[s]' of men's aggressive and uncontrollable sexuality, while women are inscribed always as passive feminine subjects (Weedon, 1987: 36). I want to extend Weedon's idea that 'redefinitions of crimes can have important implications for the forms of subjectivity available to "the criminal"' (ibid., 37) by proposing that rewriting sexual assault provisions holds similar potential. Towards this end, feminists must be concerned with two moments of textual production. First, how is women's (and men's) subjectivity constituted in, and organized through, (legal) rape text? Second, how is this subjectivity channelled to other women and men?

My point is that, if legal relations traverse extra-legal sites—including everyday life—as Hunt suggests, then feminists must destabilize all identities generated by legal structures that foreclose the emergence of new, more empowering subject positions for gender(ed) victims. In short, I am urging feminists to examine their participation in authorizing forms of feminine subjectivity oppressive to sexually assaulted women. Granted, 'victimized identities' have not been repressive unilaterally. But they have never protected women. Indeed, for many non-dominant women, victim categories, in their present form, remain politically, legally, and culturally bankrupt. And foremost, contemporary narratives about victimization enlist women in courtrooms to reiterate, rather than subvert, gender hierarchies and gender identities.

Carol Smart (1994) adopts a similar line of argument when she notes that gender constructions do not permeate law via judicial complicity in dominant ideologies, Susan Edwards's analysis notwithstanding. Rather, gendering occurs within text itself—including text not gendered specifically. Subsequently, Smart recommends that feminists shift their original focus from 'law as *sexist*' or 'law as *male*' to 'law as *a gendering strategy*', abandoning the categories of Woman and Man (ibid., 187, 191, 192). This allows us to think about gendering (as well as racializing, heterosexing, and so on) as available strategies or textually mediated processes rather than pre-discursive identities.

Towards this end, Smart proposes treating 'law as text' and gender constructions as accomplishments of pre-existing legal discourse (ibid., 230). The latter form specific identities for women—'the raped woman', 'the battered woman', 'the welfare mother', to name but three. If Smart is correct in observing that 'such discursive constructions of Woman . . . underlie the actualities which render women rapeable, vulnerable, and victimizable' (ibid., 221–2), then feminists need to rethink their own contributions to the emergence of these 'types' of women.

Post-structural social theorists, including Butler, Weedon, and Smart, all valorize the centrality of language and discourse in producing meanings, subject identities, and consciousness. And the idea that the category 'woman' is a discursive fiction resonates with many feminist claims that gender comprises a set of socially created, arbitrary differences that become fixed to sexed bodies. Nonetheless, many feminists reject post-structural tendencies to hive off discursive relations from non-discursive ones, without examining the relationship between material and discursive practices.

Non-discursive elements can never be abandoned. They denote those myriad social relations, institutions, and structural arrangements that are not formed by discourse, even though they can subsequently become objects of discourse. These relations 'happen' to us whether we think about them or not (Bhaskar, 1986). Deborah Cameron lists economic ordering, physical environment, familial relations, divisions of labour, and individual genetic constitutions as examples of non-discursive relations exerting productive and constraining influences upon us, whether enunciated at a discursive level or not (cited by Palmer, 1990: 151). Against the post-structural 'maxim' that nothing exists outside discourse, Palmer reminds us that material life sets boundaries within which language and discourse develop. In this sense, we can think about language as productive without 'descending into discourse' (ibid., 86).

Dorothy Smith, for one, insists on explicating the non-discursive social relations formative of knowledge. Without 'turning materialism on its head', Smith proposes that texts organize, and are organized by, concrete social practices. Remaining wedded to a Marxian-informed perspective, she notes that Marx could not foresee the ascendency of texts or their potential to organize both social consciousness and extra-local sites by intervening between social relations and how we experience those relations. Today, Smith explains, our knowledge of the world is rarely direct but mediated through texts that are treated like reality. Writing in the nineteenth century, however, Marx could not pursue the social relations of knowledge as externalized, textually mediated forms of discourse. Nor could he explore ideologies as socially organized and organizing work processes, simultaneously shaping local practices and linking them into extra-local relations of ruling (Smith, 1990: 51–7).

What distinguishes Smith's work from post-structural approaches is that she explicates the concerting social relations underlying the production of texts, a strategy stemming from her insistence that texts (or discourse) do not write themselves. Texts are, among other qualities, gendered, albeit written to occlude specific authorship. Moreover, for Smith, 'reality' as textually mediated creates an opening for thinking about how 'reality' might be put together otherwise. Without explicating the social relations subsumed in texts, we will be stuck always, says Smith, at the textual surface, thereby missing the social production of the text. So, following Smith, I want to think about legal subject as socially produced.

First, however, I acknowledge a theoretical debt to Sharon Marcus[1], particularly her invocation of cultural narratives or 'cultural scripts' (1992: 389) when she writes that rape is a 'scripted interaction which takes place in language and can be understood in terms of conventional masculinity and femininity as well as other gender inequalities' (ibid., 390). Conceptualizing the relationship of language to rape opens up possibilities for thinking about rescripting rape narratives, turning our attention towards language and access to language as key feminist resources for creating counter-narratives and subject positions.

Marcus suggests that a rapist 'strives to imprint the gender identity of "feminine victim" on his target'. Focusing on actual encounters between would-be rapists and their targets, she notes that rape is a script pre-existing subject identities of rapist and raped, which encourages women to recognize themselves as objects of violence and subjects of fear, never subjects of violence or objects of fear (ibid., 391, 398). Understandably, Marcus castigates feminists who think that women can be empowered by proving they have been made powerless. She writes that a 'feminist politics which would fight rape cannot exist without developing a language about rape, nor . . . without understanding rape to be a language' (ibid., 387).

In terms of her analytical framework, therefore, men acquire access to rape scripts by living in misogynist and unequal social relations. What Marcus does not say, however, is that a crucial site for producing rape scripts is the substantive sections of the Criminal Code and derivative legal proceedings. The idea that Criminal Code language circumscribes and shapes the form(s) that sexual assault/rape take is echoed in Carol Smart's remark that women's rape experiences sound ominously similar to rape narratives emerging from legal proceedings (Smart, 1994).

Unsettling Rape Narratives

Returning to Bill C–49, the language of the amended sections of the Criminal Code drafted specifically by feminists organize court proceedings and accomplish hegemonic rape scripts. Instead of disorganizing 'rape narratives', these new sections become yet another resource for anchoring and naturalizing dominant constructions of masculinity and femininity. As well, these sections derive their intelligibility by invoking contemporary heterosexual 'normality'.

We can begin by considering the addenda to section 273. Subsection 273.1(1) now reads that 'consent means . . . the voluntary agreement of the complainant to engage in the sexual activity in question.' Feminists elected not only to fix consent, but offer exemplars. The first five 'disqualifications' in section 273.1 read

> (2) no consent is obtained . . . where
>   (a) the agreement is expressed by words or conduct of a person other than the complainant;
>   (b) the complainant is incapable of consenting to the activity;
>   (c) the accused induces the complainant to engage in the activity by abusing a position of trust, power, or authority;
>   (d) the complainant expresses by words or conduct, a lack of agreement to engage in the activity; or
>   (e) . . . a lack of agreement to continue to engage in the activity.

The first three clauses, namely (a) to (c), all prefigure rape victims who have no agency or volition. The subjects anticipated are 'induced' or 'incapable', or so passive that others might extend consent to sexual relations on their behalf. Together they offer women a 'powerless' subject position in lieu of inscribing them within reciprocal power relations. These exemplars discursively produce this 'type' of woman, who now exists prior to rape itself. Ironically, these five disqualifications for consent strive to 'protect' women by codifying women's vulnerability to men's agency, thereby becoming one of the mechanisms formative of Marcus's 'rape scripts'. Despite a final qualifying statement noting that these examples do not 'limit the circumstances in which no consent is obtained', these amendments perpetuate a discourse of domination.

More specifically, these additions collude with a historically specific form of hegemonic masculinity. In doing so, they reify male sexuality as unchangeably coercive. Yet, what issues from Messerschmidt's review of historical 'rape prototypes' is that the rape narrative of our historical present—centring a masculinity materialized through sexual conquest, with its corresponding feminine resistance and capitulation—is a modern emergence. He points out also that linking (normative) femininity to a paradigm of sexual passivity, and a sexual desirability devised for a male gaze, is only the most recent form of constructed heterosexuality (1993: 49). In other words, the specific version of sexual relations, statutorily embedded now within the Criminal Code, would have been inexplicable in the early 1800s. Now, frozen in textual time, it becomes another discursive resource constitutive of the heterosexual 'norm'.

The very language of consent prefigures a specific matrix of power relations enabling the hegemonic masculine ideal. Feminist legal scholars have long recognized that law defines consent from a male perspective (see Smart, 1989). Others note the possibilities connoted by 'consent,' which are not considered by law (see Boyle, 1994b). Wendy Brown says, however, that these concerns are misplaced. Rather, the very concept of consent must be renounced for connoting a lopsided power relationship from the start (Brown, 1995: 162–3). Brown maintains that consent invokes an 'always already existing' power relationship wherein one person complies with, or permits, actions initiated by another. Arguably, this fixes the person seeking consent always as the actor, and the consenting person as the one who cedes, submits, or surrenders to the other's desires or wishes. In our statutory language, 'men are seen to do sex while women consent to it.' In this sense, rape law is gendered. As Brown writes: 'Consent is thus a response to power—it adds or withdraws legitimacy—but it is not a mode of enacting or sharing in power' (ibid., 163). For Brown, the language of consent generally, and legal consent (to sex) specifically, fails to contemplate possibilities of egalitarian agreement.

Moreover, by struggling on the discursive terrain of consent, feminists miss an opportunity to subvert the paradigmatic subject of law, which historically has been the reasonable (white) man. Instead, the subject position of 'the rapist', animated by section 273.1(2)(a to e), is instilled a priori with reason and possibilities of acting on that reason. This becomes more apparent in section 273.2, which reads that the onus is on the accused 'to take reasonable steps . . . to ascertain that the complainant was consenting'. Since most accused are men, this language centres male subjects as the locus of agency, once again entrenching their authority and echoing dominant rape narratives (see Marcus, 1992: 393). Men are ceded the choice to (mis)recognize or ignore women's consent, establishing men as agents of sexual violence. Rather than reclaiming women as sexual subjects, women are inscribed within legal language as always already acted upon. As Sharon Marcus might surmise, this pins down the rapist's status as a subject by entrenching women's subjectivity as an object of violence.

Equally troubling, this legal framing of women's passivity and lack of agency intersects with cultural narratives about women of colour. For instance, black women's embeddedness in sexualized race narratives about chronic promiscuity, uncontrolled sexuality (Collins, 1992: 178), or 'consistently . . . sexually available' (Crenshaw, 1994: 429) places many black women outside the ambit of legal redress (see Crenshaw, 1991: 1271). Put otherwise, the subject position recognized by the addenda to the Criminal Code sexual assault cannot represent the experiences of women excluded historically and today from stories about vulnerability, presumptions of chastity, or any protected 'sphere of sexual autonomy' (see Crenshaw, 1992: 430). By establishing legal subject positions of vulnerability and negations of agency, these clauses define simultaneously a 'constitutive outside' (Butler, 1994). Put otherwise, this materializes some sexually assaulted bodies as 'not raped' women.

Paralleling how evidence of battered wife syndrome (BWS) precludes many women beaten by their partners from being considered 'real' battered women, women disruptive of the dominant rape narrative are less apt to be recognizable as 'really' raped. And this is borne out empirically by examining the categories of victim's/defendant's race in American arrest, conviction, and sentencing data (unavailable in Canada). Indeed, Crenshaw (1992) points out that black women who accuse black men of rape are as likely to be construed as victimizers of more politically oppressed and socially vulnerable black men or black masculinity!

It would appear that the drafters of these amendments anticipated a framework that is not accessible directly through the actual text. For instance, returning to the 'disqualification' negating agreement to sexual activity expressed by persons other than the complainant—s. 273.1(2)(a)—this passage makes sense only if we conjure up subtext about women's lack of autonomy over their own bodies, especially in the face of other persons' (historically, male or white male-dominated) proprietary or professional claims to women's bodies. Rather than transcending narratives, such as women as men's property, this legal language depends on this imagery forever 'waiting in the wings' to give it meaning.

Restrictions on admission of evidence accomplish a similar effect. Thus, section 276(1) reads in part: 'evidence that the complainant has engaged in sexual activity, whether with the accused or with any other person, is not admissible'. To find the sense in this passage, readers must first activate interpretive frameworks—whether or not they agree with these—about women's sexuality as property of one man, (some) women's 'promiscuous' bodies as property of many men, and prior consent to sex as unretractable. Without mobilizing all these schemata, this Criminal Code directive makes no sense. To illustrate that this passage depends on readers' knowledge of, and participation in, these subjects, we can borrow the scenario devised by the American Bar Association (cited by Delorey, 1989–90: 536) and think about this section as if it pertained to robbery. It would be incomprehensible to us if the category of robbery was qualified by an addendum reading that 'evidence that the complainant had given money away willingly in the past is not admissible to infer likelihood of consent to be robbed in this case.' And so, in an attempt to insulate women from 'facts' that have no bearing on consent, we animate these subtexts each time we invoke this subsection.

Finally, section 273.1(2) anchors yet another narrative holding much contemporary conceptual currency:

(d) the complainant expresses by words or conduct, a lack of agreement to engage in the activity or

(e) . . . a lack of agreement to continue to engage in the activity . . .

In other words, rape is a (mis)communication problem. Such an account codifies one intelligible framework for interpreting, understanding, and excusing rape as an 'honest mistake'. Again, as Messerschmidt (1993: 48) says, the idea that 'no could really mean yes' is a historically specific discourse that does not exist outside those cultural relations authorizing misinterpretations of women's words or actions as available refrains. In anticipating men's misinterpretation of women's desire, this section enables that script.

The pattern I see emerging from feminist engagement with rape law reform specifically, and perhaps criminal law generally, is a propensity to entrench women's victimization by men, inscribing women ever deeper into narratives of how they are overwhelmed, in myriad ways, in the presence of power. Here we have reviewed the discursive production of a type of woman and a type of man representing the hegemonic norm. Following Sharon Marcus's analysis, this naturalizes rape as prediscursive and fixed, rather than a fluid or disruptable relationship, occurring always in time. Simply put, these sections contribute to fixing gender or gender attributes. Responding to rape, feminists superimposed a framework that reproduces, rather than disrupts, the prototypical rape script. By codifying and authorizing hegemonic rape narratives, feminists participate in the very rape scripts they seek to dispel.

Put otherwise, the problem is our 'starting point'. As Dorothy Smith (1990) notes, when we begin our investigations with existing categories and concepts, we locate ourselves within an ideological mode constructed for us by contemporary 'relations of ruling'. We thereby miss the relations of power that have formed those categories. To begin in this ideological mode, says Smith, is to participate in ruling relations. She proposes beginning at an earlier point and inquiring into categories and concepts as actual work processes in producing knowledge. Here, I have extended Smith's directive to include 'dominant rape narratives' and 'rape scripts'. In other words, feminists need to step back from those stories dominant culture tells about rape to that moment where men have been cast discursively as sexual predators and women as victims. From this starting point, we can investigate how these cultural narratives are reproduced through actual social practices embedded within systems of power relations.

Against the pattern of feminist struggle to reform rape laws, I propose that the meaning of consent and definitions of rape should not be codified, but unfixed. Thereby rape trials become forums for unsettling dominant rape narratives, not fitting women into pre-existing scripts anticipating dominant relations. Rape, uncodified, would mean that each rape trial becomes an opportunity for women to tell their stories about how rape happened to them. In turn, men, bereft of legal narratives, like consent, mistaken belief, or presumptions of reasonableness, are left struggling on terrain where they are less confident, and less assured of their a priori rational subject status. Of course, expecting that judges will be swayed by this cacophony of women's voices is naïve. But I am not concerned with punishing individual men; rather, each rape trial's role in reconstituting dominant relations must be dismantled. In addition to enabling women of colour to recount their experiences about the coercive conditions in which 'consent' is obtained, 'rape uncodified' can help dismantle racist presumptions that some women are not as injured as white women by similar forms of violence (Crenshaw, 1992: 430; Nahanee, 1994).

Moreover, this tactic is reconcilable with our contemporary common-law matrix of judge-made and positive law. Granted, over time and place a body of common law and precedent emerges. But even a cursory analysis points to disparity from case to case: across lower courts, within individual courts, and even, at individual levels, as judges (by educing different 'facts') revise their own rulings. The point is that, unfixed, judges cannot so easily invoke law, reproducing dominant discourse about rape. Obliged to hear a multiplicity of rape stories, the courts reluctantly become a resource for destabilizing and rewriting rape narratives and subject positions for women and men. And, since Marcus emphasizes that women's responses to sexual assault are as culturally scripted as men's, these discursive tactics have more potential for disrupting gendering effects than any measure of punishment, which, ironically, is also a gendering strategy.

Conclusions

> The producer of images, the Subject of representation, is a powerful actor in the real world. And the question is who produces the representations in our culture. Who is the looker? (Cameron and Frazer, 1986: 155)

Cameron and Frazer's observation that the looker has generally been male is bolstered by decades of feminist scholarship. Historically, gendered divisions of labour structured women's absence from producing 'official' knowledges (Smith, 1990). Increasingly, however, women, such as those women who revised Canadian sexual assault laws, are positioned politically as producers of texts and, by extension, subject positions for women. To date, as Marcus (1992: 389) notes, feminist legal strategies concentrate on 'post-rape events', implicitly accepting the inevitability of rape.

It is utopian to think that changing language and texts will radically transform how rape occurs. But, if sex and gender are so tenuous that they must be reconstituted and re-enacted perpetually to maintain stable subject and gender identities, then this assumes the necessary existence of gendering strategies. If sexual assault/rape is one such gendering strategy, and if language is constitutive of subject identities and cultural narratives that penetrate everyday relations and practices, then feminists can intervene in legal text to disrupt the language effects shaping both women's and men's cultural scripts about sexual assault. Put otherwise: if 'the rape victim' is not a pre-existing entity, and if sexual assault is a cultural code gleaned from legal discourse (among others), which infiltrates extra-legal sites, then quite apart from any symbolic or instrumental effect on sexual assault statistics, feminists must be cognizant about how legal texts 'work'. I suggest that feminists should screen sexual assault legislation, indeed, all official discourse, for evidence of gendering feminine and masculine subjects. After examining the gendered subjects prefigured by feminist-driven amendments to sexual assault laws, I urge feminists to develop textual strategies that fashion active political agents disruptive of dominant gendering practices. And I reiterate: feminists must re-examine their own participation in constructing disempowering subject positions for women.

Notes

I gratefully acknowledge Dorothy Chunn and Dany Lacombe's editorial assistance and thought-provoking commentaries.

1. I thank Paula Norrena for bringing Sharon Marcus's article to my attention.

Chapter 5

Victim, Nuisance, Fallen Woman, Outlaw, Worker?

Making the Identity 'Prostitute' in Canadian Criminal Law

Deborah Brock

Making the Identity 'Prostitute'

What is a prostitute? Victim, nuisance, outcast, rebel, sexual outlaw, fallen woman, worker? All of these labels are products of an ongoing struggle over the meaning of the identity 'prostitute'. These labels are far from benign because, more than in any other form of work, the woman who prostitutes 'becomes' her job, and her job becomes who she is.[1] Feminists from a variety of standpoints have challenged the conventional understanding of prostitutes as immoral disposable women, as well as their status as marginalized and stigmatized legal subjects. Feminist academics and activists have attempted, though by no means in a unified way, to effect a redefinition of the identity 'prostitute' and to challenge its organization and policing through the legal system. Some feminists regard prostitutes as symbols of patriarchal oppression and the ultimate *victims* of a gender-unequal society that privileges the interests of men. Recently, other feminists have sought to reshape the prostitute identity, asserting that prostitutes are really symbols of sexual freedom for women and, therefore, sexual *outlaws*. Still others regard prostitutes foremost as *workers*, who labour in a society permeated by class, gender, and racial inequalities, as well as homophobia. Like others who labour in this system, prostitutes' work and working conditions are shaped by these social and economic relations.

The first feminist perspective—that of prostitutes as symbolic of patriarchal oppression—has had the greatest currency. While this perspective has its roots in early radical feminism, which asserted that a revolutionary social transformation was necessary to defeat patriarchy, it has become the perspective of mainstream feminists. Yet this position contradicts the identity most often conveyed by prostitutes themselves, that is, that they are sex trade *workers* and/or independent professionals. Mainstream feminists, who believe that women's equality can be achieved in liberal societies through legal reform, regard themselves as allies of women who work in prostitution. These feminists focus on challenging the patriarchal organization of prostitution-related law, which penalizes women for the work they are compelled to do. However, in the process, they have attempted to create a new dominant identity for women who work in prostitution—as victims in need of protection (including protection from punitive laws). While the victim identity may be more sympathetic to prostitutes, it does not significantly alter their present constitution as marginal legal subjects, but rather reformulates it in a manner open to co-optation by antagonistic interests. Once again, women who work in prostitution are silenced, as they are excluded from discourses that construct their identities. This occurred in a period when feminism became a significant counter-hegemonic force and began to have an impact, however equivocal, on law and social policy.

The consequences of these differences among feminists and prostitutes have been significant for prostitutes, particularly street prostitutes, whose working conditions have become more difficult and dangerous since the mid-1980s as a result of a broadening and reaffirming of Criminal Code legislation regulating prostitution-related activities. There has been a silent reaffirmation of the Judeo-Christian morality at the heart of the Canadian legal system, which from its outset identified prostitutes as *fallen women*. I say 'silent' because this moral stance no longer has a legitimate place in Canadian criminal law. Politicians, police, and residents' organizations have been compelled to construct a new, morally neutral identity—that prostitutes, particularly those who work at the street level, are a public nuisance. Another consequence of the differences among feminists and prostitutes has been to miss an opportunity to reshape how the law is gendered, since the law embodies prostitute identities derived from these struggles over meaning. Law is gendered in a manner that formalizes and perpetuates a distinction between good women and bad women.

Far from being simply a state-imposed mechanism of social control, the way prostitution-related legislation has been produced and gendered is also the product of sometimes disparate interests in civil society. These struggles over law are one expression of struggles taking place outside of the law about the direction of social change. Social reformers, residents' organizations, feminists, and media, as well as legislators, courts, and police, have all had a role in the creation of law. These social agents, institutions, and social movements are gendering the prostitute, and hence all women, as they identify, regulate, and control behaviour.[2] The identity 'prostitute' is not fixed, but is produced, struggled over, and refashioned. How this occurs depends on the power of specific social actors and social movements in a given period. Prostitutes, or rather, representations of prostitutes, have served as a powerful symbol for social movements and crusaders.

The production of discourses about sexuality informs our understanding of the normal and the deviant, the permitted and the profane, and as such influences our identities and practices. Power cannot be simply located in 'the state', which is itself an 'overall strategy and effect' of power relations (Martin, 1988: 6). The development of new knowledges, including medicine, the psy professions, and criminology, constitutes what Foucault refers to as the 'disciplinary society', in which power is not only expressed through prohibition but is normalized, creative, and technical, and provides new modes of classification, surveillance, and regulation (see Smart, 1989). Foucault directs us to explore power-knowledge relations, to specify the processes by which these are organized, rather than relying on preconstituted and fixed concepts like patriarchy and capitalism to do our explanatory work for us.

Carol Smart, however, urges us not to neglect the power of law in the organization of social life.[3] She contends that there has actually been an expansion of the power of law in the twentieth century, in which the personal and the private have been increasingly penetrated by the law. Sexuality, reproduction, and the family are increasingly subject to legal definition; the growing 'legalization of everyday life' extends from conception to death. This has occurred both through the extension of the influence of law and through law's 'colonization' by disciplinary regimes like science and medicine. Smart concludes that we must therefore consider two parallel mechanisms of power, the 'discourse of rights' given shape through law and the 'discourse of normalization' advanced by Foucault. She directs us to examine concrete ways in which power is operative through the state, as well as through numerous disciplinary discourses and practices.

For Smart, law is a site of struggle; unfortunately, however, she regards struggle over law as a wasted effort for women. Feminist efforts to date have not significantly altered the patriarchal application of law or improved it in ways that have had a real impact on the quality of women's lives. Smart's assertion is, I think, too unambiguously conclusive. My purpose here is to assert that law *must* be an ongoing site of struggle as we document how it identifies and excludes some women while it includes others as warranting protection. Moreover, we must account for how divisions within feminism have weakened its power to influence the shape and substance of law for the benefit of women. First, however, I will present a historical account of how law, through the efforts of social agents and movements, has constructed and incorporated particular prostitute identities that identify, regulate, and control their behaviour.

Victims of Male Vice? Fallen Women?

Legal historian Constance Backhouse has determined that Canada's earliest comprehensive statute designed to prohibit prostitution was brought into effect in Lower Canada in 1839. It dealt with prostitution as a form of vagrancy and, in keeping with other vagrancy statutes, was designed to keep undesirable sorts off the streets. This particularly harsh piece of legislation dealt with prostitution as a 'status' offence; clearly, being a prostitute and found in a public place, rather than being found in the act of soliciting customers, was sufficient to lay a charge and ensure a conviction.[4] It applied to 'all common prostitutes found wandering in the fields, public streets, or highways, not giving a satisfactory account of themselves' (Backhouse, 1984a: 7). There was no question that a prostitute was always a woman, even though the law was not gender-specific in its wording. The 1839 legal statutes also made it an offence to be 'in the habit of frequenting houses of ill fame' and unable to give a 'satisfactory account' of oneself (ibid.). Being an inmate of a common bawdy house became an offence in 1852, and all of the prostitution-related statutes were extended to apply to the Province of Canada in the same year (ibid.).

The law clearly gave police a great deal of power to exercise repressive measures where community pressures demanded. However, while the legislation was harsh in theory, toleration was sometimes exercised in practice. For example, in areas where the male population exceeded the number of available women, prostitution was often regarded by judges and police as a convenient outlet for male sexual needs. Prostitution-related legislation cemented the legal identity of prostitutes as 'fallen women'; nevertheless, they were wanted women.[5] It was generally only with the emergence of more substantial urban growth and the establishment of permanent communities that police were pressured to make more frequent arrests and/or to confine prostitution to particular areas of a city. In any case, it is difficult to determine the number of women who were arrested for reasons related to prostitution throughout the nineteenth century, as women were arrested for offences like lewd behaviour and disorderly conduct in addition to common prostitution and vagrancy.[6]

The late nineteenth century was a time of rapid social change. Large-scale immigration, industrialization, and urbanization transformed the social landscape. As urban centres expanded, populated by an often desperately poor working class living in crowded and unsanitary conditions, a social reform movement developed, a primary aim of which was the elimination of vice and the attainment of 'social purity'. Strategies for the moral regulation of women included but were not restricted to those who found a source of livelihood through prostitution (see Strange, 1995).[7] Prostitution was increasingly broadly defined to include those who were casually or regularly providing sexual services in exchange for favours or for economic renumeration. The prostitute was a potent symbol not only of female degradation but of anticipated social decay brought on by rapid and uncontrolled social change.

An attack on prostitution was at the same time a defence of the institution of marriage and the family, since prostitutes counted married men among their customers (who, aside from the immorality of their actions, would spread disease to innocent wives and children), were suspected of practising birth control, and in general lowered the standing of women (even while they provided a marker for good women to be measured against). Even where a link between poverty and prostitution was admitted by reformers, it was the opinion of some that a respectable woman would rather die than submit to such spiritual and physical degradation. As Mariana Valverde comments, the social reform movement was comprised of a rather divergent set of interests, including evangelicals, feminists, physicians, and others from both left and right. They were unified around prostitution, however, and it was not uncommon to see what might appear as contradictory beliefs coexisting without challenge. For example, reformers (particularly feminists) may have regarded prostitutes as victims of male lust and the double standard of morality for women and men, while insisting that they were 'fallen women' who should be committed to a reform institution to be purified of their sins and lifted up again (Valverde, 1991).

It is not surprising that many reformers regarded prostitutes as foolish, ignorant, and by the early twentieth century, feeble-minded women who had a low moral character to begin with. Those whom they believed were forced into prostitution fared somewhat better in their estimation; the belief that many women were victims (possibly of a 'white slave trade') rather than simply social pariahs was evident between approximately 1885 and 1920 in the steady expansion of legislation aimed at procuring and bawdy houses. Then, as now, feminists contributed to the construction of a victim identity for prostitutes, which uneasily coexisted with their identification as social pariahs. However, as both John McLaren (1986a) and Valverde (1991) have pointed out, even legislation focused on procuring had less to do with the protection of women and girls than with reformers' fears concerning shifting gender, sexuality, class, and race dynamics, and had the effect of controlling the women these laws were ostensibly aimed to protect rather than the exaggerated activities of procurers.

Over the next 50 years prostitution-related legislation remained substantially the same.[8] Until 1972 street-level prostitution remained a vagrancy statute, and the wording remained almost identical to the 1839 version. Section 175(1)(c) specified that 'Every one commits vagrancy who, being a common prostitute or nightwalker is found in a public place and does not, when required, give a good account of herself' (Royal Commission on the Status of Women, 1970: 369.)[9] One significant aspect of 'Vag C', as it was known, was that it had become formally gender-specific. This and other gender-specific legislation became an important target of the Royal Commission on the Status of Women (RCSW), which was mandated in 1967 by a Liberal government to investigate the position of women in Canadian society as a result of significant pressure from the emergent women's liberation movement. Supported by the findings of the Prevost Commission,[10] as well as the general philosophy of Britain's famous Wolfenden Report,[11] the RCSW's 1970 *Report* recommended sweeping changes to criminal law and social policy.[12]

The Commission found Vag C to be blatantly discriminatory since, in addition to being gender-specific, it exhibited moral condemnation of women while restricting their activities in the public sphere, permitted the use of arbitrary police powers, and stigmatized women through the acquisition of a criminal record, thereby making them difficult to 'rehabilitate'. Prostitution, they exclaimed, was 'fundamentally a social, not a criminal problem', which would not be eliminated through punitive legislation (Royal Commission on the Status of Women, 1970: 371). The RCSW recommended the repeal of Vag C, suggesting that prostitutes who disturbed the peace be treated the same as anyone else who disturbed the peace. As well, the *Report* recommended the development of government-sponsored 'rehabilitation' programs for prostitutes, where they could be trained to perform respectable work.

Aside from the objections of feminists, the enforcement of Vag C made it a problematic piece of legislation given that police were alleged to be abusing their powers of arrest. In 1972, the Liberal government decided to repeal the existing vagrancy legislation and Vag C was finally laid to rest. It was, however, replaced with a new statute applying specifically to the act of street solicitation. Section 195.1 specified that 'Every person who solicits any person in a public place for the purpose of prostitution is guilty of an offence punishable on summary conviction' (Criminal Law Amendment Act, 1972). Justice Minister Otto Lang stated that the repeal was consistent with the recommendations of the Royal Commission. Although he had not honoured the Commission's request to keep the work of prostitutes out of the Criminal Code, he expected feminists to be appeased by the fact that the new legislation was gender-neutral. The section of the Code applying to persons living on the avails of prostitution was also revised to be gender-neutral. One MP noted that 'perhaps the recent Bird [the chairperson] Royal Commission had not thought about [the fact that] . . . an advantage that has been given to the female criminal has been removed. Several honourable members around me think this is a noble victory for man's liberation'[13] (House of Commons, 1972: 1701).

However, the identity 'prostitute' remained, if not in letter, in practice a gendered category in Canadian criminal law. It was overwhelmingly women who were charged under section 195.1 rather than their male clients or male prostitutes. Where men were charged under the section, a judge may have refused to convict on the basis of the man's sex. For example, in *R. v. Dudak* (1978) the British Columbia Court of Appeal overturned a defendant's conviction, stating that the soliciting statute applied only to the person who actually or potentially receives payment and that a client does not prostitute himself in the course of simply satisfying his desire. Four months later the Ontario Court of Appeal arrived at the opposite decision in finding that solicitations were not initiated by prostitutes alone (Hoegg, 1983: 39–42). Judicial inconsistencies also occurred in decisions about whether a man could or could not be a prostitute. For example, in *R. v. Patterson* (1972) a man was acquitted of soliciting on the basis of his sex. Summarizes Lois Hoegg (1983: 39): 'All dictionary definitions cited in the case referred to prostitutes as being female and since the accused was a male, he could not be a prostitute. Since he was not a prostitute, there could be no act of prostitution and therefore no conviction.' In 1973, however, the Supreme Court of British Columbia did find a man guilty of soliciting on the grounds that 'person' applied to both men and women, and that to uphold a statute directed to soliciting in a public place for the purpose of prostitution it was irrelevant whether or not prostitution actually took place. In 1974 the BC County Court supported this decision when it found three men, all of whom had been dressed in women's clothing at the time of arrest, guilty of soliciting (ibid., 39–40). This ambiguity was resolved when Bill C–127 was proclaimed in January 1983, specifying that either sex could be a prostitute. It clarified other ambiguous elements of prostitution-related legislation in stating that not only women but *any person* who was not a prostitute or person of known immoral character was to be protected under the procuring legislation; and that not only men but *any person* was liable to charge for living on the avails of prostitution.

A Morality Problem or a Nuisance Problem?

Formally gender-neutral or not, in practice (law enforcement) and in spirit (the intent of the law), prostitution remained fundamentally a female crime. As well, the moralist impetus for laws to control prostitution remained at the heart of the statutes and of public perceptions of prostitution itself. Prostitutes were bad women, unless of course they were forced into prostitution, in which case they were the innocent victims of bad men. However, the Judeo-Christian moralism at the heart (and origins) of prostitution law was being challenged by competing, but no less moralistic, interpretations of the activity. Since the late 1970s, residents' groups, police, and local politicians have put continual pressure on the federal government for more stringent legislation to control street prostitution.[14] A 1978 Supreme Court decision ruled that street solicitation must be 'pressing and persistent' to constitute an offence. A single proposition no longer provided sufficient grounds for arrest, nor could the interior of a motor vehicle be considered a public place (*Tremeerar's Criminal Annotations*, 1982). The pro-criminalization lobby asserted that this decision significantly circumscribed the ability of police to make arrests and allowed prostitution to run out of control on the streets of Canadian cities.

Some residents' organizations argued that they were not calling for greater control of street solicitation for moralist reasons. Rather, they argued that prostitutes were a public *nuisance* and that police had lost control of the streets. Noise, littering, cruising customers harassing women residents, and heavy traffic on residential streets were said to be plaguing urban neighbourhoods, affecting both residents' sleep and their property values. However, while the pro-criminalization lobby generally dissociated itself from the moralist rhetoric of the past through an attempt to redeploy the prostitute identity of public nuisance, their rhetoric was not entirely convincing. For example, in 1982 the Concerned Residents of the West End, a Vancouver organization whose main concern was the elimination of street solicitation from their neighbourhood, stated that 'each prostitute is like a broken window which says that no-one cares'[15] (Concerned Residents of the West End, 1982). In 1984 then Mayor Mike Harcourt of Vancouver stated that 'street prostitution is more than a nuisance. It brings in the scum bums and low rollers and the creeps that start to destroy the morale of a community and the qualities that we should take for granted—the right to be able to walk our streets in peace and safety' (Budgen, 1984: 5).

Also consider the following letter (dated 10 October 1985) sent to the Standing Committee on Justice and Legal Affairs by Toronto's Ward Seven residents:

[T]he prostitution problem in Toronto has reached *epidemic proportions* . . . the police have been totally *emasculated* by the current lack of *legal muscle.* . . . Ours is a mixed neighbourhood, consisting of expensive renovated homes interspersed with a few older rooming houses. Our taxes are the highest in Metro and still rising. . . . *Our wives and daughters* are continuously afraid to walk these streets alone after dark. . . . It is patently unfair for taxpayers to be *held hostage* in this manner while our elected representatives leisurely discuss the philosophical question of possible impingement upon the personal freedoms of these *poor creatures.* . . . Consider our freedoms also, *gentlemen.* Pass Bill C–49 and give us back our streets.[16]

As I have argued elsewhere (Brock, 1990, 1998), this letter demanded the support of the federal government in the protection of property rights that, in a formulation demonstrating that the patriarchal imagination remained alive and well in the 1980s, clearly included women as male property. In this conversation between men (which is not to say that women residents would have a different perspective on street solicitation), one population of women (prostitutes) was being held responsible for causing harm to another population of women (residents). The residents' association's call for further criminalization of street solicitation directly contradicted the virtually unanimous demand by feminist organizations for the decriminalization of prostitution. Ominously, however, it complemented the feminist pro-censorship position on pornography.

Pro-censorship feminists argued that a general community of women was being harmed by the production and consumption of pornography. Pornography made victims of all women (women who found work as porn models shared this condition of victimization). Feminist organizations argued that women who worked in prostitution were also victims, as patriarchal social conditions compelled them through force or circumstance to resort to prostitution. The men who were prostitutes' pimps and customers further victimized them, as did the law and the police. As the Royal Commission on the Status of Women had argued some years before, decriminalization was necessary to mitigate their exploitation and assist them on the road to rehabilitation.

However, the development of a campaign on behalf of the rights of prostitutes was not forthcoming; the largest and most influential feminist organizations in Canada at that time were focusing their energies towards the censorship of pornography.[17] Given these conditions, the 1985 introduction of more repressive legislation designed for control of the streets cannot be attributed only to the moralism of the Tory government then entrenched in Ottawa. Feminist organizations lobbying for the further criminalization of pornography were unintentional colluders. The new legislation (Bill C–49) specified that:

195.1(1) Every person who in a public place or in any place open to public view

(a) stops or attempts to stop any motor vehicle,

(b) impedes the free flow of pedestrian or vehicular traffic or ingress to or egress from premises adjacent to that place, or

(c) stops or attempts to stop any person or in any manner communicates or attempts to communicate with any person for the purpose of prostitution or of obtaining the sexual services of a prostitute is guilty of an offence punishable on summary conviction.

(2) In this section, 'public place' includes any place to which the public have access as of right or by invitation, express or implied, and any motor vehicle located in a public place or in any place open to public view. (Minister of Justice, 1985)

Prostitutes once again provided convenient scapegoats for public anxiety, now arising from increasingly difficult economic conditions in a rapidly changing world. As well, some downtown neighbourhoods frequented by prostitutes were in transition, as the inner-city poor and working class were being gradually supplanted by middle-class people attracted by the deindustrialization of these areas and the advantages of downtown living. In Toronto, these neighbourhoods included Cabbagetown, Parkdale, and the Church-Wellesley area, the last becoming home to a thriving lesbian and gay community. It was the residents' groups of these transition neighbourhoods that were most responsible for spearheading the 'nuisance' identity.

Mariana Valverde has noted that we must recognize a broader conceptualization of morality than its association with traditional religious thought. The decline of religious influence on Canadian society has made way for a secular, formalistic mode of moral regulation. It is 'aimed at the production of individual ethical subjectivity and the reproduction of the nation's moral capital' (Valverde, 1994: 218). 'Moral capital' is intangible; it is about *character*. The presumed character of women working in prostitution did indeed remain an issue, as the above comments reveal. It is also evident in the demand for legislation distinct from that intended to control other forms of public nuisance. Fighting, yelling, and littering are not uncommon disruptions on downtown streets, both residential and non-residential. Were the problem of prostitution only a matter of its nuisance effects, surely vigorous police enforcement of local by-laws would do much to alleviate residents' complaints.

Frances Shaver has argued that where the moralism of Victorian reformers was overt, for contemporary pro-criminalization forces it is covert: 'if *covert moralism* were non-existent, prostitution would refer to the buying and selling of sexual services and apply to both sexes regardless of their role in the exchange' (Shaver, 1994: 134). She argues that the gender-neutrality of the law has not made it any less a moralistic judgment of the conduct of women working the streets. Dictionary definitions of prostitution and public perceptions of the work remain focused on women. Furthermore, despite a significant increase in the arrests of customers for communicating for the purpose of prostitution since the mid-1980s,[18] a city by city analysis of the data indicates that more prostitutes than customers continued to be charged, and their sentences remained more severe. As well, Shaver found that men charged under the statute in Vancouver overwhelmingly came from a predominantly working-class district, indicating an inequity in enforcement practices on the basis of class.[19] Her findings reveal a persistent double standard for women and men. Shaver's purpose here is clearly not to rectify this gendered organization through equalizing the number of arrests of men, a strategy that Valerie Scott of the Canadian Organization for the Rights of Prostitutes referred to as 'equal oppression' (Scott, 1986), but to challenge the very rationale of legislation regulating communicating for the purpose of prostitution.

Why might so many spokespersons for the pro-criminalization forces insist that they opposed street-level prostitution for its nuisance effects rather than as a public moral problem? First, the development of a secular society, in conjunction with recent changes in sexual mores, has created the conditions for an ostensibly less judgmental and more permissive culture, where the commercialization of all matters sexual maintains an uneasy but growing pride of place. Having struggled against the values of their parents' generation, those who came of age in the postwar period are now struggling to make sense of it all as sexual meanings are renegotiated.[20] This may be particularly true of lesbian and gay people in the process of establishing thriving downtown communities in Toronto and Vancouver.

Second, gender relations are in the process of transformation. Mainstream second-wave feminism has had some success in reconceptualizing the meanings of prostitution. No longer the 'fallen women' who deserve stigmatization and punishment, prostitutes are foremost considered to be victims of patriarchal oppression, forced by coercion or circumstance to 'sell their bodies' on the streets or in the brothels.[21] However, the analysis of the mainstream feminist perspective that follows reveals that it is no less moralist; the standpoint has merely changed.[22]

Third, the introduction of Canada's Charter of Rights and Freedoms in 1982 changed the terms under which law could be made and enforced.[23] Dany Lacombe reminds us that the Charter was designed to overcome legislating on the basis of morality. The existence of the Charter meant that any law based on morality arguments could be struck down; hence the importance of creating a discourse of 'harm' in support of the criminalization of pornography and of 'nuisance' to support the criminalization of communicating for the purpose of prostitution. So while the arguments against prostitution remained rooted in morality, they were compelled to be 'morality in drag'.[24]

Victim, Outlaw, Worker?

As I noted in the introduction to this paper, feminism is far from providing a unified analysis of the sources of women's oppression and what is to be done about it. Some feminists regard prostitutes as symbols of women's powerlessness and degradation, and as patriarchy's ultimate victims. Others regard prostitutes as sexual outlaws who refuse to be constrained by rigid sexual mores. Still others regard prostitutes as workers whose degree of exploitation varies according to the conditions under which they labour. For high-income earners working in safe conditions, the sex trade may indeed be a source of freedom. For those women who work in potentially dangerous conditions for a low and uncertain income, sex work is one of a number of bad alternatives. However, regardless of where and how they work, the regulation and policing of prostitution remain among the most significant downsides of the job, labelling prostitutes as society's disposable women and constraining the conditions under which they can earn their livelihood. It is the worker identity, I maintain, that corresponds most significantly to prostitutes' self-identification.

The most potent and pervasive feminist perspective on the place of prostitution in women's oppression is derived from early second-wave radical feminism.[25] The primary emphasis of radical feminist analysis is on the patriarchal control of women's sexuality and fertility. Patriarchy—a sexual system in which men have power over women in all aspects of the social order—is, according to Kate Millett (1979: 33), 'perhaps the most pervasive ideology of our culture and provides its most fundamental concept of power'. Economic and political-legal relations only become significant as a product of belief systems based on biological sexual differences. Prostitution is regarded as the ultimate manifestation of women's oppression: in a patriarchal society the definition of women as sexual objects to be bought and sold provides a primary impetus for political action. Thus, as Millett (1971: 120) states, 'prostitutes are our political prisoners—in jail for cunt. Jailed for it, for cunt, the offense we all commit in just being female. That's sexual politics, the stone core of it.'

The radical feminist position posits that sex oppression is history's longest injustice, and presents patriarchy (and its structuring of prostitution) as universal and transhistorical in character. As Phyllis Chesler (1973: 138) maintains:

> Female prostitution and harems have existed among all races, in nearly every recorded culture, on every continent, and in all centuries: it predates

Catholicism and industrial capitalism. It *always* signifies the relatively power-less position of women and their widespread sexual repression. It *usually* also signifies their exclusion from or subordination within the economic, political, religious, and military systems.

Millett (1969) asserts that women are traded and regarded as currency even in societies without monetary systems.[26] It provides men with a means of acting out their contempt for women. Prostitutes are in the business not of selling sex but of self-degradation, and in so doing support ideological repre-sentations of female inferiority on both the individual and social levels (Millett, 1971). Women's experiences simply of being female, through subjection to rape, incest, and other forms of physical and emotional abuse, prepare women for an acceptance of a life of prostitution, in which woman's sexual being is not constructed for her own pleasure. Since women's essence and offence in a patriarchal culture are focused on the fact that she is 'cunt', self-contempt becomes rooted in personality structure; women are socially conditioned to accept self-denigration. Millett asserts that patriarchal social organization urges women to kill something in themselves—ego, hope, self-respect. This female masochism is, however, 'only the behaviour of accommodation, forced upon any oppressed group that it may survive' (1971: 98).[27]

This perspective was challenged in the context of the 'sex debates' of the 1980s, debates fuelled by some women's resistance to prescriptive notions about normative sex for women, as well as the entry of sex-trade workers onto feminist political turf to assert an alternative perspective about their work. The chief conflict in the debates concerned the relative emphasis on sexuality as the primary mechanism of women's oppression as a gender (sexuality as danger), which is evident in the radical feminist analysis of prostitution, or as a site for liberation (sexuality as pleasure). Gayle Rubin was a key figure in asserting an alternative 'sex-positive' perspective to that advanced by early radical feminists like Millett and Barry and later contributors such as Catharine MacKinnon and Andrea Dworkin. Rubin and others revealed that in this formu-lation, the gendered character of male and female sexuality is polarized through the idealization of the female and demonization of the male. The emphasis on differences between genders is grounded in an essentialist perspective, 'the idea that sex is a natural force that exists prior to social life and shapes institutions' (Rubin, 1984: 275). In this formulation, prostitution, pornography, and rape are the concrete expressions of a rigid and fixed mascu-line sexual power. As Dworkin illustrates, 'So many men use these ignoble routes of access and domination to get laid, and without them the number of fucks would so significantly decrease that men might nearly be chaste' (1987: 48–9).[28] For Dworkin, 'intercourse' (heterosexual coitus) is itself violence against women. As she proclaims, 'the penis itself signif[ies] power over women, that power expressed most directly, most eloquently, in fucking women' (ibid., 172–3).

The 'sex-positive' perspective recognizes that sex can be a site of danger for women but puts much greater emphasis on sexuality as an existing or potential source of profound pleasure. It calls for a recognition of sexual pluralism: that sexuality is expressed in multiple configurations of genders and practices, and calls for a recognition of female empowerment through sexual pleasure. It seeks to uproot essentialist ideas about gender and sexuality by exploring how they have been socially constructed.[29] For example, Rubin's key work, 'Thinking Sex: Notes for a Radical Theory of the Politics of Sexuality', challenges conventional hierarchical ideas about appropriate and inappropriate sexuality. Rubin illustrates this hierarchy with a 'charmed circle' where heterosexual, married, monogamous, and procreative sexuality is most privileged, while homosexuality, promiscuity, cross-generational sex, sadomasochism, sex aided by pornography or manufactured objects (sex toys), and sex for money are most heavily stigmatized. Indeed, those who have (or offer) sex for hire are categorized among the most abnormal, unnatural, and sick, along with transgendered people, fetishists, sadomasochists, and those who engage in cross-generational sex. So prostitutes face an 'erotic stigma' since 'hierarchies of sexual value—religious, psychiatric, and popular—function in much the same ways as do ideological systems of racism, ethnocentricism, and religious chauvinism. They rationalize the well being of the sexually privileged and the adversity of the sexual rabble' (Rubin, 1984: 280).

Rubin's work is important in that she links the marginalization of prostitutes to a morality-based system of goodness and badness in sexual matters, rather than simply naming it as a gendered system in which men are always privileged and women always victims. Where she errs, however, is in reducing sex workers to an 'erotic group' (ibid., 287). Rubin's perspective on prostitution begins from an emphasis on prostitution as sexual *behaviour*, which is then conflated with sexual *identity*. She virtually ignores prostitution's economic relations for women and leaves it undifferentiated from other consensual sexual practices that are socially taboo and regulated by the state. Prostitutes, like people who practise consensual sadomasochism, are identified as sexual *outlaws*. Rubin, who first conceptualized the 'sex-gender system' in 'The Traffic in Women', has reconsidered the linkage between sex and gender and determined that they must be treated as distinct systems. The sex-gender system 'is the set of arrangements by which a society transforms biological sexuality into products of human activity, and in which these transformed sexual needs are satisfied' (Rubin, 1975: 15).

Rubin asserts that the sex-gender system still remains applicable to kinship-based societies but is no longer appropriate for Western industrial societies, where sexuality and gender have acquired some autonomy from one another. Feminism can therefore provide a theory of gender oppression, but its conceptual tools are not adequate to tackle the construction of erotic desire. An autonomous theory must be developed to address the dimensions of erotic desire, which vary according to, for example, race and religion, as well as to analyse such areas of sexual practice as sadomasochism.

Rubin therefore attempts to shift the analysis of prostitution from an expression of gender oppression to one of sexual oppression. Some sex-positive writers, like Joan Nestle and Shannon Bell, have chosen to express their solidarity with prostitutes in writings that somewhat romanticize the work. Nestle expresses her solidarity from the standpoint of a lesbian, and Bell from her self-identification as a pervert (see Nestle, 1987, 1983: 468; Bell, 1994).[30] Given the vehemence of much radical feminist analysis, it is small wonder that feminists like Nestle and Bell would choose to focus on the right to fuck rather than the right to work. It should not surprise us either that the sex debates (on prostitution) became mired between the identification of prostitutes and other sex-trade workers as sexual outlaws, for whom state regulation of prostitution is a suppression of sexual behaviour, and the radical feminist emphasis on the victimization of prostitutes through patriarchal—including state—power.

The emphasis of the sex-positive standpoint on the social construction of sexualities must provide a starting point for a comprehensive analysis of sex-power relations. Sexuality varies historically and culturally, and it is organized through, for example, our gender, race, class, age, religion, and sexual orientation. As Rubin asserts, sexuality is not synonymous with gender. However, it must be recognized that it is certainly strongly linked to it in a social organization in which male dominance is foundational. Furthermore, the construction of sexuality in Western industrialized nations cannot be fully understood without reference to the economic system in which it is located. Prostitutes' oppression as women (and few women will argue that we have already achieved gender-based equality) has been shaped by the market forces of capitalism, the difference in economic conditions between women and men, and the commodification of sex. Neither a sex-positive perspective, as formulated by the libertarian-influenced Rubin, nor one that reduces women's oppression solely to the determinants of patriarchal social organization is fully capable of comprehending the organization of sex work and its regulation. The latter stance has proven to be susceptible to conservative co-optation, where 'protection' is really control and where the actions of prostitutes are regarded as causing harm to a general population of women.[31] The sex-positive stance does not significantly contribute to the building of strategies of survival and resistance, particularly for the women making a living working urban streets as they daily deal with the powers of the state, its enforcers, and customers who regard the criminalization of prostitution-related activities as a licence for abuse.

The libertarian critique of prostitution advanced in the sex debates was certainly influenced by some activist sex-trade workers, as they challenged the radical feminist perspective of sex-trade work. Some have spoken about the pleasure they derive from their work, as a means of challenging the overwhelmingly negative portrayal of prostitution and other forms of sex work (for example, stripping and porn modelling) in mainstream feminism, which has uncritically accepted the radical feminist perspective. For example, Peggy Miller of the Canadian Organization for the Rights of Prostitutes (CORP) stated in Toronto at the landmark 1985 conference, 'Challenging Our Images: The Politics of Pornography and Prostitution': 'What is so terrible about fucking for a living? I like it, I can live out my fantasies. It's being said that there's something sick if you enjoy this profession' (in L. Bell, 1987: 48).[32] Annie Sprinkle, a former porn star, feminist performance artist, and part-time whore, celebrates prostitutes because she says that they are sexy and erotic, get laid a lot, and explore their own sexual desires.[33] Some evoke the spirit of the 'sacred prostitute' in an attempt to create a 'new' prostitute identity. For example, Annie Sprinkle (Bell, 1995) and former sex worker Nickie Roberts (1993) draw upon evidence that in some ancient, pre-patriarchal societies, prostitutes were counted among the goddesses. Sprinkle insists that the spirit of the sacred prostitute resides in every contemporary prostitute, regardless of her conditions of work.

Overwhelmingly, however, prostitutes consistently represent their work as an economic activity, albeit work whose character is usually different from what dominant stereotypes (for example, the sexual slave or the hooker with a heart of gold) would suggest. They speak of work that provides much better pay and more autonomy than the other forms of work open to working-class, and even most middle-class, women. They speak in an assertive, independent voice, denying that they are simply passive victims, while itemizing the changes that must be made to improve their working conditions and their social status.[34] They contend that support for the rights of prostitutes is integral to the advancement of all women, and therefore fundamental to feminism (Pheterson, 1989: 192).

The first prostitutes' rights organization, COYOTE (Call Off Your Old Tired Ethics), was founded in San Francisco by Margo St James in 1973.[35] In subsequent years, branches of COYOTE were established throughout the United States and affiliate organizations appeared globally.[36] The year 1985 saw the establishment of the International Committee for Prostitutes' Rights and the First International Whores Congress. The Congress focused its energies on drafting a World Charter for Prostitutes' Rights. By the second Congress, as Gail Pheterson documents: 'Assembled in an official conference hall of the European Parliament, prostitutes from over sixteen countries presented violations of their human rights, realities and mythologies about their health, and the relation of their struggle to feminism. Echoing in six simultaneous languages, their voices seemed to break a sound barrier' (Pheterson 1989: 28).

As of the time of this writing, prostitutes are demonstrating in Calcutta, demanding trade union rights, public health benefits, and the elimination of police abuse. Organizer Sadhana Mukherji has been quoted as saying, 'When we have rallies and meetings like this, the girls feel power. . . . They feel part of a movement. . . . It is a long struggle but nobody will resist us. . . . That day is past' (Stackhouse, 1997: A12).

Conclusions

Feminists by and large regard the state as antagonistic to feminist demands, for good reason. However, we also need to be aware of how mainstream feminism, in both its Victorian and contemporary variants, has been complicit in the shaping of state power for the regulation of women's lives. It has launched a revolution in meaning that has influenced both disciplinary regimes and the power of law. Rather than standing outside of law, contemporary mainstream feminism in particular has become a moral regulatory force. It has managed to obtain sweeping (although by no means complete) changes in social and legal policy. In criminal law, changes have been made to the structure, meaning, and enforcement of laws regulating abortion, sexual assault, and the sexual abuse of children. The vigorous efforts of pro-censorship feminists have not yet resulted in a new law restricting the production of and access to pornography. However, a new law has been rendered unnecessary. In the 1992 *Butler* decision the Supreme Court of Canada accepted the position of the Women's Legal Education and Action Fund (LEAF) that pornography caused harm to a general community of women, thereby broadening the interpretation of existing legislation (see Lacombe, 1994; Cossman et al., 1997).[37]

When feminist organizations supporting the decriminalization of prostitution came up against pro-criminalization forces in the 1980s, the federal government responded by mandating the Special Committee on Pornography and Prostitution to come up with a resolution to the dilemma. The committee attempted a compromise solution, accepting the mainstream feminist definition of prostitutes as victims of the structural inequality of women, while simultaneously accepting the pro-criminalization alliance's assertion that street solicitation was a public nuisance with deleterious effects on city neighbourhoods. While the committee's recommendation regarding street solicitation did not become law, it certainly influenced the writing of Bill C–49 in 1985 (see Brock, 1998). Feminist interventions did not attempt to shift the identity of the prostitute from her position of social marginality, and prostitutes' rights organizations appearing before the committee could not accomplish this on their own. Most importantly, feminist organizations missed the opportunity to challenge the symbolic organization of prostitution through reformulating their demands in support of the rights of women workers in a highly stigmatized and predominantly female occupation.

Nor have subsequent efforts proven to be particularly challenging. For example, when the constitutionality of the communication law and the bawdy-house law came before the Supreme Court for review, LEAF, a feminist organization mandated to advance the legal rights of women in Canada, did not request intervener status to support the legal challenge.[38] The focus of mainstream feminism on prostitutes as victims and its linking of prostitution and pornography as forms of sexual exploitation from which women should be protected have disempowered women and ultimately benefited conservative interests, whose agenda is distinctly anti-feminist. Given the precipitous rise of the new right in Canada, we need to strategize more effectively. With the growth of the new right, social movements are focusing their critique and demands on economic conditions and employment issues. This is precisely where a demand for an expansion of the rights of women working in the sex trade belongs. Instead, the identities *victim, fallen woman,* and *nuisance* now maintain an uneasy coexistence in Canadian prostitution law. Feminists need to surmount the fear that the validation of the rights of prostitutes as working women will somehow weaken feminism and set back our struggles for women's liberation.

Notes

1. The decision to focus here on prostitution involving adult women may not give a complete picture of the trade, given the undetermined number of male and transgendered adults and male, female, and transgendered young people involved in this form of commercialized sex. Nevertheless, the 'privileged' place of women in the history of both popular discourse and regulatory strategies permits us to give prostitution involving adult women separate consideration and leave the exploration of these other aspects of the trade for different projects. I will here use the somewhat arbitrary age of 18 to distinguish between adults and youths, based on the Canadian Criminal Code's definition of juvenile prostitutes as persons under 18 years of age. For a discussion of prostitution involving young people, see my *Making Work, Making Trouble* (1998). For a more intensive analysis of young men's involvement in prostitution ('hustling'), see Visano (1987).

2. We will not be concerned with prostitution-related laws regulating procuring or bawdy-houses here, although my remarks are certainly applicable to the making and revision of these statutes.

3. Smart (1989) challenges Foucault's contention that while new mechanisms of disciplinary power are expanding, 'old power' mechanisms (i.e., the law) are diminishing in influence.

4. While being a prostitute in a public place was a status offence, it was not, nor has it ever been, illegal to be a prostitute. Canadian law has focused on circumscribing the conditions for prostitution to take place.

5. Judith Walkowitz's work on nineteenth-century Britain demonstrates that until the passage of the Contagious Diseases Acts of 1864, 1866, and 1869, which stigmatized prostitutes as transmitters of infection and ruptured their ties to the rest of the working class, prostitutes were an integral part of working-class communities. As a result of the CD Acts, which were intro-

duced to reduce the availability of prostitution around military bases (the nation's health being dependent on the soldier's health), prostitutes became an 'outcast class'. The implications of the struggles around prostitution in Victorian England for Canadian society at this time warrants further exploration. However, evidence suggests a struggle over the meaning of the identity 'prostitute' was ongoing in both countries from the mid-nineteenth century and into the twentieth. On Victorian England, see Walkowitz (1980).

6. For a more detailed analysis of the legal regulation of prostitution in nineteenth- and early twentieth-century Canada, see McLaren (1986a). For information on the enforcement of vagrancy statutes in Toronto, see Strange (1995). Strange demonstrates how vagrancy laws were used for the moral regulation of all young women in a period where an influx of independent young working women in cities was a source of considerable anxiety. The hopes and fears associated with urban growth were projected onto these young women, who were symbols of social change.

7. In his work, Philip Corrigan originally focused on moral regulation as the preserve of states and state formation (1981). Mariana Valverde and Lorna Weir have since persuasively argued that moral regulation is not the preserve of the state alone, but is organized through professional bodies and discursive regimes located within civil society (see Valverde and Weir, 1988). By 'moral regulation' I mean strategies for the social and legal control of prostitutes, exercised through community pressure, reform efforts, legislative strategies, and medical surveillance. These strategies revealed an uneasy tension between the perspective that the 'fallen woman' was the victim of economic circumstance and/or male vice and the belief that she was a social pariah who spread immorality and disease among the populace.

8. However, research into the actual regulation and policing of prostitutes during this period is due a systematic and intensive study.

9. The statute is listed as s. 164(1)(c) in the report.

10. The Quebec Commission of Inquiry into the Administration of Justice in Criminal and Penal Matters in Quebec (1968–70).

11. *Report of the Committee on Homosexual Offenses and Prostitution* (New York: Stein and Day, 1963).

12. For a somewhat more detailed analysis of the ambiguous treatment of prostitution in the ostensibly permissive Wolfenden Report, see Brock (1998).

13. The Commission had indeed considered this implication and determined that gender-neutral legislation, on the whole, created fairer treatment for men.

14. In the summer of 1995 Toronto City Council would make the unprecedented move to recommend that the federal government decriminalize street-level communication for the purpose of prostitution, recognizing that the law was ineffective and blocked local efforts to regulate prostitution through zoning and other measures. (Media reports erroneously referred to this call for decriminalization as support for the legalization of prostitution and the establishment of 'red light districts'.)

15. The reference to broken windows came from a March 1982 article titled 'Broken Windows' in *The Atlantic*, by James Q. Wilson and George Kelling, which was enclosed with CROWE's statement. The authors stated that 'If a window in a building is broken and is left unrepaired . . . all of the rest of the windows will soon be broken.' In other words, without being checked, serious crime will soon flourish. Thirty years earlier, Philip Zimbardo, a Stanford University psychologist, had conducted an experiment in which he had parked a car on a street in an affluent suburb, where it remained undisturbed for a week. He then smashed a car window. Within hours, the car had been vandalized. For more on the ongoing use of this research, see *Globe and Mail* (1997).

16. Emphasis added. Thanks to Mary Ann Coffey for providing me with this letter.

17. The preferred emphasis on pornography over prostitution was particularly evident in the submissions to the Special Committee on Pornography and Prostitution (the Fraser Committee), which was struck in 1983 and delivered its recommendations in February 1985 (McLaren, 1986b). For more on the pornography debate in Canada, see Lacombe (1988, 1994).

18. This increase cannot simply be attributed to the passage of Bill C–49. Rather, police in numerous Canadian cities realized that despite their record arrests of women using the new law, the women would be back out on the streets earning their living as soon as was possible or necessary. They therefore decided to switch strategies and focused on the buyers of the service, believing that if they cut off the demand through intimidation and fear of arrest, the supply would be taken care of.

19. In 1996, the City of Toronto initiated the 'john school', the first of its kind in Canada. The purpose of the school was to 'educate' men, with their first conviction under the communicating law, about the personal and social costs of street prostitution. Over 400 men (including one Tory MPP) graduated from the school in approximately its first year of operation. In his journalistic investigation of the john school, Gerald Hannon found that the majority of 'students' typically were people of colour, many of them recent immigrants. This numerical domination provides a further indicator of *which men* are most likely to be charged by police and convicted by the courts. See Hannon (1997).

20. On the renegotiation of sexuality in the postwar period, see Weeks (1981).

21. Following the campaign against the alleged 'white slave trade' at the turn of the century, and with the advent of two world wars (during which prostitutes were considered a threat to military hygiene and therefore national security), the perception of some prostitutes as victims had largely been lost.

22. Shaver refers to the mainstream feminist position as 'principled moralism' (1994: 135).

23. The impetus for the creation of the Charter was, of course, the same ideological, political, and economic postwar changes that fostered both the renegotiation of sexual boundaries and the rise of feminism.

24. Personal communication with Dany Lacombe, February 1997.

25. The following discussion of radical feminism was first developed in my MA thesis (1984).

26. Kathleen Barry concludes from this that pimping, not prostitution, is 'the oldest profession' (1979: 137).

27. For recent examples of a radical feminist analysis of prostitution, see MacKinnon (1989) and Dworkin (1987). Canadian radical feminists who have made contributions include Cole (1987) and Overall (1992). Overall attempts to evaluate the validity of an argument that will be elaborated below: that prostitution is a form of work like any other for women in a capitalist and patriarchal system. She concludes that it is not. Unfortunately, her argument is undermined by her a priori assumptions about prostitution, for example, that women 'sell their bodies' rather than hire out their sexual services, and that prostitution can only exist under patriarchy. For an effective critique of Overall, see Shaver (1994).

28. As MacKinnon pithily comments, 'No pornography, no male sexuality' (1989: 139).

29. For example, see Vance (1984); Snitow et al. (1983); Valverde (1985). I earlier explored this work in 'The Sex Debates' (1987).

30. Rubin does not deny that the conditions facing sex workers are in part shaped by gender oppression; however, this is mentioned only marginally and is subordinated to her focus on the sexual oppression of an erotic group.

31. For some historical parallels, see Walkowitz (1980, 1983) and a review of Walkowitz's 1980 book by Taylor (1981).

32. At this conference, the partial proceedings of which are documented in L. Bell (1987), sex-trade workers shifted the debate about their professions from one occurring between feminists to a dialogue between feminists and sex-trade workers.

33. 'Forty Reasons Why Whores Are My Heroes', at Annie Sprinkle's Web site: http://www.infi.net/ ~ heck

34. See, for example, L. Bell (1987); Delacoste and Alexander (1987); Pheterson (1989); *Social Text* (1993); Bell (1995); and *Guantlet* (1994). Numerous contributors to these volumes also emphasize that they enjoy their work, and sometimes that does involve sexual pleasure. There is certainly not a set division between those who emphasize pleasure and those who emphasize work. However, as the Toronto-based (now former) prostitute Alexandra Highcrest emphasizes in her book, for most prostitutes, prostitution is a job, not a 'lifestyle', and the prostitutes' rights movement is about securing rights for people working in this part of the sex trade, not about advancing the rights of people to live a particular lifestyle. See Highcrest (1997).

35. For a sociological account of the history of COYOTE, see Jenness (1993).

36. On the establishment of organizations internationally, see Roberts (1992).

37. For a defence of LEAF, see Busby (n.d.).

38. Personal communication with Val Scott, Canadian Organization for the Rights of Prostitutes. The Supreme Court of Canada upheld both laws, with the majority ruling that the Charter rights of prostitutes, if curtailed, were overridden by the greater social interest in restricting street solicitation (1990). (The decision was split along gender lines, with the two women justices dissenting from the ruling.) A later decision also upheld the procuring legislation. The majority ruled that while the statute presumed that anyone who lived with or habitually associated with a prostitute must be exploiting her for her earnings, thereby infringing on the individual's right to be considered innocent, the statute was justified in order to protect women and young people against a parasitical activity (*Toronto Star*, 1992).

Chapter 6

Mothers, Other Mothers, and Others

The Legal Challenges and Contradictions of Lesbian Parents

Shelley A.M. Gavigan

Introduction

My title derives its inspiration in part from the end-of-day watch sounded for my daughter by another child at her day-care centre when I arrived to pick her up: '. . . your mom's here—the other one.' As I think back to that moment more than half a decade ago, I remember with fondness the ease with which my daughter's little friends were able to assimilate that she didn't have a daddy, but rather two mommies—even the competitive little girl who said, 'Oh yeah, well I have about 10 mommies.'

Too, I recall a yet earlier conversation with one of my feminist intellectual heroes (who was then on the cusp of a post-modern turn). I shared with my colleague that I found it interesting yet odd that I, a lawyer turned legal academic, did not have what I regarded as a legal relationship with the new baby in my life. My colleague responded that perhaps that was a good thing, perhaps that was better; after all, why would I want to, need to, acquiesce to law's power to define and regulate. To be frank, as unsettled as I was by the contradictory nature of my own position, I was troubled by her response. I muttered my well-worn rejoinder that I thought legal relations and regulation were more complicated than that.

In the years following this conversation, as Brenda Cossman (1994) has noted elsewhere, brave lesbians and gay men are now taking their lives to court to challenge and resist homophobic discrimination. A community of people who scarcely, if ever, experienced the law as a shield has taken it up as a sword to advance and vindicate equality claims. To even the most casual observer, the successes and near misses of lesbian and gay litigants and law reformers illustrate that a significant social and political shift has been achieved over the last decade. In this shift, lesbians and gay men have savoured victories as often as they have endured defeats. To be sure, not every lesbian litigant would embrace the characterization of 'success' or 'victory'. In some of the litigation where lesbian former partners have squared off against each other, one lesbian's victory has been another lesbian's loss. Even more amazing, out lesbian and gay lawyers are appearing as counsel in some of these cases. Of this phenomenon, Laura Benkov has suggested that 'the past and present are colliding in the courtroom' (1994: 37). These are interesting times in which to be a student of law, gender relations, and social change. There are, nonetheless, notes of caution to be sounded at the prospect of litigating one's way to social transformation. I count myself numbered among those who are dubious about the nature and endurance of the successes that can be experienced in the courtroom (Gavigan, 1992; see also Fudge, 1991; Glasbeek, 1989; Fudge and Glasbeek, 1992).

In this chapter, I consider what is meant when we think of law as a 'gendering strategy' (Smart, 1992) in relation to lesbian parents and the varied relations and encounters with law that lesbians with children have. I identify and engage critically with two themes in lesbian legal scholarship: (1) that lesbians are 'outside' the law, and (2) that lesbian mothers are mothers just like other mothers. I examine four different forms of lesbian child custody litigation to illustrate that the characterization of 'inside/outside' the law does not fully capture the complexity of lesbians in relation to the law, as well as to illustrate the complexity (and not infrequently the fragility) of lesbian relationships to children in their lives. In this chapter, then, I hope to illustrate the importance of theorizing law when theorizing its contribution to gender relations, and lesbian engagement with both.

Theme I: Lesbians Inside/Outside Law?

At the outset, I concede that I find troubling many themes in lesbian writing and scholarship in relation to law, and here I include my own modest contribution to the literature. One theme in lesbian writing about law is that lesbians are 'outside' the law (Arnup, 1995; Robson, 1992). The evocative *cri de coeur* of the prominent American lesbian essayist, Minnie Bruce Pratt—'how I love is outside the law' (1991: 228; cited by Arnup, 1995: 378)—is powerful, haunting, almost irresistible. My response (rather too cryptic, I now see) has been to assert: 'Lesbians do not live outside the law in a kind of legal limbo, nor do they exist in a legal vacuum. They shape and are shaped by the legal and social relations in which they live' (Gavigan, 1995a: 103).

In this chapter, I hope to illustrate that *both* positions need to be revisited, rethought. After all, lesbians who have been married, lesbians who have had children with men, and lesbians who have given birth to children or who have adopted children—these lesbians are not 'outside the law'. They can't 'opt out' (Brophy and Smart, 1985: 1). They live in relation to law; even when they leave the marriages, their legal relationships do not end. Rather than have her children dragged through an ugly custody battle at the instance of their father (with her mother as a character witness for him), Minnie Bruce Pratt (1991:

231) left them with him, 'reclaiming' her relationship with them when they were older:

> I could have stolen them and run away to a place where no one knew them, no one knew me, hidden them, and tried to find work under some other name than my own. I could not justify taking them from all their kin, or their father in this way. Instead, from this marriage I carried away my clothes, my books, some kitchen utensils, two cats. I also carried away the conviction that I had been thrust out into a place of terrible loss by laws laid down by men. In my grief, and in my ignorance of the past of others, I felt that no one had sustained such a loss before. . . . I became obsessed with justice. (Ibid., 44–5)

When Minnie Bruce Pratt made the excruciating decision not to challenge her husband's assertion of custody of their sons, she had been snared already *in* the complex sticky web of family and law that touches every married woman and mother.

But for some lesbians, it may be possible to say: 'How I love (and whom I love) is outside the law.' And here, I am thinking of some of the cases involving American lesbians who have been told by former partners or their families, and then by the courts, that they are not parents to the children they have been raising. In legal terms, these lesbians, and some others who have attempted to adopt their partners' children, are told that they do not have 'standing'—no legal interest in or right to assert in relation to the children. They are not mothers; they are not parents. Their relationships do not amount to parental or familial relations. But, as I will illustrate below, even this is subject to challenge and change; the law here is uneven.

Another implicit theme in feminist legal literature suggests that lesbians have been constructed as the archetypical bad mothers of legal discourse, and as a result, always at risk in the face of a disapproving legal system (e.g., Arnup, 1989, 1995). In her recent explication of the shifting nature of maternalist ideology in law, Susan Boyd has carefully analysed how three important 'access' issues in child custody litigation have been articulated. And while the issue of sexual orientation in access is not central to her piece, Boyd intimates that law's fear of single mothers means that lesbians can anticipate 'harsher evaluations' by judges (1996a: 504). However, while the obsessive fury of husbands often seems insatiable, recent experiences of lesbians in Canadian courtrooms suggest less predictable, less certain results.

It seems to me that we can no longer assert generally or with confidence that lesbians are in or out of the law or on the wrong side of the legal tracks; it is important to identify, illustrate, and analyse the varied and changing, indeed, contradictory ways in which the law relates to lesbians and lesbians to the law. Important shifts, and the not infrequent victory, however partial, fragile, and costly it may be, need to be acknowledged (and understood). Some of the cases I discuss below are illustrative of these shifts and contradictions.

Theme II: Lesbians 'Unmodified'—Mothers or Parents?

One question that has vexed me before is: 'What makes a woman a mother?' (Gavigan, 1995a: 107). Here I modify it to ask: 'What makes a lesbian a mother?' Are lesbians 'mothers just like others' (Arnup, 1989)? Always? The commentary on the earliest reported lesbian custody cases stressed, in the face of patriarchal wrath and judicial apprehension, that lesbian mothers were not demons but mothers, 'just like others'. The importance of this contribution cannot be overstated; Arnup broke lesbian ground in feminist legal literature at a time when few scholars and lawyers could bring themselves to say the word 'lesbian' out loud. However, new and emerging forms of litigation indicate that many lesbian mothers are *not* like other mothers: there are no fathers or husbands, no lesbian mothers being aspersed because of their sexual orientation, but rather two women who have come together or who have come apart.

But what does it mean to have two mothers? The language of 'mother' is seldom unmodified: birth mother, adoptive mother, real mother, bad mother, good mother, lesbian mother. . . . The term 'mother' implicitly invites invocation of the term 'father', as if this dyad is natural and inevitable, that a child must have one of each. Lesbian couples involved in parenting and child-rearing themselves seem to cede some primacy to the (birth/natural/real) mother: the non-birth/'social' mother may be called the co-mother (Williams, 1995: 109), the other mother (Adams, 1995; Nelson, 1996: 85), the second mother (Fleming, 1995), the co-mom (Czyscon, 1995), step-parent (Rounthwaite and Wynne, 1995: 87), or stepmother (Nelson, 1996: 84). Where a child was born or adopted into a lesbian relationship, the women seem to regard themselves as mothers and other mothers. When the child comes with the mother from a previous, usually straight, relationship, the other woman may become 'co-parent' or 'co-mom'. The age and acceptance of the child and the nature of the father's involvement may also shape the lesbian co-parent's relationship with the child or children (see, e.g., Rounthwaite and Wynne, 1995). A recent case in Ontario (*Buist v. Greaves*, 1997), which I will discuss below, has pushed this issue one step further, by testing the meaning of 'mother' in the Children's Law Reform Act.[1]

Engendering Law

Law as a Gendering Strategy

In the inaugural issue of the journal *Social and Legal Studies*, Carol Smart (1992) argued that feminist socio-legal scholars ought to shift their inquiry from earlier modes and levels of analysis to think now of law as gendered (rather than male or sexist). This analytic distinction is important, she urged, because 'the idea of it as gendered allows us to think of [law] in terms of processes which will work in a variety of ways and *in which there is no relentless assumption that whatever it does exploits women and serves men*' (1992: 33; emphasis added). It is more complicated than that. This has long been a theme in Smart's work (1981, 1985), and her insights have been important and influential for many of us in Canada. In this chapter, I take up Smart's invitation to examine 'How does gender work in law and how does law work to produce gender' and to think of law as a 'gendering strategy' (1992: 35). This form of inquiry, combined with Smart's appreciation of the uneven nature and development of legal regulation (Smart, 1986) and her injunction against feminist instrumentalist analyses, is clearly a fruitful way to proceed.

One of law's contributions to gender relations, Smart argued, is the 'Woman of Legal Discourse': the 'gendered subject position which legal discourse brings into being' (1992: 34). It is here where my departure from Smart begins to form. Smart is careful to attempt to avoid ascribing (to borrow from Cain, 1994: 44) 'causal primacy' to legal discourse: she characterizes law as 'partial author' (1992: 39). Nonetheless, her illustrative exemplar (the bad mother) belies her own critique of less sophisticated forms of feminist legal analysis.

The category of bad mother, per Smart, came into being with the enactment of draconian criminal legislation that captured 'lewd women' whose newborn infants were found dead. These apparently reluctant mothers were presumed by operation of this statute to have murdered their newborn infants unless they could produce two witnesses to provide evidence to the contrary (21 Jac.I c.27 (1603)). This statute was repealed in 1803 by the same statute (Lord Ellenborough's Act, 43 Geo.III (1803)) that made abortion at any stage of pregnancy a statutory felony, thus capturing women, married or otherwise, who were trying to avoid motherhood (Gavigan, 1984). Smart (1992: 38) delineates pieces of legislation that not only 'constructed a category of dangerous motherhood' but also widened 'the net of law . . . at precisely the same time as it made it increasingly difficult to avoid unmarried pregnancy and childbirth.' There are a number of difficulties with Smart's analysis, not the least of which is the uneasy fit her discursive exemplar, the bad mother, has with her theoretical imperative. In other words, Smart's explication of the sixteenth-, eighteenth, and nineteenth-century statutes does not illuminate legal 'processes which . . . work in a variety of ways and in which there is no relentless assumption that whatever [law] does exploits women and serves men' (ibid., 33). In fact, a broader and closer analysis of the 'dangerous' mothers of infanticide law reveals that this 'legal category' in practice was always unstable and imperfectly implemented: juries often refused to convict young women indicted and many nineteenth-century judges expressed sympathy for them (Backhouse, 1984b; Gavigan, 1984). Medico-legal experts devised 'scientific' tests to determine whether or not the infant, whose birth had been concealed and whose death was alleged to have been caused by maternal murder, had breathed or not—if not, the unmarried woman was not caught by the statute (Gavigan, 1984). Leaving aside my own view that a category of (bad) Woman of legal discourse might better be illustrated by the experience of unmarried women under the English Poor Law (Thane, 1978) or by the women who were convicted of petit treason when they killed their husbands (and who experienced scant judicial or public mercy when they were burned at the stake) (Gavigan, 1989–90), I do have a deeper theoretical concern: Smart examines only one level of law (legislation), defines it as 'legal discourse', and thus imposes closure, offering but a partial image of that of which law is but a partial author.

This observation of the contradictory images of women in legal and medicolegal discourses, even in the same area of law, is not novel. In her early work on the legal construction of women's sexuality, Susan Edwards (1981) illustrated quite contradictory images of female sexuality in sexual offences: that of female sexual passivity in sexual offence legislation and female sexual precipitation in the legal process. Even in this manifestly gendered area of criminal law, there is no one Woman in the legal discourse.

Thus, I am concerned that the much criticized 'Woman' of conventional feminist discourse has been replaced by Smart's 'Woman of legal discourse', notwithstanding her own disclaimer: 'It is this Woman of legal discourse that feminism must continue to deconstruct but without creating a normative Woman who reimposes a homogeneity which is all too often cast in our own privileged, white likeness' (Smart, 1992: 39).

While I accept her admonition, I find Smart's notion of legal discourse to be too discursively unidirectional and her Woman of legal discourse to be discursively unidimensional (and relentlessly exploited as a heterosexual woman). Constituted as she is by (legal) discourse, she has neither experience nor agency: she has neither breath nor breadth. In the film *A Simple Wish*, Ruby Dee's character was rendered cartoonishly unidimensional by the flick of a hand of Kathleen Turner's wicked fairy godmother. Smart's Woman of legal discourse similarly owes her flattened fate to the *something* that has been done to her in the 'Toon Town' of legal discourse.

Again to be clear, I accept much of Smart's theoretical contribution. An attempt to identify, appreciate, and illustrate the complex, uneven, contradictory, and materially significant nature of law and of family, and of gender inequalities, informs my work (Gavigan, 1992, 1993). In particular, I continue to be interested in identifying the *images of women* in legal discourses and practices. These images, including the images of lesbians, are as uneven, incomplete, complex, and contradictory as the law itself. In my interrogation of the various lesbian parenting cases, will I find the 'Lesbian of legal discourse'? Is there a gendered subject position of lesbian or lesbian parent constituted by law? I hope to illustrate, with the aid of Smart's theoretical prescription (if not her illustration), legal relations and legal processes that 'work in a variety of ways and in which there is no relentless assumption that whatever [law] does exploits' lesbians.

Law as Practice, Process, and Institution

The discourse of law does not correspond with everyday thought except in those areas of life such as the stock exchange where the legal form has constituted what is everyday. (Cain, 1994: 40–1)

Access to justice may be defined most narrowly as access to the courts. The words uttered in judgment by a court are the product of litigation. The cost of access to justice through litigation is prohibitive to all but the most financially secure litigant.[2] Family law, as traditionally practised, is costly to private litigants and legal aid plans alike. Unlike criminal defence work, family law is 'paper-intensive'[3] and thus expensive. This may explain in part what Brenda Cossman and Carol Rogerson (1997: 785) found in their recent study:

> With the exception of child protection cases, the majority of family law cases are not litigated to a resolution. Anecdotally, it is said that between 90 and 95 percent of family law cases settle at some point in the process prior to a trial— whether by an agreement between the parties negotiated by their lawyers without recourse to the courts, or by minutes of settlement incorporated into a consent order after litigation has been commenced, in some cases prior to the hearing of the first motion or in others after the first motions, or after a settlement or pre-trial conference.

Access to the courts via litigation is also a question of access to resources, which, for many women, are diminishing with the evisceration of legal aid plans. Thus, we have a fraction of private family law cases actually litigated and resulting in a judicial pronouncement, and fewer still reported. The cases, reported or not, that go to trial are those that defy (or in which at least one party defies) settlement.

Susan Boyd has noted with concern that one problem with legal academic research focusing on reported cases in family law is that most reported cases involve white people. Boyd (1996a: 498) considers that perhaps this may derive in part from the fact that 'white people may feel more comfortable than people of colour resorting to the court system to resolve family disputes.' Yet, surely few litigants go willingly or happily to court and fewer still savour any measure of comfort from the process. Who has the resources to participate in the legal process, who takes whom to court, and who accepts the legitimacy of judicial determinations seem more relevant here. In this process, gender, race, and class, power and money, and not infrequently our old friend the state are implicated. For instance, in April 1997, family court judges reported to the *Ontario Legal Aid Review* that fully 50 per cent of litigation in matters of child support and child protection is instituted by the state (*Ontario Legal Aid Review*, I, 1997: 801). And, as Minnie Bruce Pratt (1991: 44) learned, one can experience legal 'process' without ever going to court:

> I was judged with finality. Without my climbing the steps of the courtrooms of Cumberland County, I was sentenced. Without facing the judge, since my lawyer feared that 'calling attention to my lesbian identity' would mean that I would never see my children again, I was declared dirty, polluted, unholy. I was not to have a home with my children again. I did not die, but the agony was as bitter as death. . . .

At the heart of this is the very nature of an adversarial legal system in which (formally equal) litigants commence their actions and define their issues— where these litigants want to win. The courtroom is a site less of principle than of tactics, where perceived weaknesses in either party are exploited by the other. In all of this, the influential role of lawyers as litigators cannot be overstated. The courtroom is the home playing field not only of judges, but of legal advocates, whose practice it is to translate and transform social and personal struggles and issues into legal discourse (Cain, 1994; Glasbeek, 1989). It is a lawyer who advises the lesbian litigant not to use the word 'lesbian' in her affidavit, and it surely is a lawyer who advises an avenging renegade husband to sprinkle liberally the word 'lesbian' throughout his own affidavit. Just add 'lesbian', stir, and hope for the best. It is the lawyer who advises the lesbian mother how 'out' to be or not be if she wants to win. And thus, it is often the lawyer who lacks the courage to 'raise fearlessly every issue'[4] on behalf of the lesbian litigant or who advises on matters about which she or he is less than expert.

Considered in this light, it is as much a cause for concern as for celebration that the 'past and present' collide in the courtroom—a forum in which the perspectives and experience of past and present are selected, constructed, tailored, emphasized, and ignored at the instance of the contesting litigants in their efforts to persuade a trial judge or appellate panel of the 'rightness' of their position. But, as been argued elsewhere (see, e.g., Greenwood and Young, 1976; Thompson, 1975; Hay, 1975; Smart, 1981; Gavigan, 1988, 1992; Chunn and Gavigan, 1988), and as I have argued above and hope to illustrate below, the law is filled with contradictions; it is neither unidimensional nor monolithic.

Lesbians and Their (Legal) Relations

Lesbians find themselves in four legal contexts in family court. These four contexts are not finite or exhaustive. Indeed, at the risk of appearing to invoke an essentialist image of lesbians, I am inclined to the view that the range of contexts is perilously close to infinite given the complexity and diversity of political and interpersonal possibilities that characterize lesbian lives.

Lesbians in (Heterosexual) Family Court

Lesbian and gay custody cases in which straight (former) spouses use sexual orientation as a weapon and invoke dominant notions of appropriate parenting reveal as much about the social meaning attached to biological and social parenting as they do about the wrath of the 'straight spouse spurned'. The use of 'lesbian' and/or 'sexual orientation' as a weapon hearkens back to an earlier legal era when 'fault' was an expressly relevant factor in matrimonial causes, such as divorce. In divorce proceedings, evidence of matrimonial 'misconduct' or the commission of a 'matrimonial offence' could establish grounds for divorce; this evidence was also relevant with respect to collateral issues, such as support and custody. A wife who had deserted her husband or who had committed adultery was not entitled to support. Until 1968, a wife's homosexuality in and of itself could not support a husband's divorce petition; however, it could be drawn in under the rubric of cruelty. When the federal Divorce Act[5] was enacted in 1968, the grounds for divorce were broadened considerably. Many matrimonial 'offences' committed since the celebration of a marriage (including having 'engaged in a homosexual act') were articulated in s. 3 to support a divorce petition, and even the 'marriage breakdown' provision entrenched the significance of fault: the person who deserted the marriage had to wait five years before being able to petition for divorce—s. 4(1)(e)(ii); the deserted spouse could petition after three years—s. 4(1)(e)(i). In 1985 the Divorce Act[6] was amended to eliminate many of the fault-based grounds and to limit evidence of (bad) conduct, except where relevant to that person's suitability for custody of children. Despite this attempt at formal inhibition of allegations of (mis)conduct, some lawyers and their clients continue to be of the view that they must 'make her look like a tramp' (or worse) in divorce and custody proceedings.

Susan Boyd has ably illustrated that judicial assumptions about normal families and lifestyles are firmly rooted. The English case, *C. v. C.*, upon which she comments, involved custody litigation over a seven-year-old daughter of whom the mother had been the principal parent and caregiver in the first six years of the child's life. After the parents separated, the mother became involved in two lesbian relationships, the second of which was more significant and lasting. The father remarried, and in his bid for custody argued that he offered a stable, heterosexual nuclear family and a bigger house. Each parent was found by the trial judge to have a loving relationship with their daughter, and she was happy in both homes. The trial judge indicated, says Boyd, 'if he could choose between an exclusively heterosexual lifestyle and a lesbian one, he would favour the "normal"' (1992: 278). But given the close bond between the mother and child, and the fact that the child would inevitably learn that her mother was a lesbian, the trial judge awarded custody to the mother and access to the father. On appeal, the Court of Appeal allowed the father's appeal and ordered a new hearing, which ultimately again favoured the mother. Boyd draws out the English judges' uncritical reliance on their subjective experience and beliefs and she is not comforted by their recitation of the 'now routine' declaration that the mother's lesbian relationship was not conclusive in deciding the appeal.

C. v. C. illustrates the context in which lesbian mothers most often (to date) find themselves in court: defending a custody application by a normal, remarried ex-husband[7] or (less typically in Canada) by the child's grandparents.[8] As recently as July 1992, the British Columbia Supreme Court released a judgment in a case (*N. v. N.*) in which a father relied on the fact of the mother's lesbian relationship with an RCMP constable to support his ultimately unsuccessful bid for custody of their four children. Both parents had been devout members of the Salvation Army, and while the trial judge was not certain of the precise reason for Mrs N's 'lapse of faith', the inference drawn by her husband implicated her sexual identity. The trial judge, while not unsympathetic to Mr N, noted that his 'steadfast and unrelenting reference to the gospels had just the opposite effect on Mrs N than what he had hoped. Mrs N established a relationship with another woman' (1992: 3).

The cases involving lesbians and gay men coming out of straight relationships reveal much about the gendered nature of parenting. For instance, in Canada the struggles of gay men in relation to their children tend to manifest themselves in reported cases in which a gay father has separated from his wife and mother of their children, having wrestled with the discovery and/or acceptance (after marriage) of his sexual orientation. Generally, the legal issue here concerns not custody of the children, but rather his right of access to them, and more specifically, whether he can have overnight access (see, e.g., *W. v. W.*, 1985; *D. P.-B. v. T. P.-B.*, 1988; *Saunders v. Saunders*, 1988; *Templeman v. Templeman*, 1986). Can he have them sleep in the same home where he sleeps? Can he have his lover sleep in the house, in his room, in his bed, when his children are visiting? Can he defeat the assumption that overnight access in these circumstances exposes his children to the 'harmful effects of his lifestyle' (*W. v. W.*, 1985), and where the merits and presumed 'stability of a sexually orthodox environment' (*S. (I.J.) v. S. (G.E.)*, 1989) are preferred without question, challenge, or explanation.

Often, the wife's pain at the rejection she perceives and the disruption she has experienced is palpable (e.g., *Martini v. Martini*, 1987), but occasionally the courts offer us a glimpse of the wider familial dimensions. In a 1989 decision of the Newfoundland Supreme Court, in which, as a result of the separation, the wife and children became economically dependent on her parents and lived in their home, the court expressed a particular concern:

> immediate overnight access may have a negative affect on the best interest of the children in this particular case. The maternal grandparents have openly expressed to the children their abhorrence of their father's homosexual lifestyle. The mother is economically dependent on her parents and she and the children have no choice but to reside with them at the present time. I feel a reasonable time should be given for the grandparents to get used to the idea that the father will have overnight access and hopefully this will give the mother an opportunity to find alternative living arrangements. (*A.E. v. G.E.*, 1989: 144)

Husbands, too, continue to hurl the 'lesbian' epithet, both real and imagined, at their wives; but they do so with less confidence of vindication by the judiciary. One husband in Sault Ste Marie (*Tomanec v. Tomanec*, 1993) inferred that his wife's refusal to be a 'traditional wife' was conclusive evidence of both her lesbianism and her mental illness. The court disagreed and the wife was awarded custody of the couple's two children. Another suspicious husband insisted that his wife could be on the way to initiating a lesbian relationship with their five-year-old daughter (*Korniakov v. Korniakov*, 1997). Judge Main in the Ontario Court, Provincial Division, held that Mr Korniakov was incorrect in his conclusion. Custody of the couple's two children was awarded to the mother.

In 1996, the Ontario Court, General Division, was the site of a custody application involving two girls, aged 12 and 13, who had been in their father's custody for 11 years, pursuant to a separation agreement with their mother (*Ouellet v. Ouellet*, 1997). The father's current partner had been a 'mother figure' for the last eight years. After the separation, the mother had two short-lived relationships, which produced two more children, and at the time of the court hearing, in 1996, she had embarked on her second lesbian relationship. The girls expressed a preference to live with their mother (although one of them was nervous about what her friends and others would say about her mother being a lesbian). The mother applied for custody. At the hearing, the mother and the maternal grandparents commended the father's care of the children and his ability to facilitate access. The mother won custody, with generous access to the father. The parties were to work out the details of access between themselves and were told to return to court in a year if they could not work out an agreement. With respect to the one daughter's anxiety about her mother's sexual orientation, the court noted, 'There was a need, at the present time, for support and therapy, if necessary to cope with society's sometimes uneducated reflection upon their mother's sexual orientation' (1997 WDFL O92).

This case, buried in the *Weekly Digests of Family Law*, is interesting. Here, we have an almost perfect father who, with his new wife, has raised two girls for many years. Their mother has had two other children in the meantime and is at the beginning of her second lesbian relationship. And still, the court awarded her custody of the children. Clearly, the age and expressed preference of the daughters carried weight. But we may be able to infer that the father did not make an issue of the mother's lifestyle or sexual orientation, and did not ask the court to either. The positions taken by the parties often shape, if not determine, the tone and tenor of a judge's judgment.

The wider familial dimensions in a British Columbia adoption case may open yet another window on the limits of acceptance of sexual orientation in the wider community: here a young lesbian mother was not forced into litigation by her child's father; she did not lose custody of her child to an angry father. This woman, a single parent, was pressured by her own parents to give up her child for adoption because of their insistence that as a lesbian she could not raise a child (*Adams v. Woodbury*, 1986). Some six weeks later, having been through counselling, the young mother decided that being a lesbian did not preclude being a parent; she attempted unsuccessfully to regain custody of her daughter—over the vigorous objections not of her child's adoptive parents but of her own parents.

Some of these cases involving the judicial treatment of lesbians and gay men who leave straight marriages or who run afoul of parents' expectations illustrate what others have noted elsewhere: lesbian and gay parents are at risk in the courtroom if they do not conform to dominant notions of appropriate gay sexual behaviour: quiet and apolitical. But these cases also illustrate the gendered nature of post-separation parenting: for gay fathers, as with most fathers, access is their legal issue. Their sexual orientation, as raised by their spouses, parents, and in-laws, may be constructed in a way that shapes the kind of access arrangements they may have. With respect to lesbians, custody of their children continues to be contested and litigated at the instance of the men who have been left. And, to borrow from Shakespeare, hell frequently hath no fury like a straight spouse spurned. Yet we also see judges declining to acquiesce to the husbands and a shift in which judges now not only *say* that the mother's sexual orientation is not determinative of the issue in custody, but some of them actually seem to *mean* it. The fact that they have to say it at all, of course, is due to the fact that someone has taken the lesbian mother to court, has refused to settle, and has litigated the issue. The shift? Litigating husbands can no longer be supremely confident of winning.

Lesbians Take Each Other To Family Court: Lesbian Mothers and Other Mothers

Not every lesbian relationship lasts forever. Some even unravel with pain, rejection, and recrimination. Some lesbians have resisted the label 'spouse' in order to avoid responsibility for the children of the relationship. This was the case in a British Columbia case, *Anderson v. Luoma* (see Andrews, 1995; Arnup, 1997; Gavigan, 1995), in which Arlene Luoma successfully eschewed any responsibility for the children who had referred to her as 'their Arlene'. The legal significance of this case has always been limited, as it was decided under a particular definition in a piece of BC legislation. More recently, the Supreme Court of Canada, in *M. v. H.* (1999) held that the heterosexual definition of spouse (for the purpose of spousal support) in the Ontario legislation violated M's equality rights under the Canadian Charter of Rights and Freedoms. Arlene Luoma may well be grateful that she left Penny Anderson where and when she did!

In many provinces, including Ontario, a parent is defined in family law legislation to include someone who has demonstrated a settled intention to treat a child as a child of his or her own family (i.e., 'social parents').[9] In Ontario's Children's Law Reform Act,[10] a parent or any person may apply for custody or access to a child—the neutral phrase, 'any person', helping grandparents and lesbian social parents alike. The significance of the gender-neutrality, and indeed 'familial-neutrality', of these family law provisions should not be underestimated or misunderstood. The legislation does not restrict standing in child custody cases to parents and thus allows 'third parties' to be heard. This apparently arcane legal point is a matter of some consequence to lesbian social parents who do not have a biological relationship to a child they may be parenting with a biological parent.

In Ontario, recently, a lesbian couple who had separated litigated many issues as a result of their unravelled relationship (*Buist v. Greaves*, 1997). One of the contested issues between them involved custody of a four-year-old boy conceived by alternative insemination during the course of their relationship. The biological mother had received an offer of employment in another province and she proposed to take the little boy with her. Her former partner sought to prevent her from taking the boy with her. One interesting aspect of this case is that the social parent asked for a declaration, under s. 4 of the Children's Law Reform Act, that she, too, was the mother of the child. While she did not want to displace the biological mother, she sought to have her own relationship to the child recognized as that of 'mother' as well. In declining to make the order, the trial judge had this to say:

> There is no doubt that the relationship . . . is very close; however, [he] does not consider her his mother. Ms Greaves is his mother. He calls her 'mama' while he calls Ms Buist 'gaga' which is short for Peggy. He was given Ms G's last name at birth. (1997 OJ No 2646 at para 35)

While on the facts of this case, the trial judge may well have come to a conventional and defensible conclusion on the issues of custody (to the biological mother), access (to the social parent), and child support (a modest sum to be paid by Buist), her route to that conclusion, including her identification of these indicia of 'mother', is troubling. The appellation of parents in lesbian households may bear little resemblance to or may not share the same meaning as in households where the parents are referred to as 'Mommy' and 'Daddy'. Similarly, the fact that a child is given the last name of one parent ought not, in and of itself, be conclusive of anything. If it is, every mother whose child bears the surname of its father has cause for concern.

The gender- and familial-neutral language of the Ontario legislation allows lesbians who are not biological parents to assert claims with respect to the children in their lives. And, while *Buist v. Greaves* offers an illustration of the difficulty a lesbian social parent has in asserting an equal claim to motherhood, she nonetheless has standing to be considered as a child's parent. Neither outside law nor instances of the quintessential bad woman/mother of legal discourse, these lesbian cases suggest that finer, more nuanced analytic tools need to be deployed to explicate the lesbian victories and lesbian defeats experienced here.

Other Mothers and Others: Surviving Lesbian (Social) Parents Meet Others in Family Court

Lesbian parenting cases, combining as they do birth and adoption, fostering and social parenting, and multiple possibilities for family forms, also involve risks and chances and heartbreak. It is tempting to liken lesbian social parents to tightrope artists who work without a net; a delicate balancing act is required, and sometimes everything falls.

In the Michigan case, *McGuffin v. Overton & Porter*, a lesbian social parent was told by an appellate court that she did not have standing under the state's child custody legislation to apply for custody of two boys she had helped to raise for eight years. Her life partner, their biological mother, died in January 1995. Just prior to her death, the deceased mother had executed a will naming her partner the guardian of the children. The biological mother indicated that she did not want their biological father to have custody because he had established no relationship with them. He was also $20,000 behind in child support at the time of her death. Upon receiving notice of the surviving partner's application to be appointed the children's guardian, the father moved swiftly: he obtained *ex parte* orders for custody of each of the boys, and at the end of February he collected them from school and had them in his custody. Despite the intervention of a children's law clinic urging that the boys be returned to the home they had known for the last eight years, the Michigan appeal court told Carol Porter that she did not have standing to apply for custody of the boys. She would have to recommence her application to be named their guardian (a difficult process, notwithstanding the testamentary instrument, because the biological father could claim a more direct relationship).

In another American case, this one in New York, custody proceedings involved what the court characterized as 'a unique set of facts' (*In the Matter of the Guardianship of Astonn H.*, 1995). Astonn's mother, Margo, had died a month after he was born, never having left the hospital after his birth. Astonn, a baby with many special health-care needs, was released from hospital into the care of Margo's life partner, Sofia. Sofia applied to be appointed Astonn's guardian 10 days after her partner's death. As it happened, Margo had been married to, but separated from, the father of her older daughter (who was in the de facto custody of her husband's mother). The paternal grandmother applied for custody of Astonn, even though her son was not Astonn's biological father. In support of her claim, the (not quite) paternal grandmother argued that the half-siblings should be raised together, and further that as she, Astonn's half-sister, and Astonn shared a common racial heritage, her home was the more appropriate for him. The court observed:

> In the instant proceeding the court is presented with an extraordinary combination of circumstances that must be weighed in determining who would be the best caregiver for this child. The importance of race of the caregiver, the significance of a party's physical custody of the subject child's half sibling and the lesbian relationship between a party and the deceased biological mother, including plans they made regarding the child are circumstances unique to this proceeding that the court must consider. (1995 WL)

Sofia, the surviving lesbian social parent, was named the child's guardian and awarded custody, with access to the grandmother and assurances that he and his sister would be raised as closely together as possible.

These cases suggest that biological ties between child and parent or caregiver pose the most difficult hurdle facing a lesbian parent. This hurdle is insurmountable in the absence of familial-neutral legislation (such as Ontario's children's legislation). Clearly, these (aspirant) lesbian mothers are not mothers just like others. While Carol Porter found herself *outside* Michigan's child custody law, this relegation was neither necessary nor inevitable (as the experience in Ontario law suggests).

'Playing a Different Game on the Old Court': Lesbian Couple Adoptions

In this last section, I want to examine a 1995 decision of the Ontario Court, Provincial Division, *Re K.*, which has been followed by the Ontario Court, General Division, in *Re C.(E.G.)(No. 1) and Re C.(E.G.)(No. 2)* (1995) and in several unreported lower court decisions.[11] Effectively, lesbian adoption amounts to 'playing a different game on the old court' (Cain, 1994: 42), for the fact of adoption can establish legal parenthood for both partners of a lesbian couple.

In Ontario, in the aftermath of the defeat of Bill 167 and, in particular, in response to the last ditch eleventh-hour compromise proposed by the Attorney-General (to provide that gay and lesbian couples would not be able to adopt children) (see Ursel, 1995), four lesbian couples made joint applications to adopt the children they were raising together. In each of the four cases, the biological mother consented to the application by the 'social parent'. However, the only way they could make a joint application was to challenge the hetero-sexual definition of spouse incorporated in Ontario's Child and Family Services Act,[12] as only spouses are allowed by that legislation to make a joint application to adopt. Once the 'husband and wife' dyad was struck, the lesbians had then to establish themselves as both spouses and parents.

This they did in admirable fashion. A courageous piece of litigation produced a courageous judgment and complete vindication of the position of the lesbians before the court:

> When one reflects on the seemingly limitless parade of neglected, abandoned and abused children who appear in our courts in protection cases daily, all of whom have been in the care of heterosexual parents in a 'traditional' family structure, the suggestion that it might not ever be in the best interests of loving, caring and committed parents, who might happen to be lesbian or gay, is nothing short of ludicrous. (per Nevins J in *Re K.* at 708)

The lesbian adoption cases are interesting because they have been test cases in the truest sense of the term. They have been litigated by parties who have not been hurled into court by an outraged former spouse or parent. Rather, they have been marshalled with care and, while there have been many defeats (e.g.,

Camilla, N.Y. 1994; *Dana*, N.Y. 1995), the litigation has also produced some startling judicial pronouncements. In a 1993 lesbian adoption case in New Jersey, where a lesbian couple had been in a committed relationship for 10 years, the biological mother of the child was an executive vice-president for a large communications company, the household income was in the low six figures, and the extended families of both women were described as supportive and involved in the four-year-old child's life, the trial judge concluded:

> This case arises at a time of great change and a time of recognition that, while the families of the past may have seemed simple formations repeated with uniformity (the so-called 'traditional family') families have always been complex, multifaceted, and often idealized. This court recognizes that families differ in both size and shape within and among the many cultural and socio-economic layers that make up this society. We cannot continue to pretend that there is one formula, one correct pattern that should constitute a family in order to achieve the supportive, loving environment we believe children should inhabit. This court finds that the family before it is providing a secure, stable, and nurturing environment for the child. This is to be commended. J.M.G. [the adoptive parent] is one of the two cornerstones of this supportive home, and beyond all other issues it is upon this factor that this court primarily relies in granting this petition for adoption. (per Freedman P.J.S.C., *In the Matter of the Adoption of a Child by J.M.G.*, 1993)

With respect to the issue of homophobia in the broader community, this judge observed:

> if there is ever any harassment or community disapproval, this court should have no role in supporting or tacitly approving such behavior. The court's recognition of this family unit through the adoption can serve as a step in the path towards which strong, loving families of all varieties deserve. (Ibid.)

The next year, in another lesbian adoption case, a New York judge addressed the issue of different family forms:

> This Court is aware that these cases present family units many in our society believe to be outside the mainstream of American family life. The reality, however, is that most children today do not live in so-called 'traditional' 1950 television situation comedy type families with a stay-at-home mother and a father who works from 9:00 to 5:00. . . . It is unrealistic to pretend that children can only be successfully raised in an idealized concept of family, the product of nostalgia for a time long past. The family environments presented in these adoption cases are warm, loving and supportive, well-suited for the nurturance of children. The Court is less concerned for the welfare of these adoptive children than for many of the children of heterosexual parents who

find themselves before the Court. (per Sciolino J., *In the Matter of the Adoption of Caitlin and Another (Adoption No. 1)*; *In the Matter of the Adoption of Adam and Another (Adoption No. 2)*, N.Y. Fam. Ct, Monroe County, 1994)

In these cases, however, it is not enough for the lesbian social parents to be 'parents'. In order to make a joint application, and thereby preserve the biological mother's tie to the child(ren), they must also be spouses in Ontario, and indeed in every province other than British Columbia.[13]

Thus, as profound as the challenge of lesbian couple adoptions is, it is clear that striking down the opposite sex requirement alone does not, cannot, address the constraints and familial assumptions embedded in the adoption legislation in Ontario. For the lesbian parents to be full parents, they had to be spouses, same-sex spouses to be sure, but spouses nonetheless. Perhaps then, there is after all a (new) lesbian of legal discourse: the good spouse.

Conclusion

In this paper, I have attempted to illustrate the challenges experienced and posed by lesbians who parent. There is no one kind of lesbian custody case, and no simple or easily predictable judicial response. This also illustrates the complex and contradictory nature of law—as discourse and practice—and its uneven contribution to gender relations. I have sought to illustrate that legal practice, legal and non-legal actors, and legal processes have to be factored into any analysis of law as a gendering strategy.

In many provinces, including Ontario, a parent is defined to include social parents (i.e., someone who has demonstrated a settled intention to treat a child as a child of his or her own family). In Ontario, a parent or any person may apply for custody or access to a child—the neutral phrase, 'any person', helping grandparents and lesbian social parents alike. The significance of gender-neutrality, and indeed familial-neutrality, to these family law provisions should not be underestimated or misunderstood. Unlike the experience of some lesbian social parents in the United States, lesbian partners and social parents in Canada get into the front door of the courtroom and are not denied standing, custody, or access simply because they are lesbian. I am inclined to think that, strategically, the better way for the lesbian social parents to proceed is not to press for recognition as 'mother' but rather to continue to push for legislation that has opened up the possibility for recognition of the importance of the social nature of parenting. Feminists, lesbians, and mothers ought to move away from the ideological (and patriarchal) appeal of 'mother', loosen its grip, and continue to breathe lesbian content into the 'person' and 'parent' of family law legislation.

While it is enormously satisfying to see and hear the gnashing of teeth of the self-styled pro-family right at the thought of lesbian legal victories, lesbian adoptions, and the increasing acceptance of lesbian families, it is important that we interrogate and re-examine our places in and positions on family law, especially when we (at least some of us) win our cases. This may require some rethinking of the place of gender-neutrality in the gendering of justice.

Notes

I wish to acknowledge with thanks Marilyn Clarke and Kate Matthews for their research assistance, Natia Tucci for her technical assistance, and Karen Andrews, Dorothy Chunn, and Dany Lacombe for their comments on an earlier version of this chapter.

1. R.S.O. 1990, c. C12, s. 4.

2. For instance, a lesbian parent of my acquaintance spent over $35,000 in 1988–9 in a divorce in which her right to custody of their two sons was challenged by her husband. More recently, she has spent a further $20,000 responding to his application for child support for the one child of the marriage who continues to reside with him on a full-time basis, as well as a bid for custody of and support for the other boy (now aged 16) who resides with him on a part-time basis. Although she won handily at trial (including $8,000 in her court costs), her husband appealed to the Divisional Court, where again she won so handily her lawyer was not called upon. He lost again; she was awarded a further $2,000 in costs. His annual income (as a chartered accountant) is easily twice hers (as a school teacher).

3. *Equal Justice for Women and Children*, A Report by the Family Law Tariff Subcommittee to the Legal Aid Committee of the Law Society of Upper Canada (May 1992), 8.

4. Law Society of Upper Canada, *Professional Conduct Handbook*, 1997 edn, Rule 8, Commentary 2.

5. R.S.C. 1970, c. D–8.

6. S.C. 1986, c. 4.

7. See also Katherine Arnup's thorough reviews (1989, 1995) of the early cases. For more recent Canadian cases, see *Elliott v. Elliott* [1987] B.C.J. No. 43; *N. v. N.* [1992] B.C.J. No. 1507; *Re Barkley and Barkley* 28 O.R. (2d) 136 (Ont.); *Daller v. Daller* [1988] O.J. No. 2116 (Ont. S.C.). A Saskatchewan custody case in which sexual orientation was an express non-issue involved a father who had left the marriage for a male lover; subsequent to the separation, the mother became involved in a lesbian relationship. Hence, as both parents were gay or lesbian and involved in ongoing

relationships, sexual orientation was not an issue for Barclay J. *Robertson v. Geisinger* [1991] S.J. No. 515.

8. *Bennett v. Clemens*, 230 GA 317, 196 S.E. 2d 842; *Frye v. Frye* 45 Cal App 3d 39; 119 Cal Rptr 22 (1979).

9. Family Law Act, R.S.O. 1990, c. F 3, s. 1. The Child and Family Services Act, R.S.O. 1990, c. C 11, has even broader definitions of parent for the purposes of both child protection (s. 37) and adoption (s. 137).

10. R.S.O. 1990, c. C 12, s. 21.

11. In January 1996, I was told by a social worker employed by the Metropolitan Toronto Children's Aid Society that she had seen a number of lesbian adoption cases. This social worker was responsible for obtaining the 'consents' of children over the age of seven to the proposed adoptions.

12. R.S.O. 1990, c. C 11.

13. In the province of British Columbia, The Adoption Act of 1995 allows for 'one adult or two adults jointly' to apply to the court to adopt a child.

Part III

Constructing
the Racialized Other
of Legal Discourse

Chapter 7

Theory and Practice
Clinical Law and Aboriginal People

Dara Culhane and Renee Taylor

Introduction

This chapter is the product of a collaboration between two academics: an anthropologist and a lawyer who teaches clinical law. We (Dara and Renee) are not strangers to each other. We have been friends, relatives by marriage, and colleagues for over 20 years, and we have worked together on numerous and varied professional, intellectual, and political projects. While this chapter is the product of focused discussions and research that we undertook specifically in response to an invitation to contribute to this collection, the piece represents a moment in conversations and debates between us that precede and succeed this writing.

We approached this project through an ethnographic method (Beaman-Hall, 1996; Mohammed and Juhasz, 1996). We began by tape-recording and transcribing our discussions about the questions posed by the editors; reading and discussing the transcripts; and then taping and transcribing more focused debates on issues that emerged as important in the earlier conversations. We decided first to describe the daily work of the University of British Columbia Faculty of Law's Clinical Program in Aboriginal Law ('the Clinic'), who the Clinic's clients are, and why they come. Next we conducted a review of a randomly selected sample of 50 per cent of the files opened by the Clinic up to December 1996 to check our perceptions and impressions of the Clinic's work against this documentary record. So informed, we then reflected on the central questions addressed in this volume, seeking to understand the Clinic in its social-political context as a particular 'site of struggle', and through a dialogue between everyday life and practices and analytic and theoretical concerns. Finally, we reviewed and discussed drafts of the chapter, reaching consensus on the final content.[1]

In their Introduction, Chunn and Lacombe state that the impetus for this book was to address 'the apparent conundrum confronted by contemporary feminists who teach, research, and write about law'. This conundrum results from the paradox created when disempowered groups seek social change and justice through the law: the quintessential institution that embodies and reproduces the marginalization of, for example, women and Aboriginal peoples. The moment of victory in such legal/political struggles is inevitably and simultaneously a moment of co-optation. This point is made succinctly by Pierre Bourdieu (1987: 852) when he says:

> Thus . . . the subversive efforts of those in the juridical avant garde in the end will contribute to the adaptation of the law and the juridical field to new states of social relations, and thereby insure the legitimation of the established order of such relations.

Bourdieu, we argue, is 'theoretically correct', and his analysis constitutes the limit of a critical analysis of law and the politics of legal strategies of resistance within the context of existing social relations. We take this analysis as a horizon that we do not wish to lose sight of, marking as it also does the distinction between a liberal, reformist vision of social change and a critical, transformational one. However, between our various grounded locations in an increasingly regressive, neo-conservative daily reality and that distant horizon, and any emancipated social world that we may someday create beyond it, lies everyday life and the tools at hand.

People make history, but not under conditions of their own making. This caveat is particularly relevant to the situation of Aboriginal peoples in Canada, for whom the choices of where and how to struggle for survival as individuals and as collectivities are significantly 'overdetermined' by their location as numerically small, geographically scattered, and economically, politically, and culturally marginalized minorities encapsulated within neo-colonial relations with the Canadian state. Aboriginal peoples constitute approximately 10 per cent of Canada's population.[2] The principal options for resistance and transformation are practices of daily life on the land; kin-keeping; maintaining, rebuilding, and building rural and urban communities; political negotiations with governments; litigation in courts; and civil disobedience. The movement for Aboriginal self-determination is a political, social, and cultural movement that, while it bears many resemblances to other contemporary social movements, cannot be easily or neatly fitted into prevailing theoretical frameworks.

Neither the Aboriginal population nor its political movements are homogeneous. Cross-cut by differences based in national, local, and personal histories, in gender and generational relations, in neo-colonial class location, in political philosophies, and in visions of possible futures, 'the' Aboriginal people are not univocal. Foundational assumptions, goals, strategies, alliances, and tactics that direct practices at each site both within the legal arena and elsewhere are perpetually contested (Frideres, 1994). It is beyond the scope of this paper to explore this political diversity in the depth it deserves. Our more modest objective is to contribute from a position that cautiously seeks opportunities to enhance survival with greater justice and autonomy—social change—for Aboriginal peoples through law, while simultaneously insisting that law and the legal arena can only be understood as one site among many located within a context of interrelated processes of domination, accommodation, and resistance.

Chunn and Lacombe asked that we consider the question 'How are meanings of gender reproduced, legitimized, or perhaps refashioned by law?' Our first response is that the question must be reworded to ask: 'How is law simultaneously a gendering and a racializing practice that reproduces, legitimizes, and perhaps refashions class relations?'

The Clinical Program in Aboriginal Law

The University of British Columbia Faculty of Law's Clinical Program in Aboriginal Law ('the Clinic') is located, geographically, on the edge of Vancouver's depressed inner city: the 'Downtown Eastside'. Sharing an old brick building with the Vancouver Aboriginal Justice Centre, the Clinic's north-facing windows overlook railway tracks and a busy industrial waterfront. One block to the west of the Clinic, newly gentrified condominiums and lofts are for sale. Cobblestone streets, restaurants, coffee bars, and trendy tourist stores—many specializing in Northwest Coast Aboriginal art—signal passage from the Downtown Eastside to 'Historic Gastown'. Chinatown marks the southern border of the Downtown Eastside and Japantown the eastern: inscriptions of Vancouver's geopolitical history of racialized spatial containment.

Framed by these boundary markers and lying to the south and east of the Clinic's front door is the Downtown Eastside, an area journalists like to refer to as 'Canada's poorest neighbourhood' (Mathers, 1990). Television newscasts frequently present their viewers with the Downtown Eastside as a decaying and decadent urban spectacle. Images of drug dealers and addicts, prostitutes, pimps, and johns, and alcoholics passed out on sidewalks and in doorways on 'the drag', a one-block stretch of East Hastings Street that cuts through the heart of the Downtown Eastside, have become familiar fare. These video clips are typically accompanied by shots that pan from the drag to surrounding seedy hotels, dilapidated rooming houses, dingy cafés, pawnshops, courthouses, and jails.

What the cameras fail to record, more often than not, are the brightly painted wall murals and satirical graffiti, the hard-won public housing with curtained windows, gardens, and window boxes, and the schools, drop-in centres, clinics, missions, churches, parks, and playgrounds that announce that the Downtown Eastside is a *neighbourhood* that is *home* to approximately 12,000 people (Fallick, 1987; Green, 1989). An estimated 87 per cent of

Downtown Eastside residents are unemployed. Approximately 20 per cent (2,400) are Aboriginal people, representing about 5 per cent of the estimated 42,795 Aboriginal people living in the City of Vancouver (Statistics Canada, 1991a, 1991b). Another 20 per cent are Asian or Latino, many of whom are refugees waiting in limbo for immigration hearings to determine their futures. The remaining majority are Caucasian Canadians, many elderly and disabled. 'Deinstitutionalized' psychiatric patients, now homeless and uncared for, constitute an identifiable population group in the Downtown Eastside.

Most of the Clinic's clients live in the Downtown Eastside. Many others live with their families in Native housing and other public housing projects that have been constructed recently in the adjacent working-class neighbourhood of Vancouver East. Some come from reserves within the Greater Vancouver or Lower Mainland region, others from various First Nations in rural BC, and still others from across Canada (Harding, 1994).

The Clinic is located, politically, at a nexus of emergent structures of Aboriginal self-government. The struggle for Aboriginal self-government, as noted above, takes place in many diverse locations and through many complex processes, the law and legal strategies representing only one of these. The legal arena itself includes multiple sites: international courts and quasi-judicial bodies; constitutional challenges in the Supreme Court of Canada; criminal, civil, and family law in courts at every level; and, increasingly, various alter-native forums that go under the label of 'Aboriginal justice initiatives'. Each of these sites offers diverse opportunities and constraints, and invites unique legal/political strategies. Aboriginal analysts are careful to draw links between justice, health, education, land, and culture as components of self-government, thus making change in each a necessary condition of change in the others and subverting the fragmented liberal discourse of government bureaucracy that attempts to represent each of these elements as discrete, separate administrative units (Culhane, 1995).

The Clinic originally represented a collaboration between three groups: the Legal Services Society of British Columbia ('legal aid'), which provided criminal defence services to people who are unable to afford to hire a lawyer privately and who have been charged with offences that might result in imprisonment; the Vancouver Aboriginal Justice Centre (VAJC), which offered mediation and referral services, legal aid qualification, and community outreach; and the University of British Columbia Faculty of Law, whose commitment to public interest advocacy law targeted First Nations, immigrants, and refugees as groups particularly marginalized and disadvantaged in Canadian society, generally, and in the area of legal representation, particularly. Taylor has described the emergence of the Clinic as follows:

> The VAJC was concerned that Aboriginal people, particularly in the inner-city, were appearing before the courts and administrative tribunals in such large numbers. . . . Many Aboriginal people were appearing before the courts and

other authorities without representation, tending to increase the already alarming statistics that prevail. Moreover, on Aboriginal rights issues First Nations people were not being adequately defended, if at all. In response to these needs, the VAJC approached the Faculty of Law with a proposal to open a clinic 'downtown'. (Taylor, 1996: 191)

The Clinic opened on 1 January 1995, its mandate being to represent Aboriginal clients unable to qualify for publicly funded legal aid or to hire a lawyer. The UBC Faculty of Law Faculty Council, in its motion of support for the Clinic, also noted 'the importance that the issue of Aboriginal self-government, which we see playing an integral role in the development of the First Nations theme in the Clinic, now has, and is likely to continue for the foreseeable future to have, for Canadian society' (Elliot, 1992).

Like many of its clients, the Clinic's survival is tenuous. Declining interest rates have reduced the contributions from lawyer trust funds that finance legal aid, causing rounds of cutbacks to services and increasingly restrictive qualification criteria. This has been accompanied by shrinking contributions from another funding source: the provincial Ministry of the Attorney-General. The VAJC, wholly funded by the Legal Services Society as a Native Community Law Office, secured funding only until May 1997 and has closed down. The Clinic itself is now affiliated with the Legal Services Society, with which it shares office space, and is substantively funded by the Vancouver Law Foundation.

A significant body of academic and popular literature now exists on issues concerning the relationship between Aboriginal people and law in Canada. This literature tends to fall into categories determined by the particular area of the Canadian justice system being addressed. In general, proposals or strategies for change take a two-pronged parallel approach: development of autonomous Aboriginal justice systems and an end to discrimination against Aboriginal people within the mainstream Canadian justice system. The goals in this latter sphere are equality before the law in terms of access, representation, and judgment; the linking, in practice, of legal problems to historical, social, and economic context; and, following from that, the securing of resources for non-legal solutions such as personal counselling, employment training, etc. Another objective is to increase the participation of Aboriginal people in legal professions. The Clinic plays a role in this process.[3]

Taylor: There isn't going to be a reformed system until it mirrors in some way an Aboriginal person's world. There is an almost absolute absence of Crown counsel, sheriffs, registry personnel, or police officers, and a paucity of Aboriginal lawyers doing trial work. Of the 111 Aboriginal students who have graduated from UBC's Faculty of Law since 1961, only 50 are practising lawyers, while 13 are currently articling. Three other graduates have been appointed to the bench, several are prominent politicians, a few are business people, several are bureaucrats or administrators, two are in graduate school, and three are employed by law faculties. One of the goals of the Clinic is to develop over time a cadre of Aboriginal litigators equipped to do trial work.

The Clinic builds self-confidence by teaching students to prepare cases thoroughly and to pursue aggressively their clients' interests. Standard law office procedures are followed, giving students an opportunity to hone their skills prior to the articling period. For both the Aboriginal and non-Aboriginal students, working in the inner-city area where the majority of clients reside has been an illuminating experience. To observe firsthand the degradation of poverty, racism, and substance abuse, which affect many of the clients using our services, is education in itself. Given this client base, students are forced to develop a repertoire of interpersonal skills to deal effectively with the cases.

The biggest impact, however, has been on the clients. First Nations people are generally delighted that they can access Aboriginal counsel!

Culhane: Does having Aboriginal people in those positions within the existing system significantly change anything? Do they just end up being Aboriginal people doing 'white' jobs in a 'white' system?

Taylor: I think it does make a difference. It has been my experience with students and clients at the Clinic, and certainly my own experience, that there truly is a way in which an Aboriginal person—and it does not matter whether they have grown up on or off reserve—has experienced the world in a culturally specific way. One aspect of this is the very deep knowledge we have of what the dominant society thinks of us. We have all heard things all our lives and this certainly doesn't stop when you go to law school or when you start to practise. There is, for example, the popular assumption that 'Indians get everything for nothing', and this is a strongly held view in relation to how we get law degrees. Despite the fact that we do not get any special breaks, that we take all the same courses, and write all the same exams, our colleagues as well as the general public continue to think that we have some sort of 'lesser' qualification. The fact is that if we want to specialize in Aboriginal law we are required to do *more* work and not less, to take *more* courses and not fewer. This is something every Aboriginal professional faces every day: the assumption that we are here through some sort of generosity on the part of non-Aboriginals and not as a result of our work, the struggles of our ancestors and families, our abilities and our qualifications. We also hear repeated comments in and out of court about 'what's wrong with Indians' and 'what they are like'. For an Aboriginal lawyer to acquiesce in these notions would result in a particularly painful and destructive form of schizophrenia. I haven't seen that developing as a significant problem as yet.

While the Clinic, with the VAJC, is involved in developing autonomous Aboriginal systems for the practice of justice, it is in the area of addressing issues of discrimination and inequality within the Canadian justice system that the Clinic concentrates most of its work. In 1996, the Clinic opened a total of 406 files: 177 civil, 229 criminal. In preparation for writing this article we reviewed a randomly selected sample of 50 per cent of the files: 115 criminal and 89 civil. Approximately two-thirds of clients with criminal matters were male. Among civil cases, the ratio is reversed: two-thirds were female. The 39 criminal files involving female clients included 14 charged with soliciting, 10 with theft, seven with mischief, six with assault, and two with breach of probation. All these women depended on social assistance for income.

Of the 76 files representing men charged with criminal offences that we reviewed, 23 were charged with assault, 20 with theft, 20 with narcotics offences, 10 with impaired driving, and three with Fisheries Act offences relating to Aboriginal rights. Of these 76, six had part-time employment in skilled and semi-skilled trades; the remaining 70 were, like the women, financially dependent on social assistance.

Criminal Justice

In the arena of criminal justice, numerous well-publicized cases and inquiries have established beyond the doubt of any reasonable person two facts: (1) that Aboriginal people are discriminated against on the basis of their racial(ized) identity at all levels of the Canadian criminal justice system; and (2) that Aboriginal people are disproportionately disadvantaged according to all commonly accepted indicators of sociocultural vulnerability to conflict with the law: economic marginalization, unemployment, poverty, poor education, stigmatized identity, high rates of alcohol and drug abuse, and personal histories punctuated by abuse, dislocation, and family conflict. These factors result in the disproportionate overrepresentation of Aboriginal people in Canadian prison populations.[4]

Aboriginal women, it has become a truism to say, are the poorest of the poor, the most disempowered category of persons in Canada, who are recognized as such by both the state and the populace. Like their male counterparts, Aboriginal women are found in large numbers in correctional institutions in Canada.[5]

Taylor: Where do our female clients come from? Why do they come? They come because they have been charged with crimes of poverty: theft by mothers between welfare cheques who steal baby food; soliciting by women who are really wired and support their habits by hooking. Some soliciting charges are in the category that we call grocery hooking cases.[6] These are women who are often charged a couple of days before the monthly cheque comes because social assistance simply does not provide enough to keep a family fed and sheltered from cheque to cheque. Women almost always steal for children. Assault is another common charge for women who come to see us. Ninety per cent who come in with criminal charges are impaired by alcohol and/or drugs at the time of their arrest. Or they come because they have been victims of crime: they have been beaten up by the police, or by their partners or pimps. They've been abducted by tricks or guys they've had a drink with in the bar, been taken off somewhere, and gang-raped and beaten.

Culhane: Can you outline what the Clinic's strategy is in dealing with clients charged with the Criminal Code offences you have listed?

Taylor: One of the essential parts of clinical practice that is different from general practice is that in poverty law matters you very much have to empower the client to tell her story in her own way, and not necessarily to put a gloss over it in a sociological or even a cultural or historical framework initially. Because if you do, you are not then bonding with the client and establishing a rapport. So, in the first instance you try to empower the person as much as possible. Then we look at the particulars and check to see if there was anything in the way the police proceeded that was illegal, e.g., not chartering them, searching without reasonable and probable grounds, etc. Then, in a case, for example, like a woman stealing baby food and Pampers, where the value of the item can be less than $20, it seems to me that this shouldn't be treated as a criminal offence. So in such cases, I contact the Crown, but they are often unwilling to drop charges. It may be appropriate, depending on circumstances, to discuss a guilty plea and sentencing recommendations at this point. I have found experienced Crown counsel are more amenable to taking account of the accused's circumstances and coming to an agreement on a recommendation for sentencing. Often, less seasoned Crown counsel approach their case load with zeal and rigidity, and are less responsive to opportunities to resolve issues through dialogue.

So if it's indisputable, and nothing has been done improperly, an acquittal is not likely, and Crown counsel is not agreeable to mediation, then the next thing is to try to divert it out of the court system. Diversion is very restrictive and only applies to first-time offenders. It involves a complete admission of guilt by the accused and a willingness to enter into a diversion contract, which often specifies community hours. If the diversion contract is not complied with, Crown counsel can reinstitute the criminal charge.

Culhane: Referring to the example of the woman who has stolen baby food and Pampers, let's say she doesn't get diversion and you end up in court. What is your strategy then? What's the best outcome there that you could have?

Taylor: It depends. Sometimes the matter will go to trial. If the accused has what we call a 'meritous defence', such as a strong alibi, mistaken identity, no illegal intent (*mens rea*), or self-defence, then we will have a full trial and argue the case as strongly as we can. If a client pleads, or is found, guilty, I am still looking for the best-case scenario.

Culhane: So the next stage is sentencing. What do you do at that stage?

Taylor: That's where we talk about who *else* the client is. Maybe she looks after her sister's kids three days a week. Maybe she is looking after elderly people in her family. Maybe she is known as a seamstress, or basket-maker, or cook, and is involved in community gatherings. Maybe she has been dealing with an addiction problem and is now in counselling. Maybe she has a history of abuse and has been trying to come to terms with that.

As a lawyer you may have legal strategies that enable you to present the client's story to the court in such a way as to prevent the person ending up with hollow or empty rights simply because the courts cannot categorize what they are saying. The judge only hears that they are unemployed, that they have been for years, that they are on social assistance, that they are addicts. You want the judge to see the whole person standing there.

The court is also acutely aware—and this varies from judge to judge—that the system is not working. The system is not working because people are being penalized, in truth, for being poor. Some judges are very receptive to an entirely social argument, but they can only exercise discretion. They don't write laws—those are made by Parliament or by the provincial authorities. As judges they cannot make new laws. There are some judges who are much more receptive to the particular historical circumstances of Aboriginal people, and they make it very well known in their judgments that they are bound to find guilt but they are also willing to listen to creative solutions to a problem.

Culhane: One of the questions this collection of essays is looking at addresses the contradictions that arise from the use of defences that rely on some sort of argument for 'diminished capacity' or 'diminished agency' to garner the court's mercy or sympathy. For example, one of the situations referred to a lot on this issue is the use of the 'battered wife syndrome' defence. The critique is that it may get an individual client off, and may recognize some psychological reality, but at the same time it can perpetuate the idea that battered women are therefore less reliable, less responsible, less self-determining, and less capable. And it allows the same reasoning to be used against women in other situations.[7]

Do you see similar problems with the use of defences based on fetal alcohol syndrome (FAS), or fetal alcohol effects (FAE), or residential school syndrome, or a lifetime of victimization, arguments on behalf of Aboriginal clients? Are you unintentionally contributing to a way of thinking that characterizes Aboriginal people as 'damaged'?

Taylor: If you are looking at it in a historical context of what Aboriginal people have been through, then I think it would be remarkable if there wasn't a lot of psychological and emotional damage. If, for example, you've lived in 30 foster homes and never had a bonding relationship, you are likely to have a diminished sense of self and agency from that experience. If you or your parents or grandparents went through residential school, you are likely to be struggling to gain a sense of self-worth. Contrary to the feminist critique you are referring to, we are not making an argument for simplistic determinism or passive victimization. We are talking about the *complexity* of Aboriginal people's lives. We're talking about relentless institutional, historical, contextualized oppression and resistance. We don't have to embellish, or exaggerate, or 'construct' a defence in the way that these critiques describe the process. We don't have to look beyond our client's life stories to assert without any hesitation or theoretical qualification that they have been badly treated, have experienced shocking injustices, often from birth, and that life lived in these conditions has taken its toll. And their families often have had similar experiences for generations.

Culhane: I think the problem lies not with what *you* are *saying*, but rather with what *they* (the judges) may be *hearing*.

Taylor: You mentioned FAS/FAE. Well, a lawyer can't just say that as a blind assertion. There has to be some way of making that an integral aspect of the case. There are rules of evidence. You've got to have a medical assessment. Then there's a problem of who is going to pay for the assessment. If it's done by court order then there is no cost to the person. You need a psychologist or a psychiatrist who is prepared to testify virtually without charge, and since I have been practising I have only met one psychiatrist who testified without remuneration. If the client is simply going on a roster of people who are waiting for testing, that may be well past the date at which the appearance is going to be. A poor person can't afford a lawyer, or psychologists, or expert witnesses, and they will suffer more consequences if judges can't see them as real persons, or can't understand why they have behaved in certain ways, or why they are appearing before him or her repeatedly.

So the issue you raise is not problematic for me. The problem for me is that the people I see are totally crushed. They have no self-esteem, no self-confidence, no faith, and no hope. They do not believe that they are going to get justice under any circumstances. All of their experience has told them that the system does not work for them. It works for a lot of other people but it doesn't work for them. What I see are people whose spirit has been broken. To get them to fight for themselves, or feel that they are worthy of fighting for, or worthy of just and fair treatment is the challenge. I feel this places a lot more responsibility on the shoulders of counsel. So the more difficult situation is to say [to the person to] give it one more chance with me, and I promise you it will be different.

Many of the issues clients come to us with do not begin as legal problems, and the solutions aren't legal ones either, but the law can be an entry point into the problem. We try to connect them with other resources that will help them deal with the real issues behind the immediate legal problem. We have an in-house psychologist at the VAJC. She is one of only three Aboriginals who are registered psychologists in the province and she cannot even begin to meet the needs of our clients. But for many of our clients, receiving counselling, and even a medical or psychiatric diagnosis, can be the first time in their lives that they have been offered any explanation for their predicament beyond one that labels them as inferior individuals of an inferior people, which is what many have internalized as their own self-concept.

Culhane: You have been talking about people for whom, for most of us, it is quite easy to feel sympathy: people who commit what you have described as 'crimes of poverty' and victims of violent crime. The argument that the legal system should not participate in reproducing the social injustices that led to conflict with the law in the first place is a convincing one in these cases. But what about the expectation that the law should protect the vulnerable and punish those who do harm? For example, how does the Clinic deal with men charged with domestic assault?

Taylor: That's very difficult. It's hard for an Aboriginal man to get good legal service. The Clinic's students are obliged to do their best to represent his interests according to the law. That means trying to get an acquittal. The Crown will not divert spousal assaults as a matter of public policy, and will only, with great reluctance, stay the charge, usually only if the complainant is reluctant to proceed. Upon conviction the Clinic practitioners must in some way try to create a credible client. This often means convincing the client that anger management counselling is in his best interests, and possibly addiction counselling as well where that is an issue. And it is true that a lot of the abuse happens when there is alcohol or drugs involved, and there is anger, and arguments over money, and the usual things that people fight about. I am not excusing it in any way. I am simply saying that the fact that a man has committed this crime, and that he is a First Nations man who has no money, should not be grounds to deny him the best legal representation possible. By the same token, complainants are entitled to a safe home.

Prior to working at the Clinic I had a private practice. What you do when you are in practice and you have somebody charged with a criminal offence is you spare nothing to ensure the best interests of the client are served. This is what I call a 'middle-class defence'. This is what we try to offer at the Clinic: a middle-class defence. When a woman who is a victim of spousal assault comes to the Clinic, we try to assist her in whatever way she requires. If that means, for her, peace bonds, separation, divorce, then that is what we will try to do. There is a huge lack of resources for Aboriginal women in this area. The resources that are available, like shelters and transition houses, have come out of the struggles waged by the women's movement. The women's movement has done a lot for Aboriginal women, and for society at large, and I would never say it hasn't. But we need our own resources and our own people trained in our own ways. Another achievement of feminists has been the implementation of equality provisions in the Charter. I support that because it is a legal mechanism put in place to challenge injustice on the basis of sexual inequality. I am glad it exists, and we will use it, in our own way.

But frequently these are not the instructions we receive. More often I am inundated with telephone calls from the victim saying that she won't testify in court, and she is dropping the charges for all kinds of reasons that go beyond the battered wife syndrome.

Culhane: It seems the courts can, sometimes, accommodate the liberal feminist construction of individual women as victims who are always better off out of abusive relationships. This doesn't reflect the situation of Aboriginal women who are part of an Aboriginal couple and family, who are part of a much larger collectivity.

Taylor: That's right. Exactly. At the Clinic, we try to take Aboriginal considerations into account. Such an Indian approach looks to mediation—not to mediate the violence, there's no excuse for that, but to mediate what kind of relationship the couple wants and to help both parties. The wife doesn't want to be beaten and the man doesn't want to beat her, and I think that is possible. They are often members of extended families in the same cultural group. In fact, most couples want to get back together. These Aboriginal values are professed time and time again by clients. They tell us that they want to be part of their own nations, and they want to keep their cultural ties. They are both part of a much larger kinship group that involves a whole bunch of economic, ceremonial, and spiritual practices. They are in a much different situation than the individual woman in a couple or nuclear family. There are issues of collectivities and history at play.

Culhane: So how would you respond to the critique that is made by some Aboriginal women, and Aboriginal women lawyers, who advocate greater punishment for spousal assault and are critical of these mediation models, particularly in cases of male violence against women and children. They see mediation as being an easy out for violent men. They argue that First Nations women have a right to the full vengeance of the law.[8]

Taylor: I totally disagree with the notion that Aboriginal women's main enemies are patriarchal band councils and male-dominated institutions. I think that Indian women have a harder time, though. But I don't think the Aboriginal world can be divided into men and women. I think that denies the colonial history we have all experienced. Many of our clients tell us their families' histories of generations of dislocation and abuse. Sometimes this violence turns inward. I could only adopt the model that men should be punished to the nth degree of the law if I were convinced that that's what people want, and that is what would help them ultimately re-establish the things that are important, like good, non-violent relationships. But I don't see it working that way. I don't see our men coming out of prison healthier than when they went in. I see the opposite. What I hear most from both men and women is that they want help from counselling. Frequently, both of them have addiction problems, and they want to go to addiction counselling together. And good, long-term counselling is not easy to access when you have no money. People can wait, literally, for a couple of years to get into counselling. They want their children to be safe and happy, to go to school and succeed. They want to learn how to be better parents. They want a better life.

Civil Procedures

It is not, however, criminal defence lawyers that most women who come to the Clinic are looking for. Only one-third of clients with criminal matters of concern are female. In civil cases, the ratio is reversed: about two-thirds are female, one-third male. The 60 civil files involving female clients that we reviewed included 14 appeals to the Ministry of Social Services tribunals for income assistance; 10 were tenants in conflict with landlords; 10 wanted to file petitions in small claims court; four wanted to petition for divorce; six were involved in disputes with First Nation (band) councils pertaining to reinstatement under Bill C–31; seven wished to file criminal injury compensation claims for abuse; three launched employment discrimination charges; two required advice about debt issues, one about an estate; and one each filed a name change, an Insurance Corporation of British Columbia (automobile accident insurance) claim, and a Revenue Canada income tax appeal.

The 30 civil case files we reviewed involving male clients broke down as follows: eight appeals to Ministry of Social Services tribunals for income assistance; four wrongful dismissal suits; four applications for federal pardons; two automobile accident insurance claims; two divorce petitions; two police harassment charges; one application for reinstatement under Bill C–31; two debt problems; one appeal of a federal sentence; and one application for conjugal visiting privileges in prison.

Culhane: What kinds of issues do clients come to the Clinic about that relate to problems in the workplace?

Taylor: Often, Aboriginal people feel they are not getting advanced or promoted because they are Indian. They feel they are the most marginalized people in their workplaces. Wrongful dismissal charges are common. And we hear a lot about slurs that are addressed to Indians. For example, they get called 'chief' and 'wagon burner', and if they object they are told that it is all in 'good humour'. The stereotype of the lazy, drunken Indian is still prevalent and this is reflected in demeaning comments. The unions are more often than not complicit in this. Shop stewards don't bring cases of discrimination forward and instead try to trivialize the complaint by saying 'it's just words', or 'we can move the person to another job site.' In my opinion this constitutes an accommodation of racism. We had one case where a woman went out drinking after work with several co-workers. She didn't drink very much. She had a history of problem drinking when she was younger and now she is very conscientious about having no more than two drinks. This one night, after having her two beer, she woke up to find the foreman having sex with her while she was unconscious. She reported it to the police, and the police said that everyone at the workplace said they had had drinks together, and that they were friendly, and *they* believed if she and the foreman had had sex it was consensual. The police didn't recommend charges. It is her belief and it is my belief that she was given 'the rape pill'. And it is her belief and it is my belief that they didn't take her complaint seriously at all because she is Indian. She was expected to go back to the workplace or be docked pay because they said it was her sense of shame that kept her from showing up to work, but that no crime had been committed. The assumption is that this woman, who has great dignity, is for some reason one night going to decide to go lay down in the photocopy room and spread her legs for a guy she doesn't like, and who is always calling her lewd names. And everyone buys that? That's a real problem.

That case is still open. The union was no help. The police were no help.

We have a lot of women who come in whose claims for criminal injury compensation as victims of crime have been denied. We look at the initial application and we usually find it to be woefully inadequate. It is usually done by a criminal compensation fund worker, or maybe a community organization worker. I don't want to take anything away from the good work they do, but they are often poorly trained, and weak applications that are poorly investigated and framed result in women being denied compensation. We then file an appeal. I think we've only lost one criminal injury compensation appeal, and there have been dozens since the Clinic first opened. It is another example of poor people, in this case Aboriginal women, being unable to access what rights or benefits they may be entitled to because they cannot access competent, or caring, professional help.

Culhane: Another category we identified in the file review was 'human rights violations', particularly in relation to public services. What kinds of things do your clients experience in this arena?

Taylor: A common scenario regarding social assistance is where your cheque is supposed to be issued on a certain day and it isn't. You go to see your worker and you can't get an appointment. Rightly or wrongly, many people believe very strongly that this is happening to them because they are Indian. We follow it up and are usually given the predictable bureaucratic excuses for why something that was supposed to be done wasn't. But in addition, we are often told that this person—our client—was a real nuisance, or a real problem, and the ministry worker feels justified in avoiding him or her. We have to remind them that they are *public servants*.

We also deal with a lot of landlord-tenant matters. For example, we had a case where a woman had five children. Even though she rented the place with the landlord's full knowledge that she had all these children, he decided after renting to her that the children were too noisy. He gave her an eviction notice every month for five months. They were all on specious grounds. There doesn't seem to be any sanction for that sort of thing. You would think there would be some kind of civil remedy for harassment. The woman told us the kinds of things the landlord said to her about how she was just an animal who had too many kids. Well, Indians have a lot of kids. We have the highest birth rate in the country. It was obvious you were never going to repair that situation. A solution in that case was to get her into one of the Native housing co-ops on an emergency basis where to my knowledge she still is. But this was a lucky exception—there is nowhere near enough Native housing to meet the need in Vancouver. Most people are dependent on the private market.

We've had other landlord-tenant cases that arise solely out of cultural differences. For example, when a family member from a rural village is hospitalized, relatives travel to be with him or her, and they live with family members who have a residence in the city while they are dealing with the situation at the hospital. The tenant will be told by their landlord that they can't have visitors, and they will say they don't have 'visitors', they have relatives staying because someone is sick and in the hospital.

One of the most troublesome issues that I see facing our female clients in particular is the problem of hollow rights: they have rights in law that they are too poor to activate. They cannot, for example, go to small claims court when they get ripped off by landlords and companies because they cannot pay the filing fees. They cannot afford to complete divorce and custody proceedings, etc.

First Nations Citizenship Issues

Culhane: The file review shows that you receive a lot of inquiries from people about how to go about being reinstated as status Indians and band members under Bill C–31. What issues arise in these cases?[9]

Taylor: Well, the first issue is securing the right to be registered as an Indian. Once [someone is] registered on the general list maintained by the Department of Indian Affairs, then the next problem is becoming a member of a band. In most cases, people are just automatically enrolled, but there has been a significant tendency among some bands not to accept members back. When this happens, then reinstatement results in a person having hollow rights. They are registered Indians but they can't access any benefits or resources because they are not members of bands. And they cannot live on their home reserves. We are now starting to see ludicrous situations where a woman was born Indian, lost status through marriage to a non-Indian, gained it back under Bill C–31, and is now refused band membership.

Culhane: It often comes down to land and resources, doesn't it? People living on reserve are squeezed, and are asked to accept new members without any commitment of additional resources to support them.

Taylor: Yes. I believe that not only women, but all people on reserve, need a way to appeal decisions of band councils that doesn't penalize them. Some situations are really complex, and we are working in tandem with a few band councils to try to help them sort out some of these issues in a way that is fair for everyone involved. A positive outcome in these situations is where the person gets what she or he needs and is rightfully entitled to, and the band council's authority as an institution of self-government has not been usurped.

Many band councils are very sophisticated and have legal counsel and administrative consultants, but some do not. There are lawyers who make a lot of money—literally millions of dollars—representing wealthy bands on big cases, but they are not offering any pro bono advice either to individuals in trouble or to bands without resources. We serve 'have not' individuals and 'have not' bands and nations.

Conclusion

Culhane: So, the Clinic provides legal representation and advocacy to Aboriginal people in need who otherwise would either not be represented or, perhaps, not well-represented. And you are able sometimes to connect your clients with other non-legal services that may provide them with additional support. Do you think that through the work of the Clinic you are succeeding in changing, or refashioning, the reproduction and legitimation of Aboriginal people's, and Aboriginal women's in particular, subordination? Do you think that when you fight a case in court and win that you have changed anything beyond the particular outcome of that specific case?

Taylor: On the individual cases there are little, tiny victories. But these can matter. If you change the way judges and Crown counsel see Aboriginal women, then for those who inevitably end up before them, it matters. Being treated with dignity rather than contempt is important to people. If patterns develop in the way life factors are taken into account in sentencing, then, again, it matters to people in conflict with the law, and it matters to their families. And for me that counts. For someone who has never felt respected by authorities, or who has never experienced justice, or who has never been believed and taken seriously, an experience of legal victory can be very meaningful. Our clients' scepticism about the law is based on experience, not theory.

In the legal forum the big victories are won at a court of appeal or a Supreme Court level. There is some significance because the lower courts are then bound by the judgment of a higher court. At a higher level, Aboriginal organizations lobby for parliamentary and constitutional change. If there are victories there, then the changes will be broader.

Culhane: Regarding the question of politics and political change, the experience of a lot of feminist lawyers is that the more they try to change things through the law and the courts the more they see what they initially put forward as feminist defences being reformulated by the courts in ways that backfire against women. This has led to a politics of defeatism and despair. Do you feel defeated and despairing about your work?

Taylor: We live in a society that is inherently unfair to Aboriginal peoples. In our nation-building we actually have a chance, I think, to start from the ground up and to build communities that look a lot like the world many feminists are trying to create. Will we succeed? I don't know, but many of us are working very hard at trying. I know we won't stop. We have already overcome tremendous odds by surviving this long.

Notes

1. A note on terminology. Throughout this article readers will note that the authors use the terms 'First Nation', 'Aboriginal', 'Native', and 'Indian'. There are debates about each of these labels. 'First Nation' technically refers to members of cultural groups, or nations, recognized by the Indian Act, and it is particularly current in British Columbia. 'Aboriginal' officially refers to peoples of Aboriginal ancestry, including First Nations, Métis, and Inuit, recognized as such by the Constitution Act, 1982. 'Native' is also an all-encompassing term that is declining in current usage. 'Indian' is the most controversial of these terms, arising as it does from Christopher Columbus's erroneous assumption that he had 'discovered' India when he landed in the Caribbean in 1492. However, 'Indian' remains a legal term reflected in the Indian Act. Also, in unself-conscious, everyday conversation many 'Aboriginal' people refer to themselves and others as 'Indians'. We decided *not* to artificially correct the text of the verbatim interview.

2. The question of estimates of the Aboriginal population is a contentious one. The 1991 Aboriginal Peoples' Survey conducted by Statistics Canada determined that Aboriginal peoples may make up 3.7 per cent of the total Canadian population. However, it is generally accepted that these federal government numbers represent the low end of population estimates for a number of reasons: a significant number of First Nations (Mohawk First Nations, for example) refused to participate in Census Canada counts, including the Aboriginal Peoples' Survey; off-reserve and non-status populations are difficult to document and hence are underrepresented; and an enumeration of Métis has yet to be systematically undertaken. As a result, estimates of the percentage of the Canadian population represented by Aboriginal peoples run from a low of 3.7 per cent to a high of 12 per cent.

3. For comprehensive overviews of these issues, see Goose, Henderson, and Carter (1994); LaPrairie (1993); Monture-Okanee and Turpel (1992); Royal Commission on Aboriginal Peoples (1993); Turpel (1991b, 1994).

4. See Hamilton and Sinclair (1991); Monture-Okanee and Turpel (1992); Monture-Okanee, (1993); Royal Commission on Aboriginal Peoples (1993); Turpel (1991b).

5. On the relationship of Aboriginal women and law in Canada, see Adelberg and NWAC (1993); Faith (1996); Fiske (1994); Johnson and Rodgers (1993); Kline (1989); LaPrairie (1993); Moore (1991); Sugar and Fox (1990); Trainor, Normand, and Verdon (1991).

6. In February 1997 the Vancouver police department adopted a new policy regarding the laying of soliciting charges, deciding to charge only the customers and not the prostitutes.

7. For general discussion of this issue, see Razack (1991). On the battered wife

syndrome in particular, see Noonan (1993).

8. For overviews of this debate among Aboriginal women, see Fiske (1995); Jackson (1994). For articulations of the debate itself, see McIvor (1996); Monture-Okanee (1993); Nahance (1996). Taylor's position is consistent with Monture-Okanee's.

9. Briefly, Bill C–31 refers to the Act allowing women and their children who lost their status as registered Indians under a provision of the Indian Act, Section 12(1)(b), that was repealed in 1985. Under 12(1)(b) an Indian woman was automatically removed from the registry if she married a non-Native man or a Native man who was not registered. Her children then were not entitled to be registered. Conversely, when a Native man married a non-Native woman, she and her children were automatically registered. Bill C–31 provides for two generations of these disenfranchised people to be reinstated as registered Indians. There is a complex debate surrounding the real consequences of Bill C–31, which is beyond the scope of this paper. Readers are directed to Green (1985) and Krosenbrink-Gelissen (1991) for comprehensive analyses of this issue.

Chapter 8

On Law and Hegemonic Moments
Looking Beyond the Law Towards Subjectivities of Subaltern Women

Parin Dossa

Over the last two decades, much social theory has focused on the impact of power on the construction of knowledge and the way in which human actors engage with 'practice'. Identified as a key symbol of theoretical value (Ortner, 1994: 372), practice encompasses simultaneous processes of reproduction of social institutions as well as change. While social anthropologists from different schools of thought have devoted a great deal of time and energy in explicating how systems work, only recently has attention been given to the aspect of change effected through intricate patterns of negotiations. Ethnographic research is beginning to identify alternative ways of social and cultural being that articulate with the system but also transcend it in complex ways. This approach foregrounds subjectivity (historical actors), hitherto erased in conventional ethnographic works. The issue here is not to raise subjectivity over and beyond the system but to show how subjectivity highlights the workings of power at a level where it can critique it and bring into relief concerns of sociality: patterns of co-operation, reciprocity, and solidarity. In Ortner's words, this amounts to 'views of the social in terms of sharing, exchange and moral obligations' (ibid., 401).

An appreciation of the intricate relationship between structure and change can be gleaned from law. Law is a system that encapsulates the workings of power and yet at the same time includes dimensions where power is subverted towards creation of an alternative way of life. As Comaroff (1994: ix) observes, law is a 'Janus-faced' double visage that constrains and enables, promising freedom and potential bondage, which allows us to interrogate:

> legal processes, precepts and practices precisely where they should be interrogated: in historically constituted, socially situated fields of power and resistance; the force field within which human beings live out their lives—however ordinary, however epic. (Ibid., ix–x)

Comaroff's insights form part of a 'new scholarship' in the anthropology of law that attempts to explain cultures of legality that underpin modern societies. Two moot points articulated are: (1) in modern societies, law functions in ambivalent and contradictory ways, and (2) law encompasses lives of individuals in intricate ways, the cumulative effect of which is extremely powerful (see, e.g., Lazarus-Black and Hirch, 1994). Subaltern (socially marginalized) and feminist scholarship shows that individuals are not homogeneous beings evaluated in relation to a hegemonized and normative image of white able-bodied male. Interactive social constructs of race, gender, disability provide critical insights and points of strategic intervention into social life. As I show below, these constructs provide nuanced and complex workings of power and its encapsulation in law.

The greater and more intricate the impact of law on people's lives, the greater is the need to understand law as a discourse and a code worked and reconstituted as intervention strategies. Subjectivity in this context may assume multiple and contradictory positions that ultimately lead to contestation and reconstruction of relationships. This view of law as being a marker of power/knowledge and a means of resistance also necessitates looking at the process of construction of what Vincent (1994) refers to as 'hegemonic moments', that is, subtle forms of power exercised through the civil arm of the state at specific times and contexts. While Vincent's reading of legal constructs refers merely to the process of formations of hierarchical structuring of power along the lines of ethnicity/race, gender, and class, I want to expand this theoretical construct to include discursive constructions of historical actors. A reading may then be offered of human agency engaged interactively with systems of power in subtle and not so subtle ways. To do this I examine disability within the gender/race/class complex. I agree with Stone (1984) and Ingstad and Whyte (1995) that, in the West, conceptions of disability are informed by a centralist state. Through legislation, the disabled acquire 'an existence and a consistency they never had before—definition, criteria, and degrees of severity' (ibid., 8). Legally constructed identity, entitlements, and relations are subject to intricate negotiations, more acutely so where ethnicity, gender, and disability are combined in different ways.

Using the theoretical construct of 'hegemonic moments', this chapter will demonstrate how hegemonic categories (power/knowledge) are constituted and renegotiated by those who know what it is like to be racialized/gendered and labelled as 'disabled'. Historical moments experienced by individuals in particular contexts provide an important point of entry into this subject. To show the constitution of subjectivity as practice—a practice of power-knowledge complex and a practice of resistance—this chapter is divided into three parts. The first section, on border crossing, reveals the subject's strategy of silence to manoeuvre a powerful and discriminatory legislative structure to gain entry into Canada. This entry proves to be problematic as the subject is compelled to enter into a legal-medical maze from which she emerges with a disabled identity. The next section shows the subject's negotiation of a new identity that reveals the Janus-faced nature of law: it constrains and empowers. The concluding section makes a case for a more integrated understanding of law and justice. While legislation can provide the disabled with entitlements, it does not address the moot question of what makes us human—an issue that forms an integral part of justice.

Keeping in mind that history is made up of many voices, crystallizing moments, and activities backstage (Vincent, 1994: 133), I begin with one moment that took place in August 1981 with the entry of Shayida into Canada through the Vancouver International Airport. Shayida is a 36-year-old (ethnographic present) Muslim woman with an epileptic condition. The three attributes of being a woman, 'coloured', and disabled make Shayida a subaltern woman, foregrounding two interrelated questions: Can a subaltern woman speak? And, if so, under what conditions?

Crystallizing Moments: Crossing Borders

Thousands of passengers pass through the airport booths of Canadian cities each year. Upon arrival, each passenger follows two main lanes: domestic and international. The domestic lane moves very quickly; people who are processed here do not require much scrutiny. They have not crossed any 'borders' that would throw into relief the problematic nature of 'nation-state'. This task is left to the passengers who go through the international booth demarcated into two sections: 'Residents' and 'Visitors'. Standard questions asked to those with Canadian passports are along the lines of length of stay outside the country, places visited, goods purchased. These questions may be considered to be routine and benign, yet they carry the weight of legislation in terms of who can (re)enter the country and under what conditions. Uniformed state officials have the power to stop people from crossing borders. In its heightened form, this aspect is brought into relief in the 'Visitors' lane. Here, a racialized distinction exists between whites and non-whites. The former, and especially those from Western Europe, go through the immigration booth with relative ease and facility. But an unwritten script awaits the non-whites, who undergo greater scrutiny—as is revealed in Shayida's visit to Canada. Shayida's narrative forms part of a larger ethnographic research on women with disabilities conducted in the two cities of Calgary and Vancouver in the period 1989–92.

Shayida does not happen to be just a woman. She is a displaced individual—a hybrid of post-colonialism with multiple identities: her ancestors migrated from India in the early part of the twentieth century and settled in East Africa, where they domiciled for almost seven decades. Like other Muslims, Shayida's family had made Tanzania their home until they were compelled to leave for political and economic reasons. Coming to Canada for Shayida was in many respects a move from a colonized to a colonizing country. This meant occupying a highly politicized space of the Other. Non-Europeans are differentially incorporated in Canadian society (Henry et al., 1995; Agnew, 1996), a situation that leads to a perpetual status of an 'immigrant' who can pack up and go 'home'. If an immigrant happens to cross the border with multiple categories of being a woman, coloured, and disabled, this amounts to a triple oppression (Spivak, 1988: 294).

Such a scenario potentially translates into: 'Can the subaltern speak?' This title from Spivak's work (1988) reveals a host of questions: Who is a subaltern woman? Under what conditions can she speak? If a subaltern woman does not or cannot speak, as Spivak concludes, then how do we listen to the voice that has been silenced? I am persuaded that this voice is part of a narrative that reinforces, subverts, and transcends hegemonic and legal discourses that construct her as 'subaltern' in the first place. The point of border crossing involves a hegemonic moment of interrogation by an official with power over people's lives:

Why have you come to Canada?
I have come to visit my sister.
Is your husband going to join you?
No.
How long are you planning to stay?
Six months.
I will give you a three-month visa.
Three months is too little. This is my first visit to Canada.
I am sorry, this is the best I can do for you.

With these words, the immigration official at the Vancouver International Airport stamped Shayida's Tanzanian passport on 18 August 1981. For one year and nine months, Shayida visited the immigration office in Vancouver to renew her tourist visa; each time she was granted a three-month extension, a 'faithful' enactment of the airport encounter. Shayida recounted the scene as follows:

I would go with my mum and dad—it was every three months for one year and nine months. My mother would say, 'We have to extend your visa.' Then she would give me tips with respect to what I should say. We would go through a rehearsal. He will ask you why you want to stay longer. Just say, 'I like Canada. I want to enjoy it more. My family is here. I want to spend more time with my family. Don't try to answer more then necessary.' I was so scared. What would happen if they did not give me an extension. Where would I go?

It was very difficult. Just before the visit, I could not sleep for many nights. I worried. If they did not give me the visa, where would I go? I have no other home.

Contrary to the common perception, the question 'Why have you come to Canada' and subsequent interrogations are not standard procedures applicable to all visitors. Questions asked by immigration officials, backed up by state authority with its visible trappings of uniforms and computerized access to data, are informed by a dichotomous discourse on orientalism, a Western discourse on the Orient leading to an 'us' and 'them' dichotomy (Said, 1978). The us/them category is subject to perpetual reinforcement at hegemonic moments such as that of border crossings and has a well-defined script explicated along the following lines.

Entry of non-European populations to Canada has been subject to a racialization process situated in history, institutional practices, and discourse, inclusive of moral and legal dimensions. The active role of the state in the race definition process and othering at large have been noted by Gramsci (1971), Foucault (1977), and Williams (1977) among many others. These writers show that the role of the state is not confined to economic management; rather more disturbing is the point that state control is exercised through the apparatus of civil society: media, police, social services, law, education system, and so on. An intriguing insight is that of the persistence and changing form of the Western hegemonic system, an effect brought about by the close linkage between polity and culture. Such a powerful configuration amounts to a lived process whereby routine procedures (border crossing checks) become part of what people and institutions do. This form of internalization of power posed as objective knowledge is not merely a set of values but a realized complex 'of ideas, practices, and social relations that reflect the interests of a dominant sector and which come to permeate society's private and institutional domains' (Williams, 1977; cf. Anderson, 1991: 23). European culture with its legal and civil apparatus thus has control over the definition and status of people who fall beyond the pale of 'who gets in'.

Interrogation to which non-European visitors are subject at the time of entry into the country and thereafter forms part of the constitution of 'hegemonic moments' through which the script of othering is (re)defined and (re)written in relation to each situation. While 'race' looms large in this hegemonic script, the category of gender is contextually constructed. The question 'Why have you come to Canada?' is linked with 'Is your husband going to join you?' Immigrant men get preferential treatment compared with immigrant women based on the erroneous premise that men are wage-earners and women 'stay at home'.

While one cannot comment on the specific reason as to why the immigration official wanted to know if Shayida's husband was going to join her, this question was reiterated several times. In Shayida's words:

> Every time when I went for my visa extension, they wanted to know if my husband was going to join me. I don't know why they kept on asking this question. I found this irritating. I came to Canada under my married name. I

had to do this. What choice did I have? My parents were sponsored by my married sister who has been in Canada for five years. I could not be sponsored. I am married—no—I am divorced and am not well. I have epilepsy. If I had used my parent's name, the immigration would have known that I have come to Canada with my parents. They would not have allowed me to enter the country. When we arrived at the airport, my parents stood in the 'residents' lane; I went into the 'visitors' lane. We came together but we went on different lanes.

Although Shayida came to Canada as a visitor, she had no intention of leaving the country. Her parents' migration meant that her bridges were burned. She had no 'home' to go back to. Shayida's strategy of giving minimal information to the official and coming to Canada as a visitor form part of a civil initiative through which subaltern subjects negotiate legislative strictures that restrict and confine them unduly. At this point, it is useful to chart out very briefly Shayida's narrative trajectory. My aim is to offer some of the particulars through which I tried to understand hegemonic moments when gender, 'race', and disability intersect. The following is the information conveyed to me by Shayida and her mother in *kachi*, an Indian dialect from Gujerat (India).

Narrative Trajectory of Shayida's Life

Shayida's mother described in brief outline some of the pivotal events of her daughter's life:

> Shayida was a happy and lively child. She had very high fever when she was seven years old. I rushed her to the hospital. Her fever came down but from then onward she became epileptic. We decided we would do our best to care for her. We continued sending her to school. She completed grade 10. After that we made arrangements for her to work with an optician. She would arrange frames, sort out cases, do some dusting and other little things. It was fine. At work she met Shams, who really liked her. I told him, 'My daughter is epileptic. Only marry her if you can look after her.' He promised. Within a short time, they had a son. Her husband [who took custody of their son] left her when her son was one and a half years old. We brought Shayida home and she stayed with us. We had a big house—there was lots of space. Shayida kept very busy in the house. She helped with cooking, stitching, cleaning. We went to the mosque every day. Shayida did voluntary work. She would serve water. Then we had to come to Canada. We could not continue living in Mwanza. It was hard to get licence to do business—there were all kinds of problems.
>
> The situation in Tanzania is getting worse. It is impossible to stay there. We lost quite a bit of our property to the government. We saw that there is no future. Our eldest daughter who is married in Canada sponsored us. She could not have sponsored Shayida. Shayida has epilepsy. She is not sick. She has seizures. Otherwise she is all right.

One thing was sure. We could not leave Shayida behind. There was no place for her. We decided to bring her as a tourist. She came under her married name. Once in Canada, we would try to get her permanent visas.

What else would we need for Shayida. We gave her some medication for seizures. She helped in the house and accompanied me when I went visiting. We just wanted her to be happy. We accepted her condition as there is no cure for epilepsy. Shayida is not helpless. She can do some work in the house and work part-time outside. We thought, maybe, if we came to Canada, she would get better medicine, services. We heard that there are good services that Canada offers.

'Good services in Canada' and 'Canada as the land of golden opportunity' are common phrases used by immigrants to explain their decision to settle in this country. This is also the version found in the government booklets distributed to potential immigrants overseas. In Shayida's words:

My sister wrote to me and said that there will be better opportunities in Canada. There are specialists who would help; there are special services that provide training for jobs. My hope was that I would be able to have a better life in Canada.

The question arises: What services make Canada and other parts of the Western world desirable for migration for people with disabilities and also others from the South? Within a broad framework, the script of the North having better economic and social opportunities, greater political security, and legal entrenchment of rights of the individual has been well defined. At the time of border crossing, Shayida could not relate this script to the immigration officer, at least not yet. It would be translated in the common discourse of 'immigrants (especially those with disabilities) being a drain on the system', notwithstanding the fact that Shayida's parents are working in jobs that require long hours and provide minimum wages.

Not having the social, cultural, racial, or gender space to tell her story meant staying on mute ground. Shayida maintained silence, cognizant of the fact that her larger script would not be understood and validated. Visweswaran (1994) makes the apt observation that we cannot assume the willingness of women to talk. When and why women do talk are issues that require further investigation, as women's lives indicate that there are 'strictures placed on their speech'. Thus, we should learn to 'hear' women's silences (ibid., 31), for they are pregnant with meaning. Shayida's silence at the time of border crossing—not stating that she has come to Canada with her parents, that she is divorced, that she is epileptic, and that she has come to Canada for a 'better' life because her former life has been disrupted through colonizing structures—is a form of foregrounding her agency. It also constitutes a means for meandering through a powerful legal discourse, legislated in terms of who can and cannot enter the country. Her silence gives Shayida entry into the country; this silence, with its hidden script, is a strategy of intervention, discussed below in the context of theatrical metaphor. For Shayida, then, there was no other way; little did she know that her movement from the South to the North would translate into a total change of spheres: from community and family life, where sociocentric sense of personhood is understood in terms of relationships, to a medical/legal discourse, a lethal combination for diminution of personhood.

While Shayida's visa was extended, her parents were engaged in obtaining a minister's permit to allow Shayida to stay in the country on 'compassionate grounds'. Shayida did not have 'marketable skills', an important criterion for determining 'who gets in'. According to Canadian immigration laws, concrete evidence must be produced for making a case for compassionate grounds. For persons with disabilities, the concrete evidence is nothing short of a medical certificate:

> We took Shayida to the doctors. We told him she had epilepsy and we needed a report [medical certificate]. The doctor gave us a long written report. Someone explained to us that it was a description of epileptic condition. There were all kinds of things written in there about epilepsy. They did not apply to my daughter. I do not understand why they have to make it so complicated. All that my daughter has are seizures. We even know the time of their occurrence. They happen during full moon. The lawyer told us: 'The immigration department would like a "complicated" report; otherwise, they will not give her the permit.' Shayida was granted minister's permit and thereafter landed immigrant status. Now she has a Canadian passport.

During the time she was waiting for landed immigrant status, Shayida lived with her parents in a one-bedroom apartment. Both her mother and father are working for minimum wages. Her father is employed as a security guard and her mother makes beds in a motel. Shayida regarded her stay with her parents as temporary. As a married and divorced woman she considered herself to be a guest in her parents' house. Upon becoming a landed immigrant, her first task was to find work and a place to live. This has proved to be difficult— having lived in Canada for 16 years, her search continues. She explains: 'All that I want is part-time work and a good place to live. I want my own home and a job. I will do anything to get a job. I will type, cook, sew, and babysit.' Most people would agree that this expectation is reasonable. Why should it be so difficult for a 36-year-old woman to work part-time and find a place to live?

According to Shayida's mother, without work and a lot of time on her hands, Shayida's condition got worse. She became very depressed and was hospitalized. She was put on heavy medication and her seizures became more frequent. Over the years, she has seen a number of medical specialists and psychiatrists. She has been diagnosed as schizophrenic. Currently, she lives in her own apartment in a residential complex where all the tenants are persons diagnosed with mental disabilities, and she takes the following medications prescribed by the mental health team: lithium carbonate, benztropine, perphenazine, tegretol, and sabril. A caregiver who visits ensures that Shayida takes her medication.

Taking of this medication, that is, acting 'crazy', to use Estroff's term (1981), has given Shayida the legal status on the basis of which she is entitled to:

- Subsidized housing designated for the disabled.
- Monthly disability allowance of about $790, out of which $550 is spent on rent.
- Coverage of all medical expenses.
- Subsidized bus pass.

Shayida has become a medical/legal entity, the assumption of which has led to her becoming part of the 'deserving disabled'. As several writers have noted (Wendell, 1996; Herzlich and Pierret, 1984; Estroff, 1981), a medicalized and legally inscribed identity of illness is tantamount to social exclusion. The underlying assumption is that sick people are not contributing members of our society. The irony is that through legal and social entitlements, the sick are effectively and many times brutally excluded from the labour force. Given the importance of waged work in our society, this form of exclusion amounts to 'solitude that cannot be shared' (Herzlich and Pierret, 1984: 178). In a racialized society, if the disabled are coloured women, their exclusion is compounded at many levels. As society rejects them and their bodies (women with disabilities are regarded as asexual and incapable of nurturing), they find it hard to fulfil needs that are most basic. Resistance and a search for alternative ways of being occur in situations where the most elementary pursuits, common to humankind, remain unfulfilled. It is in this context that Shayida's narrative unfolds to reveal dimensions of her life that foreground her subjectivity. The phrase 'Re: Turning the Gaze' (Bannerji, 1993) provides a useful point of entry.

Re: Turning the Gaze

This phrase is double-edged. The gaze forms part of the colonizing structure of white settler heritage with a racialized and genderized class base. The act of *Re: turning* makes women subjects of their history. An appropriate reading of such an act is contained in the dramaturgical metaphor that engages us with certain questions. How are situations framed? What stories does the subaltern relate? Who is the audience? As Lazarus-Black and Hirch (1994: 14) have expressed it, the aspect of performance associated with this metaphor 'encourages us to pay analytic attention to audiences as well as actors, to silences within and between dialogues, to nakedness as well as costume'. Here, our attention is directed towards routine encounters not contained within law courts but legally informed in entitlements and rights. Following Visweswaran (1994), I frame these encounters in the form of three acts of intervention strategies that articulate with and subvert legal/medical constructs. Let me then present the script.

Act 1, Scene 1

The beginnings . . .

Conversation with the mother:

Q: When can I phone Shayida for an appointment?

A: Anytime. Don't phone her early in the morning or late in the evening. When you phone Shayida tell her right from the beginning that you want her help. Don't tell her that you are helping her. If you don't make this clear, she will not see you.

Q: Should I phone and ask her what is a good time for her to see me?

A: Yes. Shayida is very particular about time. If she gives you the time, make sure that you stick with it. If you go late, she will not see you.

Act 1, Scene 2

First interview with Shayida:

Q: Do you feel settled in this apartment?

A: I don't know what you mean by settled. It is a place where I can be on my own. I cook here, watch TV. I have a *rim zim* radio (Indian program—aired for 24 hours), I listen to it. I go shopping from here. But it is not like 'home'. I can't have my parents for dinner. This is not the place to call home. Ask yourself: Can you live in this place?

Q: No. I do not think so. Do you see Vicki (caregiver) everyday?

A: No. I don't see too much of her. We are only supposed to see her if we need something. I take her food sometimes, to taste. But that is about it.

Q: Who else do you see here? Have you made any friends?

A: No, I don't have any friends here. I am not 'mental'—I don't know anyone here.

Q: What about David—he is your social worker. Does he help to make you feel more settled?

A: He tries. I go and report to him every week. Ten o'clock Monday morning. He has said he will help me find work. Nothing has happened so far. They talk but they don't do anything.

Act 2, Scene 1

Interview with the caregiver:

Q: You have come to know Shayida well. Do you see her every day?

A: No, I am not supposed to see her every day. The tenants are independent here. I see them when they need me. Of course, Shayida can come to my office and drop in for a chat. Others do this—but not her. She is not the kind of person who will drop in for a chat. Sometimes, she brings me some cooked food. I just taste it. I don't care for ethnic food; besides, I don't know whether it is hygienic. I have seen her leaving food on the counter.

Q: Do you think Shayida is happy here?

A.   She has a lot to learn. She is a very stubborn and difficult person. The other day, I took a bus with her as we were going to visit the Central Medical Team. I told her: 'Take out your bus pass and keep it ready.' She would not do it. Once we were inside the bus, she emptied the contents of her purse to look for the bus pass. Then she goes in front of the driver and shows it to him. She expects him to acknowledge it or maybe her.
      Do you know that she does not get into the elevator with anyone. If someone gets in, she walks out. What we are concerned about is her behaviour in the building. She is a very anti-social person. Here, people don't care. They call her and she does not respond [so] they say: 'Who do you think you are? Go to hell.'
      I want her to take her 'meds' everyday and be more sociable.

Act 2, Scene 2

Second interview with Shayida:

Q: So, what did you do this morning?

A: I had a bad morning. David did not keep the appointment. I go to see him at 10 every Monday. I went there and he said that he had another appointment. 'Can you wait half an hour?' Wait! I am not going to wait. He does not know that I am also doing him a favour by going there.

Q: So will you see him next week?

A: If he keeps his time.

Act 3, Scene 1

A meeting at McDonald's:

> I am so bored. Can you find me a job? I would like to work in the library or as a clerk. I can type and do shorthand. If this is difficult, I will do babysitting. I will do any job. I am so bored. Right now I have nothing to do.

> Should you not talk to your community worker?

> She will do nothing. If you find me a job, I will give you a gift. I will buy you a nice gift.

> You don't have to give me a gift. I will look around.

> I will give you blessings. May God bless you and your family. I need to have a job. I will do anything. You can talk to my social worker. Tell him, 'You will be doing a good deed.' Make sure what you say is said sweetly (*midhas*) and gently. Tell him that he will get blessings. Say it with conviction (*umagh*) so he takes this seriously. Whatever kind of work I do, I will keep people happy (*khus*). This is how I work—with my heart (*dil*) in it.

Act 3, Scene 2

Conversation with her mother:

Q: Shayida wants to work. What do you suggest?

A: Yes. I know. She would be very happy if she got some part-time work. That's all that she needs. To work for two or three days a week. She will be very satisfied. It will keep her occupied. Her illness (*bimari*) would disappear. She needs the kind of work where people talk to her with *midhas* (sweetly and gently) and respect (*man*) her.

Q: So why is it so hard to get a simple job?

A: I don't know. I think her social worker is not giving her a reference. Here, people do not hire without references.

Discussion and Analysis

Act 1 focuses on a conversation between Shayida and myself—the 'researcher'. Despite my constant clarification that I was an anthropologist collecting data, Shayida and her mother did not see me in this role. During our interactions, they constantly put me in the role of an advocate who would convey their perceptions to the service providers and a larger, imagined audience. The hidden script of Scene 1, then, is the 'imagined audience'. In this scene Shayida's mother establishes the parameters of symmetrical and reciprocal interactions. This aspect is necessitated by the fact that the disabled ('clients') are invariably constructed as dependent and passive recipients of social services. The demeaning and negative impact of this stance has been well noted in the literature; its concrete presence in Shayida's life is addressed through the discursive medium of '*madad*' (assistance) and 'time'.

Shayida's perception of assistance and time is not peculiar to her personality, a view adhered to by service providers. Rather, these two domains form part of the legal/medical discourse that constructs and labels people into categories. By virtue of the fact that one has become the recipient of services, one is expected to move into the professional time of institutionalized life. Hall (1961), for example, defines this form of time as linear, geared towards the accomplishment of goal-oriented tasks. In the social service sector, appointments slotted into half-hour to one-hour time frames are made to 'assist' the clients; this time is rarely used to cultivate and nourish social relationships. Time has close alliance with space. Activities in space, in itself a social and cultural construct, take place in time; likewise, time is experienced through space. This mutual interconnection between time and space has a major impact on the lives of the disabled because this structuration determines the social and the cultural constructions of disability. Spatial and temporal parameters determine the extent to which a disabled person is able to function and contribute to social life. The three acts are framed within these parameters. It is in these domains that legal and medical discourse is (re)worked and (re)constructed through human interactions. Shayida's concealed standpoint regarding time and notions of assistance is located in this context.

Scene 2 takes us into Shayida's everyday life. The elements of this life appear to be deceptively simple. What is so special about someone who has a place to live, cooks, watches TV? This is not the stuff that is written about; yet it is through everyday routine that Shayida attempts to create an alternative space that reveals the most basic needs and aspirations of human life: to interact, to remain active, and to engage in valued work.

In her apartment, Shayida watches Indian movies, listens to Indian songs, cooks, and observes regular prayers twice a day. Among the vast number of channels available on television in Vancouver, one specific channel is referred to as 'Multicultural'. Air time is given to various ethnic minorities at different times during the week. An Indo-Canadian (South Asian) program is aired on two evenings: Mondays and Saturdays. A co-ordinator of the program informed me that a vast number of South Asian Canadians tune into the program or, alternatively, videotape it for later viewing. The highlights of the program are Indian songs and dances, episodic dramas, and movies. Just before the program, Shayida's mother phones to remind her. In Shayida's words:

My mother always calls me and says, 'Shusma's program is on. Watch it.' I watch this program—I enjoy it. It is good. It is about love, and caring and relationships. It is about family. Our *dil* (heart) is filled with *khusi* (happiness). It is also about conflict, but this is part of life.

South Asian Canadians tuning into the program at the same time on a public television channel is suggestive of Anderson's (1983) 'imagined community' of horizontal comradeship. Shayida is part of this community in relation to affinities experienced through appreciation of certain common values and lifestyles, but with an additional aspect. For her, in her localized and confined setting, the meaning and value of the Indian program is both broader and deeper:

For a while I forget that I am all alone in the apartment. There are all these people out there in the film. They have sad and happy moments. They teach me the meaning of life. I like to watch family life and their stories unfold. These films remind me of some of the values of life: patience (*dhiraj*), love (*piyar*), gentleness (*ashte*).

Shayida does not remain uncritical. She engages in criticism and constructs her own stories. For example, in one particular movie where there was a depiction of a self-sacrificing woman, Shayida was quick to respond:

I think that it is time that women learn to say who they are; how they feel inside. It is no good sticking to past values. They are human beings like everyone else and they should learn to fight for their rights.

The story line of the movies is about family and relationships, an aspect that is crucial for Shayida's life and is experienced during weekly visits to her parents. When Shayida goes to her parents' house the activity of the family revolves around cooking and visits to the mosque and the Indian bazaar on Main Street. This is how Shayida recalls a typical visit:

My dad comes and picks me up on Friday evening. When I go home, we have a good dinner—my mum cooks the dishes that I like. Then we go to the mosque. Many times on Saturday morning, we go to the Indian bazaar. My mum does her shopping there. Sometimes, I buy clothes from there. We also go for masala tea and some *bhajiyas* (spiced fried food). It is a nice outing. Then when we come home, I help my mother cook. If my mother is not well, I cook the whole meal by myself. In the afternoon we sit and talk. Sometimes we go to the mosque and sometimes I just come back to my house. Quite often we go for a visit at my uncle's house or there is some community function. Last Sunday there was a social evening and so I stayed one day longer.

Social and religious activities that Shayida engages in over the weekends give meaning to her weekdays in her apartment. She re-enacts and relives moments that are meaningful and fulfilling for her. Cooking is one activity she enjoys the most. Shayida uses public transportation and does her food shopping about three times a week. She plans her menus and prepares a variety of foods, depending on what she feels like eating. Once in a while she takes some of the foods for her caregiver, who, as we have seen (Act 2, Scene 1), does not really care for the food. It is Shayida's way of reaching out and sharing.

Shayida observes her prayers on a regular basis—an activity that gives her a tremendous amount of strength and resilience. She often says:

> When I find that the world is harsh and no one cares, I pray. I know that Allah will never let me down. He protects me and looks after me. When I go out and am alone, I feel scared, I say a silent prayer and I know that Allah is with me.

This aspect of her life is muted, as religious practices and observations are regarded as private and marginalized in Canadian society. Shayida's caregiver related:

> Many times in the evenings, Shayida dresses up and when I ask her where she is going, she would say 'to my mosque'. I do not ask her any more. I think it is nice that she has a mosque to go to—it makes her feel less depressed. I am sure she meets people in the mosque.

Act 2 profiles Shayida's life as informed by the social service system. Here, the asymmetrical relationship between the service providers and client is brought to light in the form of social distance within which Shayida is othered as a disabled and racialized subject. Shayida's presence as a person is not acknowledged; for the caregiver, she is only a client who is supposed to be independent (making few demands), sociable at a superficial level of behaving well (for example, greeting others in the elevator), and organized (having her bus pass ready). Shayida's points of intervention take place within the system and also go beyond it as we learn about Shayida's continuing efforts to establish her humanness as a person who wants to be respected. This aspect is poignantly revealed in Scene 2, where Shayida decides not to see her social worker if he does not keep his time.

Act 3 reveals Shayida's desperate attempt to find work. Here, we are introduced to a discursive space through which she strives to construct a 'non-disabled identity'. By offering a 'gift' Shayida introduces the element of reciprocity—an aspect reinforced in her stating of the special qualities she has to offer. Shayida's gesture to help me through a gift and blessings forms part of a culturally nuanced understanding of *madad*. Unlike, the Western definition of help, *madad* connotes reciprocity understood along the lines that at some point there would be a return of the favour, most likely in a different form. Owing to one's embeddedness in social relationships, reciprocity can take place along a web of connectedness. Its ultimate form, *baraka*, is blessings from Allah. In this context, the distinction between the recipient and a giver is blurred. The assumption is that the giver has received the greater gift of *baraka*. The statement 'May God bless you' prevents a person from being reduced to a totally helpless and dependent being.

The three acts do not reveal the whole story. What we see and hear are parts of Shayida's life. At one level there is the all-encompassing social service discourse underpinned by legal/medical constructs. Here, Shayida's life is lived within the confined space of a 'client'. Like all performances, there are other shades and nuances that require a different kind of reading. The small acts and the discourse used by Shayida and her mother reveal a hidden script of a concealed standpoint. This script constitutes points of intervention that articulate with and partially subvert the structural parameters of her life.

While Shayida may have it three ways (woman, disabled, coloured), to revisit Spivak's (1988) phrase, she has nevertheless created a space of resistance that allows her to convey what an alternative form of life would be like for her and perhaps others. My observations reveal that Shayida's life has been compartmentalized to the extent that she lives in two domains: a legislated/medicalized world where she is constructed as a 'disabled woman of colour'; and a more muted domain of social relationships where her humanness is foregrounded in relation to her being a daughter, part of the South Asian Canadian community, and a member of the Muslim community. Her personhood is reaffirmed in the partial weekend space of social relationships.

Shayida draws on the qualities from this domain to make her weekday life in her apartment livable. Here she has created space that is beyond the appreciation of her caregivers. Through Indian movies, preparation of food, and enactment of religious ceremonies, Shayida has attempted to create a social arena, albeit an elemental one. As Folk Moore (1978: 25) has expressed it: 'Social relations constitute part of a social arena where people play out their lives in circles where their views, their actions and their reputations matter.' Shayida's social arena is not drawn into her place of residence. In her everyday interactions with service providers, she attempts to build relationships based on the basics of human interaction. In her words, 'I only want a few things: part-time work and a place to live—a place where I can be with real people.'

Shayida's life trajectory may be contextualized in two different and asymmetrical domains: Muslim community (read: other) and Western service sector (read: normal/advanced). The two domains are interconnected with the common factor of social relationships. Our inquiry into this area has led us to dramaturgical framing of acts and scenes. This stance has allowed us to capture a subaltern woman's voice. The argument I advance is that a subaltern voice cannot be recovered merely through a subject telling her story. A story takes its meaning not from its content, important as this is, but in a set of social relationships. The three acts reveal conceptual shifts within the power/knowledge/subjectivity complex that informs Shayida's life. At one level she is embedded in the medical/legal discourse of a disabled subaltern woman. Within this frame, she is constructed as passive, dependent, and helpless—attributes that are re-enacted and replayed by service providers in everyday situations. Service providers ensure that Shayida takes her 'meds' and works towards living as a model 'client' who is sociable and makes minimum demands. Their role in its visible form comes into play during times of crisis. The residential service provider informed me that Shayida is in a perpetual state of crisis, as she complains more often than what is regarded as 'normal'.

Shayida's intervention into the legal/medical discourse takes place in every-day situations in the form of a concealed standpoint. At this second level, then, Shayida deploys a creative speech genre that she draws from embodied cultural traditions. The point that needs emphasis here is that her traditions do not exist in the form of a reified and sealed package, contrary to the dominant view. Her regular watching of Indian movies, familial and community interactions, and everyday cooking and observances of prayer have given her an alternative vantage point. Raheja and Gold's observation on proverbs is relevant. They state that proverbs take their meaning not merely from overt imagery, their semantic content, and the shared understanding they presuppose, but also from the context in which they are deployed and the communicative function they fulfil within specific situations. If proverbs are strategies for dealing with situations, they entail an evaluation and perspective on a situation (Raheja and Gold, 1994: 12).

In this context, Shayida's strategy of speech imparts a certain kind of perspective in the legal/medical context within which her identity is re-created on a daily basis. I submit that the subaltern discourse is invariably discontin-uous as it weaves its way in and out of the dominant system. Thus it does not 'coalesce into a closed, unified, discrete and knowable totality', to use Raheja and Gold's phrase (ibid., 15). While contained by the legal/medical discourse, Shayida's self-perception is not reducible to this discourse. This insight points to the ongoing construction of social life and social processes in two tightly interwoven contexts: dominant discourses and the subaltern strategic points of intervention. The latter highlights the dimension of immediate, ongoing, and emerging ways of being, the impact of which is discontinuous and even contra-dictory as subaltern subjects reinforce and subvert the system. Its transforming effect is identified in the work of Scott:

> The active rebellion that may at one moment be impractical or impossible may at another moment become plausible precisely because the idea of social transformation has been nourished in proverbs, folk songs, jokes, rituals, legends, and language. (1985: 37–41; cf. Raheja and Gold, 1994: 26)

This alternative vantage point of intervention is linked to two concerns in Shayida's life—home and work.

Law and Justice: The Ultimate Question

Social interactions and valued work point to basic aspirations of humankind. These concerns are of special importance to persons with disabilities whose very struggle is for basic entitlements. While all societies address these concerns differentially, depending on how a society's resource base articulates with cultural norms, values, and notion of personhood, in Western society the issue of disability is essentially encompassed within a legal/medical framework. A person's entitlement, then, is determined by how one is defined in legal/medical terms. A medical diagnosis of epilepsy, schizophrenia, or an affective disorder, for example, entitles a person to legally inscribed rights to social security income, shelter, and other forms of assistance.

Legal/medical discourse on disabilities excludes two crucial areas of life—social relationships and work—in the sense that they are not considered as basic as food and shelter. There is no legislation in place stipulating that disabled people should have work and access to social relationships; such a course is not contemplated in liberal democracies. In a setting where law, in the form of 'rights', and medical diagnosis determine the quality of life of persons with disabilities, the ultimate question of law and justice needs to be addressed. To legislate into law the availability of social relationships and work on the same level as shelter and food would mean that a disabled person would have the opportunity to live a more fulfilling life. On the other hand, not to legislate these basic concerns amounts to people striving for their realization on their own, especially in a situation where their resource base may be minimal. As Estroff has noted, in the West we pay people to play the 'crazy' role and hire professionals to look after them so that the community can shed all responsibility to accommodate the different and alternative ways of life. If social relationships and part-time work were legislated norms, Shayida's life would include some meaningful social activity. Human relationships, work, and social activities are interlinked. There cannot be one without the other. The problem is that these have been legislated out of the entitlements for the disabled. If one is the recipient of social security benefits, one cannot work without losing these and accompanying benefits. Since a large part of what defines Shayida's life is legislated medical diagnoses, the non-legislated forms of work and social relationships translate into fragmented life. In Shayida's words: 'What do I do with this home without people; what do I do with this home without work?' Shayida receives material support but is devoid of social life.

So, how do we define law? Can a legal institution embodying and dispersing the power of the state be conceived as an alternative to state control? These questions are addressed in the work of Pavlich to foreground a congenial and informal alternative to a professionalized and institutionalized legal system. The issue, then, is whether our understanding of law is equivalent to justice. In Pavlich's words, 'justice is intimately connected with our very being. Our happiness, the "good society," the goals of human aspiration (equality, fairness, liberty)' (Pavlich, 1996: 7).

This form of deinstitutionalized justice can be beneficial in several ways. First, it can provide a viable point of entry into the power/knowledge/subjectivity configuration by validating erudite and disqualified knowledges (Foucault, 1989) of subaltern subjectivity. Second, this approach provides theoretical underpinning to those who are engaged in forging alternative ways of living and being. Following Pavlich, I maintain that 'theory' is a regional system of the struggle of subaltern subjects. Here, theory acts as a critique of existing reality, 'a challenge directed at what is' (Foucault, 1989: 114; cf. Pavlich, 1996: 7). Third, deinstitutionalized justice can contribute towards formation of meaningful social relationships.

It is only then that we can talk about justice as an integral part of our being, of a humane society where persons are not 'disabled', 'ethnic', or 'subaltern' but beings who have human aspirations and goals. In Derrida's (1992) words, 'justice is evoked as the search for an infinite aspiration beyond what is, a promise of otherness beyond the limits of that which is present' (cf. Pavlich, 1996: 7). This perspective is closer to Montesquieu's understanding expressed in *The Spirit of the Laws*. Laws, in their most general significance, are the necessary relations arising from the nature of things. They provide the 'means by which histories are made, both histories of the momentous and histories of the mundane' (Comaroff, 1994: xi). Shayida's legal/medical and alternative way of life in the form of her everyday being in the world constitutes part of the means by which her history is made.

Drawing on the life trajectory together with its (re)construction in the subaltern subject, this chapter has brought to the fore an understanding of the working of law as discourse, power, process, and subversive activity. In doing so, our purpose has been to go beyond the notion of law as at once hegemonic and oppositional. Instead, we have tried to point towards the dimension where law can be translated into justice, which draws attention to different sets of historical and social circumstances. At this level, law encompasses differential forms of knowledge and practices. The insights to be drawn from the lives and words of subaltern women like Shayida are especially poignant—in their three-way construction of multiple subordination (women, disabled, and coloured), they reveal paradoxes of law at the exact site where they should be understood: basic human aspirations to social interactions, social activity, and work.

Acknowledgements

I would like to acknowledge my gratitude for the valuable comments of the editors of this book. I am grateful to the Social Sciences and Humanities Research Council of Canada for sponsoring this research.

Part IV

Constructing the Public/Private Distinction of Legal Discourse

Chapter 9

Custody, Access, and Relocation in a Mobile Society
(En)Gendering the Best Interests Principle

Susan B. Boyd

In the spring of 1997, a series of articles and letters to the editor in the *Globe and Mail* created the impression that fathers are not valued in child custody determinations and, indeed, are the victims of a legal system biased against them and in favour of mothers (see, for example, Kruk, 1997; Laframboise, 1997; Russell et al., 1997). In contrast, in 1995, LEAF (the Women's Legal Education and Action Fund) made quite a different argument in a custody case at the Supreme Court of Canada. LEAF sought to demonstrate that current trends in child custody law undervalue women's caregiving labour and exacerbate women's inequality, with potentially harmful implications for children. I participated in the subcommittee that developed the argument and drafted the factum for LEAF's intervention in *Gordon v. Goertz* (1996) (LEAF, 1996: 469). LEAF argued that the issue of whether custodial parents can relocate is fundamentally connected to gender relations and cannot be analysed without an appreciation of gendered power relations between fathers and mothers in custody law and policy. The issue of relocation thus provides a specific arena in which the gendering practices of custody and access law can be analysed. This type of analysis provides a counterpoint to media representation of child custody and the victimization of fathers.

The gendering effects of custody law arise in two ways, both of which are significant in understanding legal arguments concerning relocation. First, there has been a trend in modern custody law to de-gender mothers and fathers as they encounter decision-making practices related to child custody (Fineman, 1992, 1995; Smart, 1991). As well, the definitions of 'custody' and 'access' have shifted and become blurred. These trends have increased the difficulty that mothers have in articulating their experience as mothers in legal terms, and in obtaining legal recognition for the disproportionate responsibility they assume for both caregiving of children and facilitating the relationships between children and their fathers (Boyd, 1996).

Second, in order to resist these problems, there is an arguably unavoidable tendency for women, and for groups representing the interests of mothers, to reinscribe gender-based discourses on parenting: to reassert the particular responsibility that women still assume in this society for children and to argue that law should take account of that responsibility. Feminists have thus developed an approach that appears to be backward-looking in contrast to the apparently forward-looking approaches of law reformers arguing for a gender-neutral approach to custody and access, a centring of the interests of children without looking to gender-based dynamics between parents, and so on (Bala and Miklas, 1993; see also Kruk, 1993). Feminists appear to prioritize the interests of mothers and to downplay the interests of children, despite their efforts to argue that these interests are intrinsically connected (see Boyd, 1989). Their arguments thus appear to fly in the face of modern custody and access law and, consequently, they are often discounted. In this chapter, I try to show why it is nonetheless important to take these arguments into account.

I first outline the broad trends in custody and access law in order to identify the gendering processes at work. I then explain how the relocation issue fits into these trends, and its gendered impact. I explore how some Canadian courts of appeal dealt with relocation in the early 1990s and why these decisions were controversial. I examine the ways in which gendering and gender-neutral discourses were deployed in the four facta presented to the Supreme Court of Canada in *Gordon v. Goertz* (1996). Finally, I analyse the two main judgments in that case, which represent the differing approaches in this field. The majority of Supreme Court justices in this case explicitly rejected the arguments of the mother and LEAF that courts should accord deference to the decision-making ability of the custodial parent. I argue that the Supreme Court's approach presents considerable difficulties for parents (mostly mothers) who assume primary responsibility for caregiving before and after parental separation. This approach can potentially run contrary to the best interests of children, whose well-being is usually intimately connected to the well-being of the custodial parent.

Trends in Custody and Access Law: Enlarging 'Access'

The somewhat contradictory gendering processes delineated above have played out in the context of custody and access in the following way. Since the mid-1980s, the meaning of 'access' has been enlarged while that of 'custody' has been diminished (Hovius, 1993).[1] Although Canada never adopted a joint custody presumption, the philosophy behind joint custody has nonetheless influenced the broader trends in redefining custody and access (Bourque, 1995) and, in some jurisdictions, eliminating these terms altogether in favour of 'parenting' plans (Boyd, 1995). In sections 16(10) and 17(9) of the Canadian Divorce Act, the so-called 'friendly parent' or 'maximum contact' rule directs courts to give effect to the principle that a child should have as much contact with each parent as is consistent with the child's best interests and that the willingness of the parent seeking custody to facilitate such contact should be taken into account in the custody decision. As the focus on access and enhancing the continued relationship between children and the non-residential parent has increased, mothers have continued to play the role of primary caregiver in the majority of heterosexual families and have continued to obtain custody in the majority of divorces and separations. When the two trends are read together, it becomes apparent that the onus of ensuring that contact continues between children and non-residential parents (usually fathers) falls mainly on mothers (Boyd, 1996; Bourque, 1995).

As Carol Smart has shown, fathers have been regarded over the past couple of decades as 'more and more central to the family in emotional and psychological terms. The father as constituted in legal discourse is no longer the paterfamilias, he is the producer of normal, heterosexual children, the stabilizing anti-delinquency agent, and the bringer of realistic values and the desire for achievement' (Smart, 1991: 485–6; see also Drakich, 1989; Smart and Neale, 1997). Dawn Bourque reports a related trend, arguing that in reported Canadian cases between 1990 and 1993, paternal access to children emerged as the major issue, superseding virtually all other considerations (Bourque, 1995: 6).

The corresponding role of mothers, now that their caregiving role is transformed, taken for granted, and less visible, is to ensure that fathers get to play these roles. Carol Smart's research showed that mothers 'prepared the children emotionally for their fathers, they consoled the children when their fathers left, they kept up the flow of information, they packed the bags and did the washing on return, and so on' (Smart, 1991: 496). If mothers do not play their assigned role of facilitating paternal contact, they are viewed as poor custodial parents and/or vindictive mothers (Boyd, 1996; Smart, 1991: 496). A subtext of these new subjectivities is the reinforcing of heterosexual 'normal' families even after the adults in them have parted (Bourque, 1995: 4). Familial ideology, therefore, is reinscribed in these processes, even as the gender-based discourses that used to prevail within familial ideology have been diluted (Boyd, 1996). The restructured nuclear family as a unit emerges as more important, for the sake of the child, than the new unit of custodial parent and child. The particular concerns and interests of women as mothers are thereby rendered invisible in the name of the best interests of the child.

Custody, Access, and Relocation: Canadian Trends

In the specific context of relocation, because mothers are custodial parents in greater numbers than fathers,[2] the move of a custodial mother will more often be at issue than that of a custodial father. Custody orders and agreements increasingly include some form of restriction on mobility of the custodial parent, or at least require that notice be given of intention to move. Yet the ability of access parents to move away from a child has not been restricted nor has it been seriously argued.[3] It has 'become the responsibility of mothers to facilitate non-custodial parent contact by not relocating, by enduring reductions in child support if permitted to move, and/or by restricting their relocation to proximate areas' (Bourque, 1995: 11).

Reviews of relocation cases in the late 1980s and early 1990s indicate that it is not unusual for a sole custodial mother's ability to relocate to be subjected to either a father's permission or a court order (Bourque, 1995; Boyd, 1996). This is not to say that custodial mothers were never permitted to move with their children.[4] However, even when they were, mothers tended to bear the burden of proof of establishing the benefits of relocating, and judges frequently reaffirmed the 'paramount importance of paternal access, despite evidence to suggest the access may not be beneficial to the child' (Bourque, 1995: 8–9, 10; Boyd, 1996).

It is now apparently common for mothers asking permission to move to another geographical location to state their willingness to remain in the current location if so ordered or if they would otherwise lose custody (*Colley*, 1991; *Fasan*, 1991). In *Oldfield* (1991), the mother received custody and was permitted to move to France, but the judge applauded her for saying, 'as most loving mothers would, that she will not leave the children—and thus, Canada—if the children are required to remain here' (237). Clearly, mothers are worried—or being advised they should worry—that they may lose custody if judges view their wish to move negatively (see *Hollett*, 1992). A 'disciplining' of mothers' behaviour is thus occurring, with women regulating their own conduct and portraying themselves as without their own concerns and interests. Because mothers have always been expected to behave in a more selfless manner than fathers, it is more noticeable if they appear to depart from this expectation (see Girdner, 1986).

The important Ontario Court of Appeal decision in *Carter v. Brooks* (1990) gave rise to various interpretations but was often credited with crystallizing the trend towards imposing a heavier burden on the moving parent (McLeod, 1991: 55; Hovius, 1993: 138). Due to its assertion that the question of relocation should be decided on the facts of each case, *Carter v. Brooks* arguably led to uncertainty and inconsistency. In other words, its flaw was its indeterminacy. In combination with the enhanced attention to ensuring children's maximum contact with fathers, this indeterminacy exacerbated the expectations that custodial mothers bear some burden in demonstrating why a move away from the non-residential parent was necessary or appropriate.

This trend shifted to some degree in cases decided by three Canadian provincial courts of appeal in the 1990s. In contrast to many judges, these courts took a realistic view of parenting in the 'post-divorce family unit'.[5] In particular, the courts in *MacGyver v. Richards* (1995) and *Lapointe v. Lapointe* (1995) rearticulated the best interests test by giving it more certainty. These decisions could thus be read as being in some degree of contradiction with *Carter v. Brooks*.[6]

Most notably, the Ontario Court of Appeal case tempered the trend towards enlarging access in the mobility context, ruling that the custodial parent's best interests were inextricably tied to those of her child (*MacGyver*, 1995). A primary caregiver mother and her child were permitted to move from Ontario to Washington state with the mother's fiancé. The onus was effectively shifted to the access parent to show that the custodial parent's decision would do harm to the child such that the custodial parent should be prohibited from moving the child or that custody should be transferred. Abella J.A. said:

> We cannot design a system which shields the non-custodial parent from any change in the custodial parent's life which may affect the exercise of access. The emphasis should be, rather, on deferring to the decision-making responsibilities of the custodial parent, unless there is substantial evidence that those decisions impair the child's, not the access parent's, long-term well-being. (*MacGyver*, 1995: 445)

In *Lapointe v. Lapointe*, a separation agreement provided for joint custody, but with the mother having responsibility for primary care and control along with ultimate decision-making power. The possibility of relocation was contemplated in the agreement. The Manitoba Court of Appeal reviewed the history of custody, access, and relocation in some detail and took the view that the onus should fall on the access parent to show cause why a change in residence should not be made (*Lapointe*, 1995: 12). Twaddle J.A. said: 'In all but unusual cases, the custodial parent is in a better position than a judge to decide what is in the child's best interests' (*Lapointe*, 1995: 12). In other words, deference should be given to that parent's decision in most cases. He added that '[t]he present access arrangements are certainly desirable, but not if they can only be maintained at the price of an unhappy custodial parent' (*Lapointe*, 1995: 15). This approach was similar to that of Abella J.A. in *MacGyver v. Richards*.

A British Columbia Court of Appeal decision (*Levesque v. Lapointe*, 1993) involved a mother who wished to move from BC to Alberta. Both parents were described as exemplary, and they had joint custody. It was clear, however, that the mother had been primary caregiver throughout the children's lives, as was the case in *MacGyver v. Richards* and *Lapointe v. Lapointe*. Significantly, the separation agreement contemplated the possibility of relocation and contained no prohibition against it. The mother could afford to facilitate access between the children and the father and offered a periodic sum of money to do so. She was viewed as reasonable and willing to facilitate contact, and was permitted to move (*Levesque*, 1993). The Court did not address the onus issue as clearly as in the other two cases, but did say that '[i]t must be recognized that one of the inevitable consequences of divorce is that one of the parents will not have as much contact with the children as the parent who assumes primary responsibility for their care' (*Levesque*, 1993: 328).

Although none of these appeal courts developed a gender-based analysis of the principles that should apply in relocation cases, their realistic approach effectively empowered parents with sole custody (mostly mothers) in their enhanced ability to make decisions about their lives and the lives of their children.[7] Abella J.A. put this approach in the context of the child's relationship with her parents:

> While it would always be preferable to attempt to find a solution which protects the child's relationship with both parents, this ideal is simply not always possible. It is practically inevitable, when two parents no longer live together, that the child's relationship with each will be different. This means that the child, and each of its parents, must adjust to the new realities. The adjustments may be painful, including the adjustment of a parent seeing a child less often than anticipated. However painful, that parent's desires cannot be paramount. (*MacGyver*, 1995: 446)[8]

A 1996 judgment of the Supreme Court of California took the same approach (*In re the Marriage of Burgess*; see also *In the Marriage of I and I*, 1995).

Given the controversy that arose after the *MacGyver v. Richards* case (Fine, 1995a, 1995b; Schmitz, 1995), the Supreme Court of Canada's opinion regarding relocation was bound to be of great interest. When the decision of the Saskatchewan Court of Appeal in *Gordon v. Goertz* was appealed to the Supreme Court, both LEAF and the Children's Lawyer of Ontario obtained leave to intervene.

Gender-Neutral and Gendering Discourses in *Gordon v. Goertz*

History of the Case

In *Gordon v. Goertz*, the parents, who had been married since 1973, separated in 1990. The mother was awarded sole custody of her daughter Samantha (born in 1988), while the father was awarded specified access. Custody of an older daughter was not in issue as she was 20 years old at the time. The mother was clearly primary caregiver of Samantha until separation (*Gordon*, 1993: 7), and, she argued, since that time as well (Factum of the Respondent, para. 7). The father argued that he had spent more time with Samantha than had the mother since the separation, even though Samantha's primary residence was with the mother (Factum of the Appellant, paras 4, 8). The trial judge on the custody issue found that the father had been physically and verbally abusive towards the mother and the elder daughter (from whom the father was estranged) and manipulative in his relations with Samantha's caregiver (*Gordon*, 1993: 7, 10).[9] No restrictions on mobility were contained in the original custody and access order, but structured access was ordered due to the continuing conflict between the parents. This order was upheld on appeal.[10]

The mother said that it had been her stated intention to pursue a Master's degree in orthodontia for some 10 years (Factum of the Respondent: para. 8). When the University of Adelaide in Australia was the only program to accept her, she planned to move to Adelaide to complete the degree. The father applied to vary the custody order so that he would have custody or she would be restrained from moving the child. The mother applied to vary the access provisions of the original order so that she could move with the child. Her application was granted, the judge relying heavily on the original trial judgment. The father was granted liberal and generous access in Australia only on one month's notice (*Gordon*, 1994). The Saskatchewan Court of Appeal dismissed the father's appeal with costs to the mother in a very brief judgment (*Gordon*, 1995) and the father appealed to the Supreme Court of Canada. He sought a change in the custody award or permission to exercise access outside Australia, where mother and child had now moved.

The Arguments

The main issue in this case was whether relocation of a custodial parent warranted a change in the earlier custody and access order. Technically, the question was the threshold test of when a material change in circumstances has occurred under section 17 of the Divorce Act, thereby enabling a court to consider a variation in a custody or access order in the best interests of the child. A second question, once the threshold test was satisfied, was whether the best interests of the child should be considered only by reference to the change in circumstances, or whether the question should be more general. A third question was what principles should guide the courts in determining the best interests of the child when relocation constitutes a material change. Only LEAF dealt with the first two questions and I will accordingly focus on the third when comparing the facta. The different approaches to the best interests test are of particular interest.

Mother: Different Position, Different Onus

Like the father and both interveners, the mother argued that the test for courts in deciding mobility issues should be the best interests of the child. This stance was predictable given the well-established principle that the best interests of the child are paramount in custody decisions (Divorce Act, sections 16(8) and 17(5)). However, in determining the best interests, the mother argued that the *differing* relationships of the custodial and non-custodial parents to the child should be taken into account. The realistic view of family breakdown enunciated by the provincial courts of appeal in *Lapointe v. Lapointe* (1995) and *MacGyver v. Richards* (1995) was argued: 'The [Divorce] Act contemplates that following a marriage breakdown new family units will be created, with the discretion given to the Court to ultimately determine upon which of either or both parents will be imposed the primary responsibility for the care of any child of the marriage' (Factum of the Respondent, para. 26). In determining best interests in the context of relocation, then, it followed that a different onus should lie on the custodial and access parents:

> The custodial parent's decision to move should not be examined in the context of whether it discloses a legitimate or necessary reason for moving. Rather, the custodial parent should be required to show some advantage accruing either to the child or the parent from the move and that he or she has given appropriate consideration to the child's best interests in the decision to move. The non-custodial parent should be required to demonstrate why the move is not in the best interests of the child. Although due consideration will have to be given to the non-custodial parent's contact with the child, the continuation of that contact should not be the Court's primordial consideration in the determination as to whether the custodial parent should be permitted to move. The non-custodial parent's contact with the child is capable of being adjusted to accommodate the move having regard to the particular circumstances of the child and the location of the child's new residence. (Ibid., para. 14)

It was also pointed out by the mother that sections 16(10) and 17(9) of the Divorce Act with respect to maximizing the contact of the non-custodial parent 'were not intended to provide non-custodial parents with the *same* involvement in the lives of their children as the custodial parent has following separation and divorce' (ibid., para. 27, 29; emphasis mine). This contact must be 'consistent with the best interests of the child', which in turn begs the question of what approach to 'best interests' should be taken. This question was answered by the mother as follows:

> It is submitted that the custodial parent would have to demonstrate that within the decision to move, he or she has taken into account the child's best interests in terms of lifestyle, physical, emotional and psychological well-being as well as the child's preference with respect to the move. Given that the interests of the child are inextricably linked to those of the custodial parent, the fact that the move will be to some advantage to the custodial parent would presumably also be of benefit to the child, unless the move can be demonstrated to detrimentally affect the best interests of the child in a very serious fashion. (Ibid., para. 34)

The mother further argued that because the custodial parent has been entrusted with many responsibilities that in turn limit and indeed burden her life, the onus on that parent to show some advantage flowing from a move 'should not be scrutinized to the extent that the legitimacy or necessity of the move is called into question by the reviewing court or the non-custodial parent' (ibid., para. 35).

Father: Equality and the Selfless Father

The father argued for a much different test. He rejected any presumptions or deference in favour of either parent and urged an analysis that focused on the perspective of the child. He invoked the indeterminate test in *Carter v. Brooks* (1990) that directed courts to weigh and balance the factors that are relevant in the particular circumstances of a case. While conceding that 'on many occasions, the best interests of the custodial parent are entwined with the best interests of the child', the father argued that '[m]any mobility cases are a striking example of when the best interests of the child and the custodial parent may be different and even opposing' (Factum of the Appellant, para. 29). Even if the move offers 'mutual benefit to the child and custodial parent . . . unlike the custodial parent who has everything to gain, the child who has a meaningful relationship with the access parent is being called upon to pay a price for the move, to experience the trauma of another physical fracturing of the family' (ibid., para. 29).

The father thus positioned himself to speak selflessly on behalf of the child, and invoked the notion of the restructured, but still oddly intact, 'post-divorce family unit'.[11] In contrast, he positioned the mother as selfishly acting in her own interests, thereby invoking discourses that Carol Smart (1991: 499) has described: 'While *fatherhood* now represents equality (an element of the higher moral reasoning) and *welfare* represents the interest of the child or weakest member, *motherhood* represents some atavistic, pre-new enlightenment claim which would drag us back into selfish emotion and a satisfaction of the sense rather than a meeting of objective needs.'

Along these lines, the father made much of the fact that the mother relied on 'surrogate' babysitters due to her busy schedule[12] and contrasted his own flexibility to spend time with the daughter and interact in her activities. He argued that 'Samantha has been isolated in a foreign country of complete strangers' and that 'the relocation of Samantha to Australia was made solely to accommodate the advanced studies of the [mother]' (Factum of the Appellant, paras 42, 43). As we shall see, the majority of the Supreme Court of Canada was persuaded by this apparently selfless stance of the father in terms of his analysis of the 'best interests' test and the approach to relocation disputes, but it did not agree to change the custody order.

Children's Lawyer of Ontario: Only the Child Matters

The Children's Lawyer of Ontario predictably positioned himself on the side of children, arguing that parental preferences and rights should play no role in the determination of custody and access disputes. The best interests of the child 'must not be assessed from the perspective of the parent seeking to preserve access but from that of the child entitled to the best environment possible' (Factum of the Children's Lawyer of Ontario, paras 4, 6). With reference to a change of residence, he argued that the courts must be satisfied that the change is in the best interests of the child, and this regardless of any agreement between the parents (ibid., paras 7, 8). No one factor of the many that are related to the best interests of the child, whether listed in legislation or in judicial decisions, should be determinative (ibid., para. 9). In general, the Children's Lawyer advocated continuing broad (and indeterminate) discretion in the judiciary (ibid., para. 14). Although custodial parents have the authority to make day-to-day decisions affecting the child without interference from the access parent (ibid., para. 16), other issues are subject to judicial review: 'In significant custody and access matters, the Court cannot evade making decisions regarding the best interests of children behind deference to the custodial parent' (ibid., para. 17).

The Children's Lawyer also stated, ignoring contradictory results in social science studies (see King 1994; Furstenberg and Cherlin, 1991), that maximum contact between child and non-custodial parent is crucial: 'It is now widely assumed to be self evident that it is in the child's best interests to ensure the access parent's involvement in the life of the child' (Factum of the Children's Lawyer of Ontario, paras 21, 22). Moreover, *both* parents should bear an evidentiary burden in mobility disputes (ibid., para. 30). *Carter v. Brooks* (1990) was said to be the correct statement of the law and to have been affirmed in *MacGyver v. Richards* (1995); in the alternative, to the extent that *MacGyver* established a new test to determine mobility cases, it was said to be wrongly decided (ibid., paras. 31–3). As with the father's argument, the Children's Lawyer positioned his argument to be on the side of children, as opposed to an approach that dealt with 'the respective rights of parents' (ibid., para. 34).

LEAF and Gendered Discourses:
Rescuing the Famous Disappearing Mother

The parties and the Children's Lawyer of Ontario never mentioned gender relations or power dynamics. This failure is not surprising in the mother's case, given how difficult it is to appear to promote an approach supporting the best interests of the child when mothers (let alone concerns about gendered power relations) are mentioned (Boyd, 1995; Fineman, 1992; Smart, 1991). The mother did raise the fact that the trial judge on the custody issue had found that during the marriage the father had been manipulative and physically and verbally abusive towards the mother and older daughter (a point ignored by the Supreme Court of Canada).

It was left to LEAF, then, to develop an analysis of the sexual division of labour and of gendered power dynamics in heterosexual families and in custody and access disputes. LEAF argued that it is artificial, and indeed impossible, to try to determine the best interests of children in isolation from a consideration of the social location of their parents, and in particular, their mothers. It pointed out that female assumption of primary child-care responsibilities after separation is a continuation of the responsibilities held by women prior to separation: the statistics on largely maternal custody are not, therefore, surprising (Factum of LEAF, paras 7, 8). It was also shown that even when a joint custody award is in place, mothers usually assume primary responsibility for child care and decision-making (ibid., para. 9). As part of the gendered context of custody disputes, studies showing the incidence of violence in heterosexual relationships were cited, as well as the fact that 20 per cent of women assaulted by their partners reported that the violence continued after separation. Men who cannot disconnect from the women they abuse can and do use the legal system, and children, as 'a new arena of combat' (ibid., para. 18).

In developing its arguments about women holding primary caregiving responsibility for children, LEAF documented the disproportionate labour that women still assume in the domestic sphere regardless of their employment status and referred extensively to research in this field. It emphasized that this sexual division of labour is linked to the lack of public support for child care and the unresponsiveness of the work world to family needs (ibid., paras 3–6).

Like the mother, LEAF emphasized the difference in positions of the custodial and access parents, noting that the 'high level and constancy of the responsibility for custody is far greater than that of the parent who sees the child intermittently and exercises access' (ibid., para. 35). LEAF pointed out that the child's best interests were not only intimately intertwined with the well being of the custodial parent, but also with any new family unit: 'The custodial parent and the child are a new family unit on separation. The court must consider the effect on the mother, and thus on the family unit, of restricting where she can live' (ibid., para. 37).

Moreover, LEAF developed an analysis and critique of the direction in which access law has been moving. It asserted that while the goal of maintaining present access may be desirable, it should not be at the cost of the well-being of the custodial mother and the child in her care. Access was to be in the best interests of the child, not in accordance with the needs and desires of the access parent: 'Custodial parents are expected and obliged to make decisions and to conduct their lives consistent with the child's best interests, not with the needs and desires of the access parent' (ibid., paras 37, 38). LEAF went on to deconstruct various myths and assumptions about access, such as the benefits of maximum contact, showing that these benefits are highly contingent on circumstances. As a result, principles determining relocation should not be based on an assumption that maximum contact must in most instances be preserved or that it can be preserved only by close physical proximity (ibid., para. 39).

For all of these reasons, LEAF endorsed the approaches of the *Lapointe*, *MacGyver*, and *Levesque* cases discussed earlier, that deference should be given to custodial parents' ability to determine and act in the best interests of children (ibid., para. 33). 'As the person responsible for exercising judgment on a daily basis, who is most familiar with the child's needs, and who will live with the reality of decisions, the custodial parent is better situated than a judge to determine what is in the child's best interests, including residence' (ibid., para. 34). LEAF argued for even less judicial discretion in reviewing relocation decisions than the mother/respondent did. When sole custody (with access) was involved, as in this case, the test submitted by LEAF was as follows:

> Where a parent with sole custody seeks to relocate, the move, in and of itself, is a material change in circumstances with respect to access only, but not with respect to custody. Accordingly, a sole custodial parent's decision to relocate is not subject to the court's review, as the relocation decision is an incident of custody. However, access may be restructured by the court. (Ibid., para. 59(a))[13]

LEAF also argued that deference to the relocation decisions of custodial parents is consistent with the modern philosophy of family breakdown, 'which aims at encouraging and facilitating the ability of former spouses to get on with their lives' (ibid., para. 43). In order for custodial mothers to do so, they may need to move to obtain employment or better employment; child care; support from family or friends; housing; and so on. In a highly mobile society where government fiscal constraint and economic restructuring are occurring, the need to move may be greater (ibid., paras 17, 42).

In its use of language such as 'primary caregiving',[14] LEAF drew on Canadian cases that have increasingly adopted this terminology without asserting a presumption in favour of the primary caregiver having custody (e.g., *Levesque*, 1993; see Boyd, 1990; Pask and McCall, 1991). LEAF also cited feminist literature on the primary caregiver presumption (Boyd, 1990; Munro, 1992; Pask and McCall, 1991), although it never used the language of 'presumptions'. This literature has been criticized from within feminism (as well as without). Feminists are concerned about its tendency to overlook the particular circumstances of mothers with disabilities (Mosoff, 1997) and mothers who parent in extended family settings and/or who experience racism in assessments of their parenting (CACSW, 1994; Kline, 1993). As a strategy, it has also been based mainly on an analysis of the experience of women who have raised children in a heterosexual family context; its applicability to lesbian co-mothers remains unclear.[15] Finally, it arguably exacerbates trends to privatize social and economic responsibility for children, which in turn may reinforce women's inequality (see Pulkingham, 1994).

In making its case for judicial deference to the custodial mother's decision-making responsibility, LEAF arguably developed a gender-based argument that left these complexities of race, sexuality, disability, and poverty to one side. Moreover, due to the fact that the parties in this case were quite well-off, poverty and class could not be raised as factual issues. LEAF did identify the particular difficulties and discrimination that women of colour, Aboriginal women, immigrant women, and women with disabilities experience in the labour market (Factum of LEAF, para. 13), as well as the links between lack of employment and the poverty of single mothers (ibid., paras 14–15). It was then noted that these difficulties are magnified for custodial mothers who are socially isolated or geographically removed from family and community (ibid., para. 16). By implication, it may be particularly important for women facing multiple discrimination to relocate in areas that offer greater employment opportunities and/or support networks. LEAF never dealt directly in its factum with the (white, professional) parties in this particular case, focusing instead on painting a picture of the impact of restrictions on mobility on women, particularly women affected by racism, poverty, or disability. The more complex ways in which race, sexuality, and disability may intersect with gender in the custody and access field were largely unstated.

The Supreme Court of Canada Decision(s): Gender Nowhere in Sight

Far from the complexities mentioned immediately above being considered by the Supreme Court of Canada, a gender-based analysis was not even attempted in the judgments.[16]

Madame Justice McLachlin for the Majority

McLachlin J. began by stating that '[w]hen parents separate, one typically enjoys custody of the child, the other access', but she never mentioned the fact that this pattern is highly gendered (*Gordon*, 1996: 185). The majority of the Court[17] endorsed McLachlin J.'s analysis, which firmly rejected the arguments of LEAF and of the mother on deference to the custodial parent's decisions, and reasserted a highly indeterminate and individual case approach to the best interests of the child principle argued by the father and the Children's Lawyer. Indeed, McLachlin J. rejected critiques of the indeterminate approach (such as that raised by Abella J.A. in *MacGyver v. Richards*), saying that '[a] more precise test would risk sacrificing the child's best interests to expediency and certainty' (ibid., 192). However, all members of the Court agreed that the mother should retain custody and be permitted to move with the child to Australia. The only change to the earlier order was that access could be exercised in Canada instead of only in Australia. Although the result in this specific case was therefore positive for the custodial mother concerned, questions can be raised about the impact of McLachlin J.'s reasoning for mothers in future cases.

McLachlin J. not only reasserted a highly indeterminate version of the best interests test, but also stated that where a material change in circumstances has occurred, courts should consider custody '*afresh* without defaulting to the existing arrangement' (*Gordon*, 1996: 191; emphasis mine). The inquiry is not to be limited to the *change* in circumstances alone; rather, all factors relevant to the original order are to be considered in light of the new circumstances (ibid., 191–2). Her definition of material change opens the possibility of many fresh assessments of the initial custody award, which in turn will likely give rise to increased conflict and re-litigation of custody. Indeed, McLachlin J. shocked many family lawyers by saying that '[t]he short-term pain of litigation may be preferable to the long-term pain of unresolved conflict. Foreclosing an avenue of legal redress exacts a price; it may, in extreme cases, even impel desperate parents to desperate measures in contravention of the law' (ibid., 197).[18] Her remark appears to come dangerously close to sympathy for parents who abduct children.

In discussing the threshold condition of a material change in circumstances that permits a court to consider an application to vary a custody or access order, McLachlin J. held that a judge must be satisfied of:

(1) a change in the condition, means, needs or circumstances of the child and/or the ability of the parents to meet the needs of the child;
(2) which materially affects the child; and
(3) which was either not foreseen or could not have been reasonably contemplated by the judge who made the initial order. (Ibid., 190)

She added that a relocation will always be a 'change' and often, but not always, a change that meets the first two requirements above. Although '[a] move to a neighbouring town might not affect the child or the parents' ability to meet its needs in any significant way' (ibid.), it appears that many moves would satisfy the requirement of material change:

Similarly, if the child lacks a positive relationship with the access parent or extended family in the area, a move might not affect the child sufficiently to constitute a material change in its situation. Where, as here, the child enjoyed frequent and meaningful contact with the access parent, a move that would seriously curtail that contact suffices to establish the necessary connection between the change and the needs and circumstances of the child. (Ibid.)

In an environment where maximum contact between fathers and children is given high priority, despite studies showing that the value of this contact is less certain than the link with the custodial parent and the custodial parent's well-being (see, e.g., Furstenberg and Cherlin, 1991: 71–2; King, 1994: 963), McLachlin J.'s approach means that many relocation cases will now involve a material change in circumstances, allowing a court to review the custody order. Relocation can mean a material change not only in cases where joint custody orders or mobility restrictions are in place, but also where 'frequent and meaningful contact' would be seriously curtailed. The likelihood of this change giving rise to a fresh custody review is exacerbated if the possibility of relocation was not mentioned at the time of the original order (see point 3 above). Yet many mothers seeking custody may choose not to mention a desire to move for fear that it may prejudice their ability to persuade a judge that they are committed to maintaining the child's connections with the father and any extended family in the location where the family had lived before separation. Or they may fear that raising the issue of relocation (for example, by putting a provision on notice about relocation in an agreement) will be too dangerous due to the possibility of the access parent then asking in turn for a restriction on relocation.

McLachlin J. explicitly rejected the use of 'presumptions' in favour of custodial parents[19] that would place an onus on the access parent (to show why the move is not in the child's best interests) and discounted the notion that greater certainty would result from the use of presumptions:

> The argument that a presumption would render the law more predictable in a way which would do justice in the majority of cases and reduce conflict damaging to the child between the former spouses also founders on the rock of the *Divorce Act*. The Act contemplates individual justice. . . . Even if it could be shown that a presumption in favour of the custodial parent would reduce litigation that would not imply a reduction in conflict. (*Gordon*, 1996: 197)

While McLachlin J. may well be right that some conflict in custody and access would continue despite presumptions aimed at reducing it, any greater certainty in the law would assist parties in settling disputes out of court (Neely, 1984). However, her conclusion seems to ignore the unequal bargaining power that typically exists between mothers and fathers at the time of family breakdown (ibid.; Neave, 1994; Poirier and Boudreau, 1992). Moreover, given the serious consequences of the sexual division of labour for women in both public and private spheres, it seems surprising that the following statement could be made, apparently in response to LEAF's argument: 'Nor does the great burden borne by custodial parents justify a presumption in their favour' (*Gordon*, 1996: 190). She did concede that the custodial parent's views were entitled to great respect; but both custodial and access parents should bear the evidentiary burden of demonstrating where the best interests of the child lie (ibid., 198). The benefits of the child remaining with the parent to whose custody it has become accustomed must be weighed against the continuance of full contact with the access parent, extended family, and community (ibid.: 202). The playing field has thus been levelled as between access and custodial parents, with custodial parents (mainly mothers) being given little credit for the responsibility they have borne in the past for caregiving and decision-making.

Neither did McLachlin J. give guidance as to how judges should balance the many factors that can be seen as part of the best interests test. She listed several factors that a court should consider in determining the best interests of children. These included the existing custody arrangement and relationship between the child and custodial parent; the existing access arrangement and relationship between the child and the access parent; the desirability of maximizing contact; the views of the child; the reason for moving in the exceptional case where it is relevant to the custodial parent's ability to meet the needs of the child; disruption to the child of a change in custody; and disruption to the child consequent on removal from family, schools, and the community (ibid., 201–2). How to balance these factors, which often conflict with one another, was left up to individual judges.

Madame Justice L'Heureux-Dubé: A Minority Opinion

L'Heureux-Dubé J. (with only La Forest J. agreeing with her in full) took a much different approach, similar to that argued by the mother. Without mentioning the gender-specific analysis of LEAF, she followed the deference approach of *Lapointe* (1995), *MacGyver* (1995), and other recent cases in Canada, the United States, and Australia. She agreed with McLachlin J. that a change of residence like this one, which involved moving to another country and which was unforeseen at the time of the original order, was a material change of circumstances. But she did not agree that once that threshold test had been passed, a reappraisal of the whole custody situation was necessary (ibid., 205–6). Only if the original order was irrelevant or no longer appropriate would this be true.

L'Heureux-Dubé J.'s ability to take this position rested, as she herself said, on her view of the notion of custody, which differed from that of McLachlin J., as their earlier judgments in *Young v. Young* (1993) revealed. L'Heureux-Dubé J. quoted from her judgment in *Young* and that of Twaddle J.A. in *Lapointe* (1995) to the effect that at common law an order of sole custody vested full parental authority to one parent to the exclusion of the other. However, that power was not a 'right' granted for the benefit of the parent, but rather was 'designed to enable that parent to discharge his or her responsibilities and obligations to the child.' Determination of the place of residence of a child was included in this power (ibid., 208).

L'Heureux-Dubé J. then demonstrated that the Divorce Act had not changed the common law in any material way, and drew support for her position from international law and several other jurisdictions, including England, France, the United States, and Australia. She concluded that any application for variation must begin with the proposition that, 'absent an agreement or court order restricting the incidents of custody, such as the place of residence of the child, it is within the powers of a custodial parent to decide such a change of residence' (ibid., 215). The onus of showing why the move is *not* in the best interests of the child therefore lies on the party who opposes the move (ibid., 215, 218).[20]

L'Heureux-Dubé J. said that where an agreement restricts mobility, the court can always review such restrictions based on the best interests test (ibid., 216). Moreover, because restrictions should be imposed only in the best interests of the child, not 'for frivolous reasons, for the sole purpose of insuring the non-custodial parent's access, to frustrate the custodial parent's mobility, as a bargaining tool, etc.', then 'restrictions on incidents of custody, such as the right to determine where the child should live, should not be inferred, for instance, from generous or specified access provisions without more [clearly specified restrictions]' (ibid., 217). However, where an agreement or order did expressly restrict a change of residence, the custodial parent would have the onus of establishing that the decision to relocate was not made to undermine the access parent's rights and that she (or he) was willing to make arrangements to restructure access (ibid., 218).

L'Heureux-Dubé J. noted that although parental agreements should be encouraged in the interests of minimizing ongoing conflict and litigation between parents, in some cases courts will be called upon to decide an issue, which is 'never an easy task and sometimes courts can only choose between the lesser of two evils' (ibid., 222). She thereby adopted the 'realistic' approach to family breakdown of the courts of appeal in *Lapointe, MacGyver*, etc.[21] On the question of what standard should apply in relocation cases, L'Heureux-Dubé J. delineated the following factors relevant to a consideration of the best interests of the child. One such factor was maximum contact, but she also noted that the experts are divided on the weight to be given to maximum contact in assessing best interests (ibid., 221). 'The desirability of maintaining maximum contact between the child and both parents is but one of those numerous factors, albeit a very significant one.' Another factor was 'a consideration of the particular role and emotional bonding the child enjoys with his or her primary caregiver' (ibid., 225).

Moreover, where no express restrictions on custody exist, 'it must be assumed that an existing custody order or agreement reflects the best interests of the child and that such interests lie with the custodial parent' (ibid., 222–3). She added:

> The basic premise according to which the custodial parent must be assumed to carry out his or her decision-making responsibilities in the child's best interests is in no way attached to a particular incident of custody, but rather stems from the inextricable link between the significant decision-making responsibility entrusted to the custodial parent and the best interests of the child. (Ibid., 223)

Quoting from Abella J.A. in *MacGyver*, she added that 'where, as here, a decision of the custodial parent is challenged by the non-custodial parent on the basis that it is not in the child's best interests, "[t]he emphasis should be . . . on deferring to the decision-making responsibilities of the custodial parent, unless there is substantial evidence that those decisions impair the child's, not the access parent's, long-term well-being"' (ibid., 224). Therefore, in most cases, the relocation will imply a restructuring of access, rather than a change of custody, which would be 'a more violent disruption in the life of a child' (ibid., 226).

Conclusion

In the end, the majority of the Supreme Court of Canada in *Gordon v. Goertz* has reasserted a wide power of judicial decision-making in the custody realm, despite abundant evidence that judicial discretion often leads to contradictory and sometimes highly problematic results due to the indeterminacy of the best interests test. McLachlin J. for the majority could not get beyond the argument that deference to the custodial parent would shift the focus from the best interests of the child to the interests of the parents (ibid., 200). She felt that these interests could be severed and were not relational. L'Heureux-Dubé J., on the other hand, took a more realistic approach to post-divorce parenting, that ultimately, one has to trust that custodial parents will usually do what is in the best interests of their children and these decisions should not be subject to too much second-guessing. She felt that a principled approach to the best interests test, such as the one she outlined, reinforced the test rather than contradicted it. For her, this approach 'provides much needed clarity and certainty in this difficult area of the law and minimizes the need to resort to protracted acrimonious negotiations [*sic*] or, even worse, traumatic and costly litigation which, ultimately, cannot but injuriously affect the children' (ibid., 229).

The one concession that McLachlin J. made, although it fell short of a presumption, was that the custodial parent's views were entitled to 'great respect and the most serious consideration' in determining best interests in a relocation context. She added that '[t]he decision of the custodial parent to live and work where he or she chooses is likewise entitled to respect, barring an improper motive reflecting adversely on the custodial parent's parenting ability' (ibid., 201). Thus, the custodial parent's reason for moving was generally not to be considered by a court unless it was relevant to that parent's ability to meet the child's needs. (However, subsequent cases indicate that reasons for moving may play a role in determining the best interests of the child.) Also, while asserting the significance of the 'maximum contact' factor in ss. 16(10) and 17(9) of the Divorce Act, McLachlin J. noted that it is:

> mandatory, but not absolute. . . . The reduction of beneficial contact between the child and the access parent does not always dictate a change of custody or an order which restricts relocation of the child. If the child's needs are likely to be best served by remaining with the custodial parent, and this consideration offsets the loss or reduction in contact with the access parent, then the judge should not vary custody and permit the move. (Ibid., 193)

Presumably it was on this basis that McLachlin J. decided that the mother in *Gordon v. Goertz* should be permitted to move. McLachlin J. also noted that factors that might negatively affect the child due to the move were 'somewhat attenuated . . . by the fact that the father has the means to travel to Australia' to see her and that both parents have 'ample means' to facilitate access notwithstanding the move (ibid.: 203). Some commentators have pointed out that the practical effect of the Supreme Court of Canada's ruling is therefore unclear, despite the difference in emphasis between the judgments of McLachlin and L'Heureux-Dubé JJ. (see Simpson, 1996). In other words, it may well be that some form of respect for custodial parents will occur, at least where they appear to have carried out their responsibilities properly and there is no clear evidence that they have in some way been 'unreasonable' with respect to the other parent.

The problem lies in the ways that reasonableness and responsibility will be interpreted. There is evidence that due to the potential for bias and value judgments inherent in an indeterminate best interests standard, permission to move will be granted to some but not others (see Bourque, 1995; Boyd, 1996). Cases decided since *Gordon v. Goertz* suggest that economic issues especially may influence judges, for example, where lack of economic resources may prevent the exercise of access. Moreover, due to the increased uncertainty in the field, litigation may well increase, thereby exacerbating conflict between parents, which is never good for children. More worrying, it is likely that many cases where relocation is disputed will never make it to court: mothers will simply 'choose' to stay put rather than have the custody question reopened, at what cost we will never know because these cases will remain invisible. The problem will be perceived to have disappeared.

In the end, the voices of access parents (mainly fathers) have been elevated to a position of equality with those of custodial parents, regardless of any differential caregiving responsibility. These voices have also been aligned with a moral stance of deference to the perspective of children. The voices of custodial mothers have been aligned with selfishness and gender-specific 'rights' claims, and therefore discredited. LEAF's effort to enunciate a principled position of deference to the custodial parent's decision-making, based on an analysis of the social context of caregiving in Canadian society, has been implicitly denigrated as a rights-seeking move by narrow-minded women's groups. Despite Karen Munro's caution (1992) that in the custody field any 'rights' analysis is misplaced and instead the analysis must focus on caregiving, the majority of the Supreme Court of Canada has been unable to hear the difference between 'caring for' and 'caring about' (Smart, 1991) and the continuing gendered nature of that difference. The voices of caregivers, largely women, have been rendered silent in the process. The very indeterminacy of the best interests test (re)asserted in *Gordon v. Goertz* means that, in practice, some judges will still give weight to past caregiving. This possibility remains unpredictable, however, and means that custody decision-making will be subject to the same biases that feminists have identified in the past.

Notes

This paper was presented at the International Society of Family Law North America Regional Conference on Parent and Child in North American Family Law, Quebec City, 13–15 June 1996. Thanks to Gillian Calder and Kim Stanton for invaluable research assistance, to Dorothy Chunn for comments, and to the Social Sciences and Humanities Research Council of Canada (Women and Change) for research support.

1. Section 2(1) of the Divorce Act defines custody broadly as including 'care, upbringing and any other incident of custody'. 'Accès' is defined in French as 'le droit de visite' (the right to visit). The Divorce Act, s. 16(5), says that unless a court otherwise orders, the access parent has the right to make inquiries, and to be given information, as to the health, education, and welfare of the child. Until recently, custody and access were thus thought to be quite different things. See Madame Justice L'Heureux-Dubé's discussion in *Gordon* (1996) at 210-11.

2. In 1991, mothers were awarded sole custody of children in 73.6 per cent and fathers in 11.8 per cent of all custody decisions made in divorce court. Joint custody was awarded in 14.3 per cent of these decisions: Statistics Canada (1995: 18, 25, Table 2.8). These partial figures include only cases decided by the courts and not those in which custody arrangements were decided outside of court or by courts dealing with non-divorce situations: ibid., 20 n. 3. This pattern of custody awards had remained relatively constant since 1978, when 78.7 per cent of mothers, compared to 15.6 per cent of fathers, received custody: ibid., 18, 25, Table 2.8. However, figures from 1994 indicate an increase in joint custody awards (20.5 per cent), while mothers received sole custody in 69.6 per cent and fathers in 9.8 per cent: Statistics Canada (1996: Tables 8, 9).

3. In the course of oral argument (December 1995) in *Gordon v. Goertz* (1996), McLachlin J. did suggest that she would be interested in hearing such an argument. In contrast, in a case of the Court of Appeals of New York, Titone J. suggested that in some relocation cases, a court could consider whether the access parent was willing to make a parallel move to the new location as an alternative to restricting the custodial parent's mobility: *Tropea v. Tropea*; *Kenward v. Brown* (1996).

4. Bourque (1995: 9 n. 27) reports that the cases she studied were roughly evenly split between denying and allowing a mother's move.

5. The phrase the 'post-divorce family unit' appeared first in Canadian jurisprudence, seemingly out of the blue, at the Supreme Court of Canada level of *Thibaudeau* (1995), a case on the taxation of child support payments. There it was used by Cory and Iacobucci JJ. in their concurring judgment to deny the claim that the custodial parent was discriminated

against by the Income Tax Act, s. 56(1), which requires that tax be paid on child support payments received. They used the term to describe the restructured nuclear family unit of access parent, custodial parent, and children, and decided that the inclusion/deduction regime of s. 56 in fact conferred a benefit to the 'unit' as a whole. Contrast McLachlin and L'Heureux-Dubé JJ. in dissent, defining the relevant groups for comparison purposes to be custodial and non-custodial parents.

Interestingly, 'post-divorce family unit' has been used in United States courts for some time, especially in the context of relocation. However, it is used to describe not the restructured nuclear family, but rather the single-parent family unit typically consisting of separated/divorced mother and children. See, for example, *Tropea v. Tropea*; *Kenward v. Brown* (1996). Some authors used this imagery to support arguments in favour of laws deferring to that unit. See Wexler (1985). I find this usage to be more in accord with reality.

6. McLachlin J. tried to reconcile the *MacGyver* and *Carter v. Brooks* decisions in *Gordon v. Goertz* (1996); L'Heureux-Dubé J. viewed them as taking significantly different approaches.

7. It is, of course, possible that this approach might lead to greater litigation over the initial custody order itself, given that the decision-making power of the custodial parent would effectively be enhanced while the veto power of the access parent would be diminished. Parents who might otherwise see themselves as access parents might choose to fight for sole custody, joint custody, explicit restrictions on mobility, or shared decision-making.

8. In *Tropea v. Tropea*; *Kenward v. Brown* (1996) at 740, Titone J. said: 'Like Humpty Dumpty, a family, once broken by divorce, cannot be put back together in precisely the same way.'

9. Evidently the father had used corporal punishment on the older daughter, including severe spankings that left marks.

10. Saskatchewan Court of Appeal, 14 Mar 1994, docket #1482.

11. See the discussion of 'post-divorce family unit', note 5 above.

12. See, for example, paras 8, 12, 40 of the appellant's factum. Compare the discourses employed in the *Tyabji v. Sandana* (1994) case where an 'ambitious' female politician lost custody to her former husband, who, according to the court, had more time for the children.

13. Different tests were laid out for arrangements of 'true' equal parenting and where relocation restrictions were contained in an order or agreement: Factum of LEAF, para. 59. Only in true equal parenting situations should custody *per se* be re-examined, as opposed to the decision to relocate. Where restrictions were in place, the relocation restriction could be reviewed but not custody itself, and an onus should be on the access parent

to establish that the move is contrary to the best interests of the child.

14. The mother also used the language of primary caregiving in her factum, as did the father. He argued that the role of primary caregiver had changed from the mother to himself, although the facts on this point appeared to remain in dispute and unresolved by the Supreme Court of Canada.

15. See, however, *Buist v. Greaves* [1997].

16. I hasten to add that this is not surprising, given the lack of gendered analysis in most of the arguments and the fact that LEAF, while presenting a gendered argument, clearly stated that its suggested principles for decision-making were gender-neutral and would apply to any custodial parent, whether male or female. It is striking, however, that the abusive behaviour of the father documented in the original custody judgment of Carter J. and mentioned in the mother's factum and her lawyer's oral argument was not referred to at all by the Supreme Court of Canada.

17. Lamer C.J., Sopinka, Cory, Iacobucci, and Major JJ. concurred with McLachlin J. Gonthier J. concurred with McLachlin J.'s reasons but said that he also agreed with 'L'Heureux-Dubé J.'s explanations of factors pertinent to assessing the best interests of the child and that they are to be considered in doing so' (*Gordon*, 1996: 235). However, he then said that he did not share L'Heureux-Dubé J.'s view on onus of proof. La Forest J. concurred with the reasons of L'Heureux-Dubé.

18. L'Heureux-Dubé J. criticizes this part of McLachlin J.'s judgment at 230.

19. Presumptions *per se* were not mentioned in the factums. However, in arguing for an onus on the access parent and deference to the decisions of the custodial parents, something close to a presumption was urged by both the mother's lawyer and LEAF. Moreover, Abella J.A. referred to a 'presumptive deference' in *MacGyver v. Richards* (1995).

20. L'Heureux-Dubé J. quoted extensively from the recent decision of the Supreme Court of California, *In Re Marriage of Burgess* (1996), on the onus question.

21. See also *Gordon v. Goertz* (1996) at 232.

Facta Cited

Factum of the Respondent (unpublished)
Factum of the Appellant (unpublished)
Factum of the LEAF (the Women's Legal Education and Action Fund) (LEAF 1996: 469–91)
Factum of the Children's Lawyer of Ontario (unpublished)

Cases Cited

Buist v. Greaves [1997] O.J. No. 2646 (Q.L.) Ont. Gen. Div.
Carter v. Brooks (1990), 30 R.F.L. (3d) 53 (O.C.A.)
Colley v. Colley (1991), 31 R.F.L. (3d) 281 (Ont. U.F.C.)
Fasan v. Fasan (1991), 32 R.F.L. (3d) 121 (Ont. Gen. Div.)
Gordon v. Goertz (1993), 111 Sask. R. 1 (Sask. Q.B.)
Gordon v. Goertz (1994), Court File No. 1035 of 1990 (December 30, 1994) (Sask. U.F.C.)
Gordon v. Goertz (1995), 128 Sask. R. 156 (Sask. C.A.)
Gordon v. Goertz (1996), 19 R.F.L. (4th) 177 (S.C.C.)
Hollett v. Collins-Hollett (1992), 102 Nfld. & P.E.I.R. 145 (Nfld. S.C.)
In the Marriage of I and I (1995), 19 Fam. L.R. 147 (Fam. Ct. Austr.)
In re the Marriage of Burgess (1996), 51 Cal. Rptr. 2d 444 (S.C. Calif.)
Lapointe v. Lapointe (1995), 17 R.F.L. (4th) 1 (Man. C.A.)
Levesque v. Lapointe (1993), 44 R.F.L. (3d) 316 (B.C.C.A.)
MacGyver v. Richards (1995), 11 R.F.L. (4th) 432 (Ont. C.A.)
Oldfield v. Oldfield (1991), 33 R.F.L. (3d) 235 (Ont. Ct. of Justice-Gen. Div.)
Thibaudeau v. Canada (M.N.R.) [1995] 2 S.C.R. 627 (S.C.C.)
Tropea v. Tropea; Browner v. Kenward, 1996, 87 N.Y. 2d 727 (N.Y.C.A.)
Tyabji v. Sandana (1994), 2 R.F.L. (4th) 265 (B.C.S.C.)
Young v. Young (1993), 49 R.F.L. (3d) 117 (S.C.C.)

Statute Cited

Divorce Act, R.S.C. 1985, c. 3 (2nd Supp.)

Chapter 10

Limited by Law?
Gender, Corporate Law, and the Family Firm

Mary Condon

Introduction

The business enterprise is central to the operation of the Canadian capitalist economy in that it is a vehicle for the accumulation of profit, as well as a significant social location of employment. It is therefore one of the key mechanisms through which inter-class relations are mediated. A number of feminist scholars have pointed out that those class relations cannot be understood in isolation from gender relations. As Folbre and Hartmann (1988: 192) note disparagingly, 'the rhetoric of class interest simply subsumes the possibility of gender interests.' In their historical study of the English middle class between 1780 and 1850, Davidoff and Hall (1987: 13) begin their analysis from the proposition that 'gender and class always operate together'. The development, and claim to moral superiority, of the middle class in the period they studied 'was articulated within a gendered concept of class. Middle-class gentlemen and middle-class ladies each had their appointed place in this newly mapped social world.' Indeed, they argue that gender played a strategic role in the development of the middle class in that 'A heavily gendered view of the world was utilized to soften, if not disavow, the disruption of a growing class system as the master and household head was transmuted into employer on the one hand and husband/father on the other.'

In the contemporary period, the intersection between gender and class has been examined by feminist scholars in the context of women as workers (Fudge, 1991), but less in the intra-class context of women within the ownership class. One significant aspect of an examination of the potentially gendered nature of business ownership would be the extent to which women's role in, and membership of, that class is mediated by their position within the family (Zeitlin, 1989; Davidoff and Hall, 1987). As Folbre and Hartmann (1988: 191) point out, in the context of working-class women, 'members of families are assumed to have the same class membership and class interests as their male wage earner.' Yet women who do not have access to a wage themselves are dependent on a wage-earner, or are possibly more dependent on state benefits. Women who do work for a wage may still be expected to assume greater responsibility for family well-being. This latter point may still hold true even if women are themselves property or business owners (Belcourt, 1991: 67). One important social location where the intersection of class, gender, and family relationships can be observed is the family business,[1] in which women may have the opportunity not just to be workers in the enterprise but also to be owners or managers. Indeed, the family business is a location where analytically distinct class positions, of owner on the one hand and worker on the other, become blurred. Further, investigation of the role of women in family businesses may provide insight into the manner in which two spheres of liberalism's 'private' realm—the business enterprise and the family—intersect (Boyd, 1997; Davidoff and Hall, 1987).

If the question of whether and how women's participation in family businesses is 'gendered' has been neglected by feminist researchers, even less an object of attention has been the contemporary significance of legal rules in the constitution and maintenance of that gendered family business enterprise. This chapter seeks to make a contribution to that assessment. In accordance with the theme of this collection, law will be examined as a 'gendering strategy', that is, a process that produces gender identities and 'insists on a specific version of gender differentiation' (Smart, 1992: 34). An attempt will be made to assess the continuing importance of the rules of *corporate* law in maintaining gendered identities and opportunities for women in family businesses. Historically, of course, as Davidoff and Hall (1987: 275–89) demonstrate, law played a largely restrictive role in that women were limited in the forms of property they could legally hold and what they could do with that property. It is useful to ask whether corporate law now plays a more facilitative role for women. Does it constitute differences between the roles of women business owners and those of their male counterparts? Are the 'subjects' of corporate law gendered?

It should be emphasized that the examination of corporate law from a feminist perspective is in its infancy. Such work as has been done has by and large focused on a preliminary demonstration that the fundamental premises of corporate law, though ostensibly gender-neutral, in fact are permeated with gendered understandings and discourses (Lahey and Salter, 1985; Bauman, 1991). This feminist rereading of corporate law can usefully be linked to a recent and broader feminist project of critiquing the premises of economics (Nelson, 1996; Folbre and Hartmann, 1988; Ferber and Nelson, 1993; McCluskey, 1996), since the economic perspective on law is one of the more enduring, and contested, intellectual perspectives on law in the North American context (Easterbrook and Fischel, 1991; Cheffins, 1997; Trebilcock, 1991; Williams, 1991). The first task of this chapter, therefore, is to outline some of the key premises of corporate law, along with the critique from feminists about their gendered underpinnings. The purpose of doing this is to demonstrate how the doctrines of corporate law may operate at a symbolic level to constitute gendered understandings of the appropriate structure and operation of business enterprises.

However, this chapter is in part a plea to move to the second stage of feminist engagement with corporate law. This is to specify, using the admittedly limited sources of empirical information that currently exist, the actual influence of corporate law in structuring gendered business *practices* and producing gendered material effects for women within firms, recognizing the variation in types of corporate enterprises. It will be argued that in the specific context of the family firm, there is a need to be sensitive to other constitutive practices that may be at work in this domain. Thus, care must be taken in attributing primacy to the specific role of corporate law in the gendering of family business enterprises.

Corporate Law, Economics, and Gender

Business enterprises can be operated through a variety of legal forms, such as sole proprietorships, partnerships, co-operatives, joint ventures, and corporations.[2] These different legal frameworks for doing business allocate the risks, responsibilities, and benefits of enterprise in a variety of ways. One implication of this is that these different legal forms may create different legal resources, opportunities, and restrictions for the mediation of class or gender relations in the context of the business enterprise. One legally authored form of enterprise, the corporation, is popularly regarded as the most pervasive mechanism for doing business, despite the fact that in Canada, as in other jurisdictions, many small enterprises are not actually incorporated (Freedman, 1994). Corporate law is best understood as a set of rules governing the structure and organization of a business entity and as a device for allocating responsibilities for action within the organization. From the law and economics perspective, the purpose of corporate law is to allow a business or firm to function in the interests of efficiency. From this perspective, corporate law provisions are a cheaper alternative to an individual market-based negotiation of terms on which to invest, work, manage, supply raw materials or resources, and so on. As Easterbrook and Fischel (1991: 34) put it, 'corporate law fills in the blanks and oversights with the terms that people would have bargained for had they anticipated the problems and been able to transact costlessly in advance.' Thus, the major ways in which the legislated rules of corporate law are said to facilitate the operation of business enterprises are the following.

Separate Legal Entity

Section 15 of the Canada Business Corporations Act (CBCA) provides the corporation with a separate legal personality that is autonomous from those who own it (shareholders) and those who run it (directors). Corporate law thus creates a new category of legal 'person'. Its personhood enables the corporation to 'act', in legal terms, independently of those who own and/or run it. It can have legal relationships with 'outsiders' to the corporation, such as creditors, suppliers, customers, and clients, as well as with its own shareholders and directors. Its individual personhood allows it to make contracts, to sue and be sued, and to have rights.

One strand of feminist theorizing would focus on how this emphasis on carving out spaces and categories of separation and autonomy, which is played out in liberal philosophy and scientific discourse as much as it is in corporate law, is associated with masculinity and valued on that basis, while femininity is associated with the connectedness and altruism that allows the (male) autonomy to exist (England, 1993: 40). More specifically, Hall (1995: 173) argues that the separate legal entity doctrine 'operates to split both the involvement and responsibility of directors from the acts and relations of a corporation. It starts with the assumption that directors . . . are not primarily responsible for the acts they undertake on behalf of or as a corporation.' This feminist theme that the norms of corporate law operate to displace responsibility for the consequences of action from where it 'rightly' belongs, in this case with the directors, is one that will recur when we look at the other fundamental contribution of corporate law to the organization of a corporation, that of limited liability for shareholders.

Specialization and Hierarchy

Corporate statutes establish specific roles to be played by actors within the corporation. These legally established roles are then allocated different rights and responsibilities. The most significant roles are those of shareholder, director, and officer (CBCA, ss. 24, 102, 121). Corporate law thus establishes one type of legal distinction between the identity of 'owner' and that of 'worker' in a business enterprise. Shareholders make the investment of capital that, pooled together, allows the enterprise to function (Ireland et al, 1987). Should the enterprise make a profit, shareholders will likely see the market value of their shares increase and possibly get paid dividends on those shares. Many corporations contain a number of 'classes' of share ownership, each of which bestows a set of corporate 'rights'on the holder. The most significant distinction among classes of shareholders has to do with whether the shares are assigned voting rights at shareholder meetings. Holders of voting shares are considered to 'control' the corporation in the sense that they are the shareholders who elect the board of directors and also make a number of significant corporate decisions requiring their approval (CBCA, ss. 24, 173, 183). As shareholders, they have no particular obligations to the firm and, indeed, remedies are available to them if actions taken by the company or its directors are not in their best interests. Discussion of some of these remedies, including the inaptly named 'oppression' remedy, will form a significant part of the second half of this chapter.

On the other hand, directors are elected by shareholders to run the company on their behalf. Their legal responsibilities are not particularly clearly specified in the corporate statutes, beyond an admonition to take some care in running the corporation and to act in its 'best interests', a formulation known in corporate law as the fiduciary duty, or the duty to be loyal (CBCA s.122). Much debate has surrounded the question of whether these statutory responsibilities mean that they have to act in the best interests of the shareholder-owners only, or that they can take into account the interests of constituencies other than shareholders, such as workers, consumers, the environment, and so on.[3] Officers are full-time employees who are appointed by the board of directors to run the company, ostensibly with oversight by directors. The reality in small corporations such as family businesses, however, is that all these legal roles actually may be filled by the same people, a fact that makes the accountability devices of voting and requiring loyalty, established by the corporate legal rules, somewhat redundant.

From an economic point of view the establishment of legally distinct roles within the corporate structure is justified by the virtues of specialization and comparative advantage. As Easterbrook and Fischel (1991: 11) put it:

> The separation of risk-bearing [via investment] from employment is a form of the division of labor. Those who have wealth can employ it productively even if they are not good managers; those who can manage but lack wealth can hire capital in the market; and the existence of claims that can be traded separately from employment allows investors to diversify their investment interests. . . . Investors bear most of the risk of business failure, in exchange for which they are promised most of the rewards of success.

Further, as Cheffins (1997: 34) points out, 'The hierarchical organization of a firm offers another important advantage which is that joint production can be organized on a more effective basis.'

A feminist perspective would counter, at the most obvious level, with the empirical observation that despite the fact that these legally established categories are formally gender-neutral, comparatively few women perform these roles. One of the difficulties with drawing conclusions here is that the actual extent of women's *shareholding* in corporations whose shares do not trade on public markets (i.e., most family-run corporations) is hard to conclusively establish. But case law dealing with family businesses tends to reveal anecdotally that if women are shareholders, the classification of shares they hold are the non-voting shares. In other words, while they may be owners, they do not necessarily share control (*The Queen v. McClurg* 1990; *Re Ferguson*, 1983). This makes Davidoff and Hall's (1987: 277) historical point that 'It was primarily women who were the beneficiaries of "passive" property yielding income only: trusts, annuities, subscriptions and insurance' of continued contemporary relevance. On the other hand, with respect to the larger, publicly traded corporations, one of the recurring liberal feminist criticisms of the corporate sector in Canada has been the paucity of women directors. At the moment 9 per cent of public Canadian corporations have women directors (Carlyle, 1995).

At another level, feminists would be attentive to the fact that these legally established categories of shareholder, director, and manager have the effect of assigning power, control, and inequality in specific ways. Hierarchical organizations, both commercial and non-commercial, have long been subjected to a feminist critique for their tendency, not only to exclude women in the interests of particular versions of 'social cohesion', but to express masculine values (Ferguson, 1984; Elson, 1994: 39–40; Gabaldon, 1992: 1429). Even more significantly, it is necessary to be attentive to what happens once women come to play these roles in particular corporate hierarchies. Although the empirical evidence we will later consider deals only with one corporate sector, the family business, one of the important research findings in this respect is that women owners or decision-makers in these enterprises do not necessarily *exercise* the power or control the legally defined categories of shareholder or director accord them. Understanding why this is so is crucial to our ability to draw conclusions about the role of corporate law in reproducing gendered social and material relations in the context of the family business.

Limited Liability

It has been noted that the allocation of specific legal risks and liabilities is closely connected to the creation of specific corporate roles. The establishment of limited liability for corporate shareholders (CBCA, s. 45) is often seen as *the* fundamental feature of corporate law. This principle means that, generally speaking, shareholders are not personally liable for any debts incurred by the corporation that it is unable to pay. All that a shareholder stands to lose in making a corporate investment is the value of the investment that she or he has contributed. This occurs despite the fact that the shareholder, depending on the number of shares held or other roles performed, may be in a position to cause the corporation to incur the debt in the first place. Nor, as a matter of corporate law, are directors usually personally liable for the debts of a corporation, either, although a number of recent statutes will assign specific responsibilities to directors, such as in the environmental law area. But directors can be sued by the corporation, or its shareholders, for failure to abide by their duty of loyalty to the corporation.

Law and economics scholars have an elaborate set of justifications for the doctrine of limited liability (Easterbrook and Fischel, 1991; Cheffins, 1997; Gabaldon, 1992). Among the most popular arguments from this perspective are that the rule allows investors to diversify their risk and so promotes further investment, since they know in advance how much risk they bear in investing in a corporation (that is, they know the maximum they can lose). The rule also allows the stock market to value shares appropriately, since it does not have to take into account, in assigning values to shares, the wealth of, and likelihood of recovery from, individual shareholders. This enables the stock market to work efficiently. Furthermore, limited liability reduces the need to monitor or oversee the decision-makers in the firm (assuming the owners are not themselves the decision-makers), because the shareholder's exposure to risk is not unlimited. The apparent problem with monitoring is that, first, it is costly, especially in large corporations with many shareholders, and, second, shareholders with only an insignificant holding have no incentive to engage in monitoring that would benefit shareholders generally (the 'free rider' problem). In this sense, allocations constituted by the limited liability doctrine privilege the interests of shareholders over those creditors who lend the company money, or who supply it with goods, but do not thereby obtain an ownership interest. In response, law and economists argue that limited liability actually equalizes the position of shareholders and creditors since both groups stand to lose only what they invest. Shareholders, of course, stand to *gain* more than creditors should the corporation turn a profit.

As we can see, these justifications revolve around ideas of promoting efficiency generally, and more specifically, of shifting risk to where it is most efficiently borne. Theresa Gabaldon has engaged in an extended critique of the law and economics justifications for limited liability from a feminist perspective. She points out that while the economic analysis of limited liability 'permits particular actors . . . to calibrate the economic gambles that they are willing to take' on the basis of a profit/loss calculation, it does not 'address the responsibility-culpability characterization'. She argues that 'liability limitations artificially distance individuals from the real-life effects of the enterprise in which they invest, thus decreasing their acknowledged personal responsibility.' She further asserts that the 'key difference between economic and feminist reasoning on this point is . . . the feminist belief that interest in monitoring is a social good, rather than a duplicative waste' (Gabaldon, 1992: 1424). This argument presumably cannot be taken to the somewhat essentialist length of saying that if women ran corporations, they would be more likely to accept personal responsibility for their actions. It is rather to acknowledge that the legal rule on limited liability constitutes understandings of the appropriateness of risk displacement and the need for accountability for corporate 'harms' in particular ways, which may, at least in part, be related to the interests of those with superior economic power within the corporate enterprise. For a particular strand of feminist analysis, participation and accountability are valued in and of themselves, irrespective of whether they contribute to the efficient operation of a corporate enterprise.

Finally, it should be pointed out that law and economists are generally more sanguine than are feminists about the possibility of unlimited liability for shareholders in the case of small corporations. This is because in those contexts, the connection between the capacity of the shareholder to control the corporation and its ultimate actions is a closer one. This position, of course, is based on an assumption about shareholder control that would benefit from being supported by empirical investigation, particularly where women fill those shareholding roles in family businesses.

Profit Maximization

While profit maximization is not unique to the corporate form of business enterprise, there are various ways in which the norms of corporate law lend particular support to this goal. For example, the judicial interpretation of the fiduciary duty of directors to act in the best interests of the corporation has emphasized the interests of shareholders in corporate profit maximization at the expense of attempts by corporations to engage in 'socially responsible' behaviour (*Dodge*, 1919; *Parke*, 1962; *Varity*; *Teck*, 1972; Tolmie, 1992). This is why corporations that attempt to be socially responsible usually use as a justi-fication the fact that such behaviour is in the shareholders' interests. Another example of corporate law support for the goal of profit-making is the rule with respect to shareholder proposals, which is that shareholders can only request the corporation to act, or refrain from acting, in order to achieve the economic interests of the corporation as opposed to other, more 'social' interests (CBCA, s. 137).

The singularity of this goal of corporate enterprise is justified by economic theory at a number of levels. At one level, the rational actor who is the core of economic theorizing is assumed always to act in his or her self-interest so as to maximize his or her 'utility'. An economic system, and the legal rules that support that system, must seek to allow individuals to pursue their particular self-interest in the course of their interactions with others, since to do other-wise would be to impose a particular set of preferences on them. As England (1993: 45) points out, although self-interest need not imply *selfishness*, or specifically in the context of corporations, profit maximization, 'in practice, most economists do assume selfishness in markets.'[4] England sees this as flowing from the 'separative model of self', which is at the core of economic reasoning. With respect to the fiduciary duty of directors in the corporate law context, however, loyalty (often considered antithetical to selfishness) to the corporation *is* expected, but this loyalty is required to be exercised in the inter-ests of profit-making for shareholders . At another level, economists argue simply that a singular goal is more efficiently accomplished than a multifaceted one. Furthermore, it is argued to be undemocratic to require or expect unelected directors of corporations to achieve socially responsible or distribu-tive outcomes by their decision-making.

In assessing whether this focus on self-interest and profit maximization is a gendered one, scholars such as Folbre and Hartmann (1988: 193, 195, 197) caution against a potential feminist response that women 'are not as econom-ically rational or self-interested as men'. They characterize the argument that 'women altruistically choose' to put the interests and well-being of others, such as family members, ahead of their own economic interests as 'ideological'.[5]

They argue that a more fruitful approach would be to bring 'the traditional boundaries between self-interest and altruism into question' and to 'develop a more complete theory of economic interests, one that can encompass concepts like cooperation, loyalty, and reciprocity'. A family business is, of course, an important place to see a multilayered economic rationality at work. Anderson's work (1993: 34–5) contains an example that nicely illustrates, in a business context, this effort to develop an expanded understanding of economic rationality. She describes the couple who 'struggle for years to . . . establish a family restaurant' and who are offered a buy-out from a franchise operation. She argues that 'A concern for the narrative unity of their lives, for what meaning their present choices make of their past actions, could rationally motivate them to turn down the offer.'[6] In other words, despite presumed financial benefits to be gained from selling out, an expanded definition of economic rationality would instead result in a continued commitment to, and satisfaction with, an enterprise to which they had devoted a significant part of their lives. Fehlberg's study of women involved in family businesses, discussed in more detail below, found that 'involvement in the family business reflected "the often passionate belief that marriage and business were intimately intertwined"' (1997: 14).

To summarize, then, an attempt has been made to articulate the ways in which corporate law may operate at a symbolic level to 'engender' the corporate form, by privileging values of efficiency over accountability, hierarchy over inclusiveness, risk displacement over responsibility, and profit-making over social responsibility. But it is important to investigate empirically the extent to which, and how, this discursive framework of corporate law actually structures practices within the family firm. It is a truism of socio-legal scholarship that the 'fit' between the 'law in the books' and the 'law in action' is not usually a complete or smooth one. It is to this issue that we now turn.

Women, Corporate Law, and Family Businesses: Some Empirical Evidence

I have noted that the family business provides one empirical entry point into the question of the opportunities for, and characteristics of, women's involvement in business enterprises as owners or directors. Research into how the participation of women in this realm is structured is relatively new, but still a few trends may be observed. Again, there has been little empirical consideration to date, especially in Canada, of how the role of women in family businesses has been mediated by law, though a number of Australian feminists recently have embarked on such a project. The goal is to use this empirical evidence to assess the power of corporate law in 'gendering' the participation of women in these enterprises.

The first two of the following empirical studies described did not, in fact, have the role of law as a primary focus. In an English study titled 'Entrepreneurship, Ethnicity, and Gender', Phizacklea (1988) examines the contemporary relationship among class, gender, and race in the context of the family firm. In answer to the question, 'Do members of a family firm share an identical class situation or not?' she responds in the negative. Her study of the operation of the clothing industry in the West Midlands demonstrated that 'All female members and young male members of the family are working under patriarchal relations of production, they remain dependent for their maintenance on the 'boss' who is usually also the head of the household, in return for their efforts' (Phizacklea, 1988: 31). She concludes that while it has been well documented that 'access to "family" or community members as low-wage workers is a key competitive advantage for many ethnic businessmen', what has been less evident is 'the extent to which this "family" and "community" labour is female and subordinated to very similar patriarchal control mechanisms in the workplace as in the home.'[7]

In a 1991 groundbreaking study conducted for the Canadian Advisory Council on the Status of Women, Belcourt et al. investigated the 'struggles, challenges and achievements' of more than 200 women business owners across Canada. One of the main purposes of the study was to 'consider how public policy might facilitate the work of female entrepreneurs and thus help to harness the economic benefits of this form of business development' (Belcourt et al., 1991: 1). In a telling example of the absence of corporate law as a variable studied, it is not completely clear that the businesses surveyed were in fact incorporated, although the study contains a table (ibid., 11) entitled 'company start up', indicating that 60 per cent of the women surveyed founded their businesses themselves, 29 per cent bought them, and 5 per cent inherited them.[8] The overall conclusion of the study was that in addition to the usual difficulties facing all entrepreneurs in making a success of a new business venture, 'a woman entrepreneur faces conditions that appear to be attributable almost completely to the fact that she is a woman in a non-traditional occupation. . . . Surrounded by opportunities but hemmed in by circumstances, the woman entrepreneur sees her ability to realize business and personal success limited by a number of obstacles' (ibid., 65).

In proceeding to identify those obstacles, the study enumerates issues such as: discrimination,[9] clustering in business sectors with low financial pay-off, limited relevant work experience or management training, shortage of peer support networks or an inability to make use of them because of being 'overloaded with business and family responsibilities' (ibid., 67) and insufficient financial return. Included in the list of obstacles were those of the 'conflicting demands of managing a business, a home and children' and 'no operational support from husbands'. With respect to the former, the study notes that 'the double shift is standard', with most of the women entrepreneurs they studied, unlike men entrepreneurs, assuming 'complete responsibility for home and children'. With respect to the latter, few of the study's respondents 'were able to rely on their husbands for anything but token help'. The help given by husbands was characterized as 'one-shot', but 'nothing close to the continuing responsibility taken on by many wives of male small business owners'. Significantly, Belcourt et al. conclude that 'although some have broken new ground in the business world, thus far they have not renegotiated the traditional division of family and household tasks' (ibid., 69–70). Thus, while this study did not set out to examine the effects of corporate law rules on women's experience of entrepreneurship, what is striking about its conclusions, as well as those of the Phizacklea study, is that the most influential practices in the gendering of entrepreneurship have to do with the intractability of the traditional familial roles played by women rather than being attributable to what business law rules 'allowed' or required women to do. This suggests that corporate law's gendering role may be less significant than that of traditional family organization or familial divisions of labour.

Australia has been a more fertile location for feminist legal consideration of the role of women in family businesses. For example, Dodds Streeton (1994) examines the liability of women as company directors or guarantors for the debts of their spouses or the companies of which they are directors, in a process now widely characterized as 'sexually transmitted debt' (Fehlberg, 1994: 475). She argues that women directors became liable for company debts because they 'share the hallmarks' of a surety, who guarantees the debt. Yet, 'Although formally appointed as directors, these women will often have little opportunity for actual involvement or input into the business because of their 'traditional' role in the patriarchal family and their exclusion from matters of business' (Hall, 1995: 175). Dodds Streeton (1994: 16) ultimately concludes:

> The fundamental problem of women's vulnerable position in personal and family relationships with men, and their relative exclusion from commercial experience and control cannot be solved by law. . . . If the law attempted to address the problem of the pervasive vulnerability of women as a group by absolutely precluding creditors from access to their assets, it would effectively destroy their legal capacity, restrict their access to credit, and totally undercut the achievement of equal and independent status.

In similar vein, Fehlberg describes two studies of women's involvement in family businesses, one conducted in Australia by Singh (1995) and the other conducted by Fehlberg herself in England (1997). These studies found that although the women surveyed tended to be very 'involved' in the family business on a day-to-day basis, they were 'likely to view themselves as less powerful than their husband or de facto partner in the family business context' (Fehlberg, 1997: 2). Interestingly, one of the findings of the Fehlberg study was that women who described themselves as having no role in the family business often held the legal positions of company director, company secretary (officer), or shareholder. Yet, 'they had never considered exerting their formal legal rights as directors or shareholders in order to obtain a direct financial benefit from the business. Similarly, women who held shares invariably did not know the extent of their shareholding' (ibid., 8). The Singh study contained one example of 'Mrs. A not being "allowed" to see the books, even though she was the company secretary, [which] indicates strongly the discrepancy between formal legal rights and practical realities.' Fehlberg concludes that 'these findings challenge the accuracy of contractual assumptions that legal rights are readily acted upon and translated into practical benefits.' Furthermore, even women who were involved in the 'financial operation' of the business had 'no role in strategic decision-making', a position Fehlberg characterizes as 'informed powerlessness'. Thus, 'the business emerges in these studies as ultimately the province of the male decision-making authority. Women may be very involved in family businesses without sharing the strategic decision-making power' (ibid., 15).

To what extent does this empirical material shed light on the feminist critiques of corporate law doctrines described above? In the first place, it suggests that the analysis of the doctrine of limited liability of shareholders as being responsible for the passivity and non-involvement of shareholders in the direction of corporate activity is incomplete. Rather, the picture that emerges here is that women as owners or directors of family businesses continue to be enmeshed in power inequalities that derive from the practices of traditional family relations. As Grbich (1987: 329) puts it in the context of taxation laws, 'Positions for women appear never to be secured by rights to income or to property so long as her position is part of familial relations.' Furthermore, we have seen that one of Singh's findings was an 'often passionate belief that marriage and business were ultimately intertwined' (Fehlberg, 1997: 14), suggesting again that the formal legal characterization of a company as a separated and independent actor has no particular resonance in the context of family businesses.

From Oppression to Corporate Power?

The material discussed in the preceding section arguably suggests some limitations on our ability to impute a significant power to corporate law to accomplish unaided the 'gendering' of family businesses. Another striking feature of the picture painted by this empirical material is that, while the extent of corporate law's contribution is arguably unclear, women appear vulnerable in the family business or entrepreneurial context, victims of their lack of commercial experience or their position in the family. But a rather contradictory impression emerges if we consider some examples of the use by women shareholders of the shareholder remedies provided for in various provincial corporate statutes and the Canada Business Corporations Act. The most controversial remedy is that known as the oppression remedy, which allows shareholders and other 'complainants' to seek a judicial remedy if their interests have been 'oppressed' or unfairly prejudiced by actions taken by the corporation or its directors.

Another is the winding-up remedy which allows a court to order a company to be wound up or liquidated, and its assets dispersed to shareholders, if a shareholder has legal grounds for such a request. An interesting feature of the cases considered below is precisely the use of these remedies in the context of *family* dissolution, a situation where women's economic interests are considered by family lawyers to be particularly vulnerable.

One of the best-known Canadian shareholder oppression cases is *Ferguson v. Imax*.[10] Here the mobilization of the corporate law remedy had the effect of allowing the complainant shareholder to achieve recognition for her contribution to the business enterprise and to remain a shareholder despite significant opposition from another powerful shareholder, her ex-husband. The case involved a business (Imax) owned by three heterosexual couples, the Fergusons and two others, both of which couples were previous associates or friends of Mr Ferguson. All three women involved held non-voting preference shares, whereas the men held voting shares (meaning, as we have seen, that they had control of the decision-making). Only Ms Ferguson, of the three women, actively participated in the company. The Ontario Court of Appeal found that 'she worked hard in the company's interest and was one of its founders together with the three men.' In fact, the three men 'were each employed in other endeavours and could not devote their full time to the company.' In 1974, Ms Ferguson divorced her husband on the grounds of his infidelity. The issue we are interested in revolved around her contention, which was accepted by the court, that from the time of the divorce Mr Ferguson did his utmost to squeeze her out of her shareholding in the company. He first tried to prevent the declaration of dividends to the class of shares that she owned and ultimately used corporate procedural devices to attempt to pass a resolution that would have had the effect of forcing redemption (repurchase) by the company of her class of shares, thereby eliminating her involvement as a shareholder. Ms Ferguson was pressured by other shareholders to sell her shares because, according to them, her former husband would not countenance the declaration of dividends while she would share equally in them.

The court held that the conduct of Mr Ferguson on behalf of the company was oppressive. Thus (p. 135), 'I am satisfied that what she says is true. The company could pay dividends. Mr. Ferguson set out to stop the payment because he did not want Mrs. Ferguson to share in the benefits in the growth of the company and wanted to force her to sell her shares to him or to one of the other men in the company. . . . In my opinion this conduct was oppressive and unfair to her.' Significantly, the court concluded that when dealing with a 'close' corporation (a small company with few shareholders), the court 'may consider the *relationship between the shareholders and not simply legal rights as such*' (emphasis added). Even though evidence was provided that there were economic advantages to the corporation of doing the reorganization of the share classes, the conduct was oppressive because the 'reasons that motivated management' were unfair. In rather disturbing language, the Court of Appeal characterized the attempt to pass the corporate resolution to redeem Ms Ferguson's shares as 'a final solution to the problem of the ex-wife shareholder'. On the basis of the evidence, the court was unwilling to accept that the company had a valid business purpose in attempting to squeeze her out. She was thus able to mobilize to her advantage norms of corporate law requiring directors to have valid business reasons for their actions on behalf of corporations. In view of our earlier discussion about the need articulated by feminists for a broader conception of economic interests, it is also significant that Ms Ferguson's interest in this company, as recognized by the court, was one that came out of her loyalty to and history of participation in it. The result ultimately allowed her a continued interest in the company's affairs and prosperity rather than resorting to the family law approach of dividing of property and severing ties.

Another example of the strategic use of corporate law by women shareholders comes from the more recent *M. v. H.*[11] case. Here a lesbian couple were separating. One of the couple applied for interim support from the other under the Family Law Act, which was denied on the ground that she did not come within the definition of 'spouse' in the Family Law Act. She also claimed interim relief from oppression under s. 248 of the Ontario Business Corporations Act. She made this claim because of the alleged oppressive actions of her former partner with respect to the company of which they were both 50 per cent shareholders. The latter began operating the company as though she were the sole owner. The plaintiff was refused access to the company's books and her signature was imitated (with her knowledge) on cheques that required joint signatures. Epstein J. concluded (p. 100) that 'the evidence here strongly supports a conclusion that the defendant, particularly in excluding the plaintiff from any meaningful participation in [the company] during the past 5 years and then closing the business down after the parties separated, was in violation of the plaintiff's expectations that could be said to have been (or ought to be considered as) part of *their compact as shareholders'* (emphasis added). The court therefore used the plaintiff's expectations as a shareholder to establish a standard of corporate conduct to which the defendant was expected to adhere. Significantly, the court ordered money to be released from a corporate account to the plaintiff by way of a loan, to be non-interest-bearing, and to be available to the plaintiff until the ultimate resolution of this action. Thus the judge awarded her support under corporate law rather than family law principles. The norms governing relations among shareholders in a small business were ultimately more effective for the lesbian plaintiff, in the context of relationship dissolution, than those acceptable within a family law context.

Finally, *Belman v. Belman*[12] is particularly interesting for the insight it affords into the differing legal implications of behaviour depending on whether the context is marital or corporate. The case dealt with a claim for division of assets following divorce. The judge's treatment of this claim explicitly separated the 'family law' issue from the 'corporate law' issue. The first of these involved a claim by the former wife for a payment of $250,000 over and above the equal division of the spouses' property on the basis of her 'extraordinary contribution to the marriage' (p. 64). The husband had agreed to this in 1990 'after much discussion', but withdrew his agreement on hearing about an alleged affair between his wife and one of her business associates. This was consistently denied by the wife, though the court found that the husband had a 'sincere belief that it was true'. Because the wife's claim to the $250,000 was based by her on 'a moral obligation that arose out of her extraordinary contributions to their marriage', the court concluded that the 'alleged affair was relevant to that rationale' (p. 68). Further, Spence J. considered that he 'would have difficulty concluding that Mr. Belman's reaction was unreasonable'. Mr Belman was therefore released from the obligation to pay the money to his former wife.

However, what was considered a reasonable reaction in the context of marital obligations was regarded otherwise in the corporate context. The corporate law issue arose from a claim by Ms Belman for a transfer to her of her former husband's 50 per cent ownership in the corporation. This claim was made on the grounds that there was a 'loss of mutual confidence' between the two owners such that the business could no longer be conducted effectively. In response to this, the husband claimed that he had not lost confidence in his former wife (having forgiven her for her alleged conduct), so that the grounds for a mandatory transfer of his shares were not present. In his consideration of this issue, the judge again relied on the response of the husband to the information he received about his wife's alleged affair. Mr Belman's denunciation of his wife following his accusation about the affair, and his statement that 'he did not wish to see her again or to continue to work with her' (p. 78) meant that *her* loss of confidence in their ability to carry on together in the business 'was entirely appropriate' and could not be said to be 'arbitrary or unreasonable'. Mr Belman had requested that the court consider his wife's concerns about continuing to work with him as a business partner as being 'exaggerated or without foundation'. Significantly, Spence J. concluded that this was 'in effect an invitation to the court to substitute its business judgment for that of Ms. Belman and should accordingly be treated with the greatest caution' (p. 79). The result of this, therefore, was that Ms Belman's business judgment was deferred to by the court even though her interpretation of her 'moral obligations' was not. The privilege that courts tend to award to the business judgment of directors in running corporations as they see fit prevented the former husband in this situation from being able to characterize his wife's wish to dissociate him from the business as exaggerated and unreasonable.

As we have seen, the remedy sought by Ms Belman was an order that would direct the transfer to her of Mr Belman's shares for fair market value. The latter wanted, instead, a court-ordered shareholders' agreement relating to the direction and management of the business, which would allow him to remain a shareholder in the business. In choosing between these two proposals, Spence J. favoured that of the wife, ordering a mandatory transfer of Mr Belman's interest in the company to her at fair market value. The demands of running a business effectively, it seems, preclude any tolerance for ongoing disputes and loss of confidence in a partner's business acumen.

The significance of these cases is only partly that they show, in contrast to the Australian material referred to earlier, how women in family-run enterprises can use corporate law principles to their advantage.[13] Even more important is a specification of the corporate law logic that proves compelling in these cases. This logic has to do with a privileging of judgments about how to run a business effectively and requirements for 'valid business purposes' in making decisions, as well as for demonstrations of loyalty to a company. It seems that as long as they formulate their claims in terms of these corporate logics, plaintiffs in cases such as *M. v. H.* or *Belman* may escape the potentially negative effects of how *family* law norms reinforce prevailing understandings of 'appropriate' family relationships.

Conclusion

It may well be premature to draw conclusions on the basis of such preliminary data. But the data so far suggest that there is no easy answer to the question of the extent to which corporate law is complicit in, or furthers, the oppression of that class of women who are business owners or managers. The answer depends in part on a close consideration of the relationship between the role of corporate law as discourse and its importance in structuring actual business practices. While the discourses of corporate law may have general social effects in privileging particular sets of values, it is crucial to develop a nuanced understanding of how these discourses actually operate in a variety of contexts. Further, it is arguable that corporate law is not solely responsible for bringing into being gendered subject positions within family firms. It is clear that those women who seek to use corporate law to their material advantage are required to formulate their claims in terms of particular arguments about loyalty to a corporation and the efficient running of business enterprises in order to be successful, as they sometimes are. But it is also arguable that the gendering of women's role in the family firm by corporate law cannot be understood in isolation from the family relationships and familial practices in which those women are implicated. If, in fact, women do not routinely exercise the economic power the legal categories of corporate law give them, the reason for this may have to do with the gendering practices of these traditional family relations and, particularly, the *family law* that supports those practices. In this sense the gendering effects of corporate law and family law may in fact be contradictory or at odds with each other. This suggests that, in order to draw conclusions about the importance of law as a gendering strategy, it is necessary to be sensitive to the ways in which different discourses of law, such as those produced by family law and corporate law, interact with each other to produce gendered subjects and material consequences, and to appreciate that different arenas of law may support a multiplicity of outcomes for women.

Notes

I would like to thank the editors of this collection, Dany Lacombe and Dorothy Chunn, for their useful comments on an earlier draft of this paper, and for their patience and support of this project. I am also grateful to my colleague, Shelley Gavigan, whose paper in this collection assisted me in thinking through my own contribution, to Suzanne Kennedy and Elizabeth Valentina for their capable research assistance, and to Maureen Boyce in the York University Law Library for her help in gathering materials.

1. It should be noted that 'family business' is a term of art; there is no specific legal definition of this concept.

2. In this paper, the terms 'corporation' and 'company' are used interchangeably.

3. Of course, directors are supposed to abide by all regulatory requirements with respect to consumer and environmental legislation.

4. See also Cheffins's contention (1997: 156) that 'The mainsprings of capitalism tend to derive from what many think of as baser human motives, such as self-interest and the desire for personal profit.'

5. See the feminist literature (Waring, 1990; Boyd, 1997) on how business profit-making is subsidized by women's unpaid labour.

6. Interestingly, Anderson does not tell us whether either or both of this fictitious couple was a woman, or whether there was any dispute between them about what decision to make!

7. The mediating effect of race on the gendered nature of participation in family businesses is an extremely significant issue in the Canadian context, raising as it does the further question of the role of law in that process. Unfortunately, these intersections cannot be pursued here.

8. The complication here is that another 'ownership' table in the study indicates that some women owned their business in conjunction with 'major' or 'minor' partners (partnership being a separate form of business enterprise). The authors also quote a 1988 study by Lavoie that appears to indicate that the choice of the legal form of a business enterprise (e.g., a sole proprietorship or a corporation) is itself gendered. Thus, 'Lavoie noted

the tendency of women to operate their businesses as sole proprietorships, although she observed that women in traditionally male sectors tended to follow the organizational structure preferred by men owners (incorporation)' (Belcourt et al., 1991: 12).

9. This included differential treatment by creditors, suppliers, customers, and even employees. It seemed that 'being married and having children contributes to the perception of stability in male applicants, but these same factors are taken to suggest unreliability in women applicants' (Belcourt et al, 1991: 66).

10. *Re Ferguson and Imax Systems Corp.* (1983) 43 O.R. (2d) 128 (Ont. C.A.).

11. *M. v. H.* (1993) 50 R.F.L. (3d) 92 (Ont. Ct., Gen. Div.).

12. *Belman v. Belman* (1995) 26 O.R. (3d) 56 (Ont. Ct., Gen. Div.).

13. It should be recognized that the ability to advance these corporate law remedies may largely be a function of the legal advice obtained by the plaintiffs.

Chapter 11

If Choice Is the Answer, What Is the Question?

Spelunking in *Symes v. Canada*

Rebecca Johnson

Introduction

To set the stage for the discussion that follows, a discussion that plays with metaphors of spelunking and of exploring caves deep below the surface, I begin with a poem that plays with the same metaphors of visions above and below the surface.

The Summit
by Kelvin Johnson

The railroad ribboned
Across Canada
To reach
The Rogers Pass.

And the grandeur
Of the glaciers
In their summit glory
Caught and held
The summer sun.

But what brought
Continental tourists
Were the caves,
Now closed,
Almost forgotten.

Forgotten too
The shift from sky
And heaven
To a strange
Earth centred myth.

Something of
An alien eternity
Hung delicately
From the darkness,
And crystal fingers
Struggled upwards
Through time trapped
Drops of silence.

There were European names
For all these things
That made them feel at home;
But nothing
To relieve the shock
Of pilgrim bones
In shaman beads and buckskin
Deep within
Those cavern walls.

I would like to take you on a voyage with me, spelunking in *Symes v. Canada*. Why spelunking? Because spelunking—the exploration of underground caves and rivers—is all about changing focus. Spelunking is about making 'the shift from sky and heaven' and 'summit glory', to the less immediately visible terrain, to the caves and rivers that run below the summit. Spelunking captures the sense of the search for points of access that allow one to explore territory that lies beneath the surface. In the pages of this text I use 'choice' as an entry point to explore caves lying below the summit in the realms of law.

The point of this spelunking excursion is the exploration of this book's claim that law is a gendering practice. There are two dimensions to this claim. The first is that gender is not a biological given, but a social construction. That is, women are made, not born (de Beauvoir, 1952). The second dimension is that law is not simply an objective venue of judgment, but is also an active participant in the 'creation' of gender. Central to the argument that gender is a social construction is the assertion that language matters. Language is not just a transparent tool for expressing facts, but is also the material in which facts are constructed (Weedon, 1987: 131). Language is central to the construction of knowledge. Discourse matters because it is in discourse that power and knowledge are joined together (Foucault, 1978: 100).

Law is one of the many sites of struggle in which competing discourses and practices dovetail with and build upon discourses and practices in other social, economic, and political institutions in ways that construct (and reproduce existing) social relations of power—relations of power that are deeply classed, racialized, and gendered. These social relations are constituted hegemonically through the mobilization and consolidation of some discourses and the exclusion of others. Power plays a significant role in these processes of consolidation and exclusion. Still, as Foucault reminds us, 'power is tolerable only on condition that it mask a substantial part of itself. Its success is proportional to its ability to hide its own mechanisms' (ibid., 86). When it is at its strongest, power best hides its mechanisms.

On this spelunking expedition, I will explore one of the mechanisms that serves to obscure the workings of power in the constitution of gender: the discursive practice of invoking the rhetoric of choice. Prevailing orders of inequality are maintained in part through the shaping of beliefs about an order's legitimacy or immutability (Gaventa, 1980: 42). The rhetoric of choice, I will argue, is one of the mechanisms used by those who participate in shaping beliefs about the legitimacy of current constructions of gender.

In exploring this claim, I will focus the deployments of 'choice' in the legal arena, and particularly, in contexts where there are ongoing struggles over the reconstruction of social meaning. In such contexts, choice is deployed as a mechanism of conflict resolution that deflects attention away from underlying struggles about the racialized, classed, and gendered dimensions of meaning. Instead, the invocation of choice directs attention to specific choices made by specific individuals. By suggesting that individual choice provides the answer to the problem, those using the rhetoric provide an answer to a simpler question. Questions about that which lies in the caves of meaning below are answered by reference to the summit of individual choice above.

By directing attention to individual choices, those using the rhetoric of choice in the arena of law simplify their task. By individualizing the problem, they deflect claims that the law should explicitly participate in reconstructing the meanings of gender, of race, of class. The irony is, of course, that through the practice of deploying the rhetoric of choice, law participates in exactly that which it ostensibly seeks to avoid: the construction of social meaning. In the assumptions they make about the conditions under which choice is exercised, those deploying the rhetoric sustain and replicate specific constructions of gender, race, class. Choice itself becomes a thoroughly and complexly gendered, racialized, and classed concept. The deployment in law of this socially constructed rhetoric of choice is an important moment in the ongoing construction of a system whose interweaving of gender, race, and class systemically leaves different groupings of people with different and less desirable ranges of choices than those available to others.

My argument will not be that any invocation of choice unremittingly reconstitutes harmful gendered, racialized, and classed relations of power. Clearly, feminists have used the discourse of choice to some positive effect. In certain contexts, choice has been successfully employed as a rhetoric of freedom, liberation, and empowerment. However, in many other contexts, non-feminist or even anti-feminist meanings of choice have had greater resonance with legal decision-makers. Thus, choice poses something of a dilemma. It is not surprising that many feminists are left asking whether it is possible to use choice to advance feminist claims, or whether its potential has been exhausted or even co-opted. One answer to the question might be found through focusing on the ability of power to hide its mechanisms.

My argument will be that the rhetoric of choice tends to obscure the workings of power. Intentionally or not, those using the rhetoric participate in the (re)construction of social relations of power. Those who seek to challenge and reconstruct social meaning would be well advised to pay close attention to the ways in which the rhetoric is deployed. Closer attention to the practice of deploying choice can provide insights into the ways that legal struggles over meaning are reproduced, legitimized, and perhaps refashioned. In the discussion that follows, I will pursue this claim by exploring the deployment of the rhetoric of choice in the multivalent context generated by *Symes v. Canada*.

Symes v. Canada: The Case and the Context

In 1994, the Supreme Court of Canada released its judgement in *Symes v. Canada*. The legal question in this case was simple: Could child-care expenses be fully deductible as business expenses under the Income Tax Act?[1] This deceptively simple question caused a certain amount of consternation for feminists across Canada; the question was one in which difficult struggles over the meaning of gender intersected with equally complex struggles about class privilege and disadvantage.

The issue at the centre of the case was the interpretation of several sections of the Income Tax Act, specifically those related to child care and business expenses. Beth Symes, the mother of two children, was a partner in a small law firm. The significance of this fact in tax terms was that, according to s. 9 of the Income Tax Act, she would be taxed on profit from a business rather than on wages from employment.[2] The calculation of 'profit' is in principle rather simple: business revenues minus business expenses. The difficulty is to figure out which expenditures qualify as business expenses. Section 18(1) of the Income Tax Act provides some guidance, specifying that the expenditure must be 'incurred for the purpose of gaining or producing income from business' and that it cannot be a 'personal or living expense'.[3]

Symes had employed Mrs Simpson to look after her children while she worked, and argued that the salary she paid to Mrs Simpson was a business expense, deductible from her business revenues in calculating her profit. The Minister of National Revenue disagreed, saying that child-care expenses were not made for the purpose of gaining income, but that even if they were, they were non-deductible because they were personal expenses. The Minister of National Revenue allowed instead the limited child-care deduction in s. 63, a deduction available to business people and wage-earners, male or female.[4] The amount under the deduction was considerably less than the actual child-care costs Symes had paid, and which she would be able to deduct fully if her child-care expenses could fit within the test for a business expense.[5]

The matter went before the courts with two issues to be resolved. The first was an interpretation question that was fundamentally about the meaning of child care. Was it merely 'personal' or could it also be related to doing business? The second issue was a Charter question: though the business expense sections were worded in gender-neutral language, would a restrictive interpretation of business expenses result in adverse impact discrimination against women?

The seeming simplicity of the two legal questions was belied by the controversy the case generated. And generate conflict it did. The case raised questions about gender, parenting, the needs of children, the world of business and work, race, and the ties between family, economy, and the state. The case was multiply cathectic, located at a juncture where many discourses, interests, and visions intersected and interacted in complex ways. Not surprisingly, a great deal of ambivalence existed within women's communities about the stance to take *vis-à-vis* the case.[6] As Isabel Grant, a law professor at the University of British Columbia, aptly put it, 'It's not a case on which feminists are necessarily in accord.'[7]

Many women supported the case, both politically and financially. At the same time, Symes did not have the official support of large feminist organiza-

tions like the National Action Committee on the Status of Women (NAC) or
LEAF. Against a history of seeking universality in day-care provision, some in
these groups were troubled by the class-based implications of the case. If
successful, the case could extend child-care benefits through tax relief, but
only to business women. Wage-earning women would see no benefit.
Businesswomen, argued some, were already relatively privileged *vis-à-vis* other
women. The case might have the effect of increasing class-based gaps. This
was a difficult issue since, despite the relative privilege of some businesswomen, it was also clear that businesswomen in general were still subject to
the disadvantaging effects of gender.

Some feminists were persuaded by the message in *Symes* that the traditional
public/private boundary needed to be challenged, but they were troubled by a
strategy that did so via taxation. According to Martha Friendly, 'Using tax
breaks to pay for child care doesn't satisfy the requirements of social equality.'[8]
Certainly, there was a history of lobbying efforts designed to create a national
day-care system of some sort, and women's groups had long pointed out that
tax deductions were the least desirable and equitable method of government
involvement in child care (RCT, 1967; RCSW, 1970; SWC, 1986; HWC, 1987). If
the government were to subsidize child care, should it do so through taxation
or through other more direct means? There were also strategic concerns. For
example, would tax deductions for businesswomen split the child-care lobby
and reduce the likelihood of a more equitable day-care system?

Because both Symes and Mrs Simpson were white, questions of race privilege and disadvantage were rarely foregrounded in the public discussion. As a
result, some women were worried about the inability of the case to foreground
the racialized dimensions of child-care provision in Canada. The relationship
between (often) white upper-middle-class female employers of (often)
economically and politically vulnerable women of colour or immigrant women
was one that required attention (Silvera, 1989). Would the courts neglect or
erase the very real issues of white privilege that often were threaded through
the private child-care relationship? Women were left struggling with counter-
vailing concerns about child care, parenting, gender, equality, public rights,
and private obligations.

How did the courts deal with the host of complex and troubling questions
engaged by the case? At trial, Symes won ([1989] 3 F.C. 59). Mr. Justice Cullen
referred to the expert evidence about the impact of child-care responsibilities
on women's ability to participate in the paid workforce and concluded that the
meaning of business expense must account for the business needs of both men
and women, and thus could include child care. A contrary interpretation, he
found, would violate the guarantee of sex equality in s. 15 of the Charter.

On appeal, however, Symes lost ([1991] 3 F.C. 509). According to the judges
of the Federal Court of Appeal, despite the influx of women into the workforce,
the circumstances relating to business expenses had not changed. Business
was business and child care was something else altogether. The Court drew a

sharp line between objective 'commercial needs' of business and the 'particular' non-business needs of individuals (p. 523). Further, the Court interpreted the limited child-care deduction in s. 63 of the Income Tax Act as a complete mini-code for child care, finding that child care could only be deducted under this section. Such an interpretation, the judges found, produced no discrimination. Writing for the unanimous Court of Appeal, Mr. Justice Décary stated that he was 'not prepared to concede that professional women make up a disadvantaged group' suffering from s. 15 discrimination as a result of this interpretation (p. 531).

What about the Supreme Court? In a much remarked upon 7–2 gender-split decision, the male majority dismissed Symes's claim ((1993) 110 D.L.R. (4th) 470). On the 'interpretation' question, the majority spent many pages discussing past case law about the meaning of business and the characterization of child care as a personal expense (pp. 527–44). Rather oddly, after this big build-up, the majority came to the somewhat surprising and anti-climactic conclusion that it was not necessary to revisit these questions because (following the Court of Appeal) s. 63 was a complete code for child care (p. 548). And what about the Charter? The Court avoided any engaging discussion of the problem of equality in the case with a second anti-climactic sleight of hand: lack of evidence. Symes, they claimed, had proven that women carried the disproportionate burden of child care. What was required, however, was evidence 'that women disproportionately pay child care expenses' (p. 558). In the absence of this evidence, no discrimination had been shown.

As far as the ratio goes, this is really all the Court said: lack of evidence. Against this background, a decision based on supposed clarity of statutory language and the supposed lack of appropriate evidence, I will explore the deployment of the rhetoric of choice.

The Rhetoric of Choice

'Choice' is of central symbolic value in Western societies and has great power as a signifier of liberation, freedom, and empowerment. These symbolic dimensions of choice are explicitly mobilized, for example, in cases concerning abortion and reproductive rights. But the rhetoric of choice also has great power as a signifier of responsibility and blame. And questions about 'who is responsible' are often at the centre of law.

The rhetoric of choice provides a simple framework for resolving claims about individual behaviour and responsibility. Boiled down to its essence, the rhetoric suggests three general alternatives: first, a given situation is the result of a person's own choosing, and so there will be no intervention to minimize that person's suffering; second, a given situation is not the result of a person's choosing (i.e., she or he has been forced or coerced) and so intervention is appropriate to minimize that person's suffering; third, a given situation is not the result of a person's choosing, but there is nothing that can be done to remedy the situation (i.e., the problem is one of nature, or society, or simply outside the jurisdiction of the court). In short, the possibilities are 'you made your own bed', 'it was somebody else's fault', or 'it is not my department'.

I am not suggesting that the practice of deploying this rhetorical model is the exclusive domain of the courts. The model is deployed in all kinds of social and political contexts where responsibility is at issue. Nor am I disclaiming the utility of the model. Certainly, it has proven useful where the questions for resolution are ones of responsibility, and further, of responsibility in contexts where there is fairly widespread consensus about the meaning of behaviour. Where one's concern is with allocating blame or responsibility, the rhetoric of choice provides a simple decision-making mechanism.

My argument, rather, is this: the simplicity of the model obscures the role played by the model in shaping beliefs about the legitimacy or immutability of the reigning order. It is often via this rhetoric that the law participates in the construction of gender. The rhetoric deflects attention from the ways in which power shapes the outcome of 'choice' while allowing the chooser to believe that, in fact, a choice has been made (Gaventa, 1980: 63). The rhetoric functions most powerfully in this way when it suggests that 'choice' is a neutral arbiter of responsibility.

The rhetoric of choice is rarely neutral. On the contrary, it rests on a series of strongly gendered, racialized, and classed presumptions. Joan Williams argues that the language of choice is often employed in ways that presume and thereby reinforce the current and unequal distribution of paid work and family responsibilities (Williams, 1991). In other words, the attribution of responsibility based on choice depends on other assumptions about gender, class, and race. In discussions purporting to be determined by questions of individual choice, we see the sediment of previous and ongoing struggles over meaning and the social distribution of power—struggles conducted in political, social, economic, and legal realms.

Perhaps a concrete example may serve to illustrate the point that the rhetoric of choice rests on unarticulated gendered presumptions. Consider the following anonymous comment, which was published in response to a public survey about the *Symes* case.[9] In response to the question, 'Should business women be able to deduct child care expenses as a business expense?', this person said:

> No, I don't think they should deduct it as a business expense because if a couple decide to have children that is their problem and if she chooses to work they should have to pay for it.

This comment both captures and typifies some of the ways in which the discourse functions. There are a host of assumptions and presumptions nested in the comment. One set of presumptions relates to the decision to have children. First, there is the presumption that children emerge into the world as the result of an affirmative decision: 'if a couple *decide* to have children'. This assertion skates over the complexity of conditions under which children are both conceived and carried to term: it is not so clear that children are always the result of a 'decision', unless one collapses the distinction between deciding to engage in sexual activity and the bringing of a child into the world. Invisible here are systemic barriers to some women's ability to make the kinds of reproductive decisions they would more happily choose (Fried, 1990).

Also nested in this comment about decisions is the further presumption of heterosexual partnership: 'if a *couple* decide'. Invisible here are problems in the attribution of both decision-making power and consequences to 'the couple'. Any couple is composed of two individuals, each of whom may have different interests and may differentially experience the results of 'the decision of the couple'. A focus on *the decision* obscures power differentials and differential impacts. Attributing the decision-making power to 'the couple' also glosses over the many situations where—*if* decisions are made about birthing—those decisions are made by single women, by homosexual or lesbian couples, or by the families of pregnant (sometimes teen) women.

The comment also presumes that the decision to have children (along with the ramifications of having made that decision) is a private one: 'if a couple decide to have children *that is their problem*'. This use of the rhetoric of choice both invokes and reinforces the traditional liberal public/private divide. This divide has been central to the ways liberal societies have determined where and when the state should intervene and where and when people should be free from such intervention. Without completely disclaiming the need for both public and private spaces (Gavison, 1992), it is important to note that the public/private divide has not been gender-neutral: men have been more strongly identified with the public realm and women with the private (Elshtain, 1981). Public violence and exploitation have merited state attention, while private violence and exploitation have been seen as less susceptible to state intervention, if they have been visible at all. The result has been state inattention or blindness to those forms of injustice disproportionately suffered by women in those realms seen as the private, and the family is quintessentially within the private (Okin, 1989). The state is generally not to interfere with family decisions, but neither is the family generally entitled to make a claim on the state for that which is a family matter. In saying that the couple's decision 'is their problem', the respondent asserts that the decision to have children is a private one and that any costs resulting from that decision are also private ones. The fact that such 'decisions' may place undue burdens on women is not a matter of public concern. The respondent leaves no room for the possibility that the public as a whole may have an interest in children, let alone that the public is implicated in reproductive decisions.

The comment reveals a second set of assumptions about the appropriate gendered division of the labour that results from the couple's 'decision': fathers are to provide primary economic support, while the primary task of caring for the child belongs to mothers. It is significant that the response says, 'if *she* chooses to work *they* should have to pay for it.' The statement is not 'if *he* chooses to work' or even 'if *they* choose to work'. The implication here is that a father's responsibility is to work. It is not a matter of choice; it is a responsibility. The other half of this gendered division of labour is the mother's responsibility for the physical care of children—a responsibility that locates her in the home. The statement 'if she chooses to work' implies that women's work outside the home, unlike men's work, is a consumer or luxury good of sorts. Mothers, unlike fathers, have a choice to make. They can stay at home or they can seek employment, but their work outside the home is characterized as a luxury item. If a couple decides to buy the consumer good of women's work, then the couple should have to pay the cost of that good. Fathers do not 'choose' to work; if they have children, they must be employed. If a mother chooses to work, then the couple has the private responsibility for the child-care costs resulting from the woman's decision. The 'choice' of whether to work or not once children are involved is a choice of the woman. A woman should undertake employment knowing that the couple will have to carry the costs of this luxury good. It is the woman who must carry the burden of a decision whose economic consequences will be felt in the collective.

The point I wish to emphasize is that the rhetoric of choice, while privatizing the problems of women by attributing them to individual choices, does more than this. It participates in the construction of gender itself, relying on and reproducing gender by asserting different expectations and responsibilities for men and women—for fathers and mothers. The gendered presumptions that slide in through this example are further shaped by additional presumptions about marital status, socio-economic class, and sexual orientation. The gendered division of labour and responsibility presumed by the response is one possible only for some kinds of people in specific contexts. But the need for express contextual specificity is made invisible by the seemingly universalizing rhetoric of choice. The rhetoric's simplifying logic participates in the practice of gendering, sustaining very specific constructions of gender while appearing to rely on neutral and universal principles of choice.

The response deconstructed above is one that appeared in the social world of the daily news media, not in the courtroom. However, the very same kind of reasoning was articulated throughout the case, including by Mr Justice Major when the *Symes* case was heard at the Supreme Court of Canada. Mr Justice Major asked J.J. Camp (lawyer for the intervening Canadian Bar Association) about the role that choice played in his submission. Here, as in the newspaper quotation above, 'choice' seemed to have been raised as a trump card, as if choice rendered irrelevant the host of other complex issues in the case. The interchange went as follows (SCC transcript: 63–5):

Major J.: Let me ask you, to what extent does it matter that the question of having children is a matter of choice? The woman in the work force has a choice. Does it make the society have an obligation to encourage her to make the choice to have children, compared to her counterpart who wants a career without children?

Mr Camp: No. I don't think society encourages one way or another, but society should not disadvantage her from doing so.

Major J.: No, but who are they disadvantaging? Not all women. It is women who elect to have children.

Mr Camp: Yes.

Major J.: Isn't that a matter of their choice, knowing that having a child is going to bear some costs in time and money?

Mr Camp: Mr. Justice Major, I am tempted to say and I will say it is the future of our society at stake. We cannot enjoy a future unless we have children, we cannot enjoy it unless those children are properly cared for. They are us, they are our future.

Major J.: But surely there is an element of personal choice in a decision to have children. It serves two purposes: one may be the future that you describe, the other is whatever comfort may arise out of having children. My simple question is: To what extent does the element of choice play any part in your submission?

Mr Camp: The element of choice as you have described it plays no part in my submission.

In this discussion, one can hear echoes of the presumptions in the early media response: that women can choose to have children or not and that women are responsible for children. J.J. Camp's comments about the inequality suffered by women is deflected by the response that 'not all women' are disadvantaged. The only women who suffer disadvantage are those 'who elect to have children'. Questions about 'the future of our society' are set aside in the interests of the more immediate question of 'individual choice'.

Mr Justice Major, perhaps drawing on discourses from economic theory, appears to subsume questions of disadvantage in a cost-benefit model. That is, the woman who makes the choice to have children does so 'knowing that having a child is going to bear some costs in time and money'. On the other side of the equation is 'whatever comfort may arise out of having children'. Thus, we can assume that women who choose to have children have done so rationally, having weighed the costs and benefits. Starting from this perspective, Mr Justice Major views societal intervention as problematic—as interfering with the preconditions of choice. To allow a woman to deduct the cost of child care would be unfair. It would be like providing an unearned benefit to these women, a benefit not available to other women in the workforce who want 'a career without children'. To give this benefit would be 'to *encourage* her to make the choice to have children'.

Even the reference to the woman 'who wants a career without children' obscures as much as it reveals. Certainly there are women who want a career without children. Just as certainly, there are men who want a career without children. But this is beside the point. To compare those who want children and those who do not deflects attention from the differential costs that may influence these decisions. The evidence in front of the court indicated that women with children were less professionally mobile than their female counterparts without children.[10] At the same time, it appeared that having children had no impact on professional mobility for men. That is, the constraints on men who want to have children are significantly different from those on women who want to have children. But in reducing the question to one of 'want' or 'desire' or 'choice', questions of gendered constraints disappear.

Interestingly enough, the backgrounding of gendered constraints on choice has the effect of subtly re-enforcing an age-old choice for women: to be constructed as 'selfish' or 'selfless' (Williams, 1991; Duffy et al., 1989; Keller, 1986). Questions about the unequal gender-based costs of being responsible for children, about the societal interest in caring for children, about the disadvantages attendant on being a parent—these questions are reduced to the question of whether or not women choose to have children, whether they choose to be selfish or selfless. It is significant that men are absent from Mr Justice Major's question. It is only the career woman who is required to make a choice. Her male equivalent is excused. It seems unnecessary to look at his choices or to hold him responsible in this context. Mr Justice Major uses the rhetoric of choice as a tool of decision-making, and does so in ways that import elements of other gendered social, political, religious, and economic discourses.

These two examples, neither outrageous nor uncommon, serve to illustrate the point that the rhetoric of choice is not a neutral or ungendered tool. Deployments of the rhetoric that proceed as if choice were neutral suggest that it is not necessary to turn attention to differentially gendered, racialized, and classed dimensions of meaning and experience. We can see how a number of issues (the social division of labour, the notion of the ideal worker as not responsible for child care) seem to vanish in an equation that focuses on a woman's 'choice' to have children. It is this vanishing that leads Williams to argue that the rhetoric of choice is essential to the construction of a gender system that leaves women with a different and less desirable range of choices than those available for men. Those using the rhetoric are able to deflect challenges to the disempowerment of women by invoking choice, by drawing attention away from the constraints within which women's choices occur.

Drawing on Ani DiFranco's insight that 'every tool is a weapon if you hold it right',[11] I want to emphasize that the rhetoric of choice is not a monolithically dangerous tool. The danger lies in uncritical use and acceptance of the rhetoric. The challenge is to learn how to 'hold it right'. To do this, one must study how the rhetoric is deployed. To what extent are the assumptions upon which it rests made explicit? What meanings are assumed by those using the discourse? Uncritical deployments of the rhetoric, to the extent that they draw on beliefs that sustain current societal power relations, participate in the reinforcement of those relations.

In the next section, I will examine the deployment of the rhetoric in the *Symes* case. The case involved fundamental struggles over the social meaning of motherhood and parenthood, and over the value and meaning of employment of and by mothers of various socio-economic classes and racial/ethnic groupings. The rhetoric was sometimes deployed to displace explicit struggles over gender—to shift the terrain of struggle from the complex caves of socially constructed meaning to the simpler peaks of individual choice. We will also see the rhetoric of choice used by those seeking to challenge the social construction of meaning. We see explicit challenges to the assumptions grounding the rhetoric. These challenges direct attention back to the struggles over the meaning of gender and over the meaning of meaning itself.

The Rhetoric of Choice as a Gendering Practice

The Cross-Examination

In giving evidence at trial, Beth Symes stated that she carried the burden of responsibility for the care of her children. John Power, the lawyer for the government, argued that the government had statutorily decreed that child-care responsibilities were to be shared equally between parents. How was the court to theorize the actual burden carried by Symes in the face of laws dictating that child-care burdens should be shared equally between parents? Power deployed the rhetoric of choice: if Symes was carrying an excess portion of the burden, it was because she chose to carry it. There was thus no reason for the court to intervene or shift the costs of this burden. In his cross-examination, Power returned time and time again to the question of choice (trial transcript: 91–8):

> 'Who made that decision?' 'Who said that it was your responsibility?' 'Was that your choice that [the burden] rest with you?' 'Did somebody force that upon you?' '[It was] at your own choice.' 'Who imposed that burden upon you?' 'Who decided that?' 'And you accepted that course of events?'

In the face of this onslaught, Symes agreed that the burden of responsibility rested on her, but continually rejected Power's assertions that this was at her own choice. She refused to use the notion of choice to explain her situation. Instead, she kept turning attention back to the preconditions of choice and the circumstances under which working mothers exercised their choices.

But Power's cross-examination remained tightly focused on Symes and her ability to make a choice. Power asked specifically whether the Minister of National Revenue required her to carry the burden of child care in her family (trial transcript: 96). The question, on the surface, could only be answered in the negative: clearly, the minister had not forced Symes to carry the burden. But does the absence of physical force leave the Minister of National Revenue unimplicated? Power's superficial question obscures the role that taxation has always played in consciously directing the behaviour of taxpayers (Blumberg,

1971; McCaffery, 1993). A rhetoric of choice that focuses on identifying 'the chooser' obscures the ways in which many factors (i.e., tax codes) are strongly implicated in the actions taken by individuals.

Power did not foreclose the possibility that Symes was coerced, that she was forced to carry the burden of child care. In leaving room for this possibility, he turned his attention to her husband (trial transcript: 93–8):

> 'You mean your husband was not willing to share with you in that responsi-bility?' '. . . you are saying that your husband does not share in the duties of bringing up children?' 'Do you have any reason to give to the Court why he did not pay part, half or all [of the expenses]?' 'Are you saying under oath today that your husband would have refused or did refuse to pay any of those expenditures?' 'Did your husband say he would not share?' 'Did anybody impose that decision on you and your husband except you and your husband?'

Under this line of questioning, Power used the rhetoric to suggest that if Symes was forced, she was forced by her husband. In effect, Power was suggesting that the Court accept the following train of thought: 'Symes did not choose, but was forced to carry the burden, therefore she is entitled to redress. That redress should be directed not against the government, but against the husband who forced her.' He seems to suggest that Symes can choose from two alternatives: she can accept that the burden she carries is carried at her own choosing, or she can name her husband as the source of her oppression. We can see how the rhetoric of choice is structured in a binary form: either one chooses or one is forced. The binary model seems to allow only for total choice or its total absence. Such dichotomization, a defining characteristic of much liberal thought, draws attention away from the complexity of the middle ground between force and freedom. When articulated in this fashion, the rhetoric makes it hard to get at processes resulting in decisions that are neither chosen nor visibly forced. We also see how the rhetoric presumes gender equality. It allows for the persistence of gender imbalances by pushing them into the private realm. If there is gender inequality here, Power suggests, it is a private individual matter that is not of concern to the collective whole.

Symes tried to get at the complexity of the problem, but the model of choice used by Power made it difficult for her to illuminate the reality she was trying to describe. In response to Power's question, 'Did somebody force [the burden of child care] upon you?', Symes replied that she was required to carry the burden by 'circumstances'. Circumstances. She had some difficulty in putting her finger on precisely what those circumstances were, saying simply, 'Perhaps that I was willing to do it.' I think she gets very close to the problem when she says, 'It's difficult to answer because it is a matter of how families operate.' Here, she touches on the deep interwoven social structures that have a shaping influence on the matter of choice, and that themselves are in the process of flux and transformation. In her reply, we see an honest struggle with her own unexplored discomfort with 'circumstances'. She seems at least to be aware of the 'cave' in which she found herself, even though she clearly had not been able to provide a good analysis of it.

While one might remain critical of the ways in which a full class analysis was not present in the case, one can also appreciate that the case directed a quite radical challenge to some of those forces that construct a gendered world. In Power's response to this challenge, we see the rhetoric of choice deployed in a defensive counterstrike. Rather than engaging in a dialogue about 'circumstances' and the gendered implications of the public/private divide, Power offers the following (rather scathing) response to Symes's most realistic admission of difficulty (trial transcript: 96–7):

> Excuse me, Mrs. Symes, you're a professionally trained lawyer. . . . You have indicated this morning the range of your professional experience as a litigator, etc. Are you suggesting to me that you had no choice but to bear with your income the raising of these children during the years in question—the child care expenditure—and that your husband had no responsibility for that? And did not share in it? And you accepted that course of events?'

Here, we see the rhetoric of choice deployed as a mechanism of shaming. Power suggests that a professionally trained litigator could not possibly have accepted a deal as lousy as the one she is describing. Her professional credentials are held up and found to be wanting. If she really were any good as a professional litigator, she should have been able to work out a better deal! There are many interesting dimensions to this 'shame attack'. Note that the shaming response ties gender with class. Why is being a 'professionally trained lawyer' relevant to the 'choosing' of child-care burdens in the first place? Are we to understand that such bad choices would be understandable if they came from a woman who was not a lawyer? Also intriguing is Power's implication that litigation models are appropriate in the context of an ongoing relationship between two parents with respect to their children. In directing attention to the negotiation between Symes and her husband, Power glosses over other participants, enforcing the presumption that child-care responsibilities are a private matter to be partitioned between only two parties: a husband and a wife. This deflects attention from Symes's claim that the Canadian taxation system itself is implicated in the so-called private realm of family and children. It deflects attention from her assertion that tax provisions and practices help reinforce and police the gendered division of child-care labour and responsibility.

We see here how the focus on choice deflects attention away from the conflict surrounding this case. Explicit struggles over the construction of gender are displaced by a framework that focuses on determining 'who made the choice?' The simplifying model of choice/no choice flattens out the case and makes it difficult to engage explicitly in the reconstruction of gender. At the same time, the simplifying model imports and reinforces current assumptions about gender, work, and the public/private divide.

Eberts's Response

We see a quite different deployment of the rhetoric of choice in the final comments made at the Supreme Court hearing by Mary Eberts, lawyer for Symes. In these comments, she returned to Mr Justice Major's concern that having children was 'a matter of choice' (SCC transcript: 154–5):

> The last point that I wish to make addresses the questions of my lord Mr. Justice Major and of my lord Mr. Justice Gonthier on this issue that having children is a matter of choice.
>
> It is unfortunately true that if a couple chooses to have children the woman must bear them. There is no option. There is no choice there. Our social arrangements are such that women, by and large, also must rear them. In spite of the contention of counsel for the Attorney General of Quebec that men and women now, by statute, are equally responsible for the expenses of child care, I would ask that you not take the statutory prescription for the factual reality. There is ample documentation in this record that women still must bear the responsibilities for child care.
>
> She has no choice, or at least a false choice, if she wants to participate in the labour market. If she puts her child care responsibilities first, she chooses either to stay out of the work force or to work part time, because it is simply not possible to stay in it, or she chooses to pay a higher proportion of her income for child care than a man would have to do.
>
> On the issue of childlessness, it is not a choice for a woman to be childless in order to participate in the work force. Men do not have to choose to be childless in order to participate in the work force. It is a false and cruel choice to say that a woman voluntarily chooses to be childless. She is in fact responding to the structural inequities of the labour market that make it very difficult for women to participate in it while they have child care responsibilities.
>
> This Honourable Court has recognized that in recognizing the ability of women to choose reproductive freedom, because often women are in a situation where they cannot afford to raise children, so they will seek abortions. Until we have a society where women are equal and can equally afford to raise their children in the same circumstances as men do, that 'sombre choice'— and I put it in quotation marks—must all too unfortunately still be available to them.

Eberts, like Power, deploys the rhetoric of choice. But Eberts uses the rhetoric as an entry point for an explicit challenge to the social construction of gender. She makes a clear distinction between the biological reality that women bear children and the social reality that has made women also responsible for the care of children after they are born. She challenges the statutory prescription of equality, drawing the court's attention back to the factual reality of inequality. She also draws attention to the forces that constrain and shape women's 'choices', emphasizing that the structure of the labour market makes it very costly for women with child-care responsibilities to participate. She also points out that men are not required to make the choice between having children and participating in the labour market. Her comments in fact seek to displace a rhetoric of choice, which is blind to these constraints, and substitute one that accounts for the ways that larger social structures interact to restrict and channel choices.

In short, this deployment seeks to draw the Court's attention to the complexities posed by talk about women and choice, illustrating the ways that a focus on the question 'didn't she choose?' tends to take attention away from the constraints shaping women's choices. Her use of the rhetoric seeks to prevent decision-making based on unarticulated but nonetheless present assumptions. Here, talk about choice occurs in a context where the preconditions of choice are themselves challenged. Attention is directed away from individual choice and back towards structural inequities distributing the palette of options.

The Majority Judgment

Richard Terdiman reminds us that 'No discourse is ever a monologue' (Terdiman, 1985: 36). The truth of the comment is reflected when we look at the Supreme Court judgment. In deploying the rhetoric of choice, the Supreme Court reflects some of the arguments expressed by Eberts in her reply. Recall that Power had asserted that Symes had chosen to have children and that this was a 'personal choice'. He followed this route because the Income Tax Act precluded the deduction of 'personal expenses'. Writing for the majority, Mr Justice Iacobucci considered the arguments about personal choice. He concluded (p. 541):

> Pregnancy and childbirth decisions are associated with a host of competing ethical, legal, religious and socioeconomic influences, and to conclude that the decision to have children should—in tax terms—be characterized as an entirely personal choice, is to ignore these influences altogether.

This passage makes explicit reference to the kinds of forces to which Mary Eberts referred. This certainly can be seen as a positive shift in use of the rhetoric. The Court does not conclude that Symes 'chose' to have children, or that she 'didn't choose'. However, the Court nonetheless is able to avoid an explicit consideration of the exclusionary and harmful gendered presumptions built into the law's treatment of business expenses by using the rhetoric in its third formulation: 'not my department'. The Court agrees that it might be time to reconceptualize the gendered relationship between the business class and the changing social structure, but finds that the language of the Income Tax Act is sufficiently clear that the Court is precluded from intervening. Parliament has made clear its intention that child-care expenses not be addressed through the business provision sections (p. 548):

> the *Income Tax Act* intends to address child care expenses, and does so in fact, entirely within s. 63. It is not necessary for me to decide whether, in the absence of s. 63, ss. 9, 18(1)(a) and (h) are capable of comprehending a business expense deduction for child care expenses.

It is irrelevant to consider the gendered content of business expenses, according to the majority's interpretation, because the legislature has spoken clearly: child-care expenses can only be deducted through the s. 63 limited child-care deduction. Iacobucci uses the rhetoric of choice to draw tightly circumscribed limits on the Court's powers to intervene. Here, he makes use of the classic liberal solution, one mandated by liberalism's strict separation of spheres: the public from the private, the legal from the social, the judicial from the legislative. Because the legislature has spoken clearly, the Court can do nothing. Symes must take her grievances to her elected representatives, not to the courts. This rhetoric of deflection is particularly interesting because it enables the majority to evade any responsibility for intervening or failing to intervene while allowing them to appear supportive. In short: 'We have no choice. We see your pain but are powerless to help you.'

After having determined that the legislative body intended s. 63 to be a complete code for child care, the majority is required to ask whether the government's intentional action resulted in adverse impact discrimination against businesswomen with child-care expenses. Yet again, we see the rhetoric of deflection, and again an invocation of the public/private divide. Symes had argued that women carried the burden of child care. But the burden of child care, according to Iacobucci, has a social and a legal dimension. The Court can act only where discrimination involves the legal dimension. Parents are viewed as having a joint legal responsibility to care for their children, but one must be careful to identify correctly the content of this legal responsibility. As Mr Justice Iacobucci elaborates: 'the law will impose the legal duty to share the burden of child care *expenses*, if not necessarily a duty to share the child care burden itself' (p. 558).

After reviewing all the evidence before the court, Mr Justice Iacobucci says: 'I have no doubt that women disproportionately incur the *social* costs of child care' (p. 558). However, he does not find that this disproportionate burden constitutes adverse effect discrimination under the Charter. In Iacobucci's words, 'We must take care to distinguish between effects which are wholly caused, or are contributed to, by an impugned provision, and those social circumstances which exist independently of such a provision. . . . social costs, although very real, exist outside of the Income Tax Act' (p. 559). In other words, child-care *expenses* are 'legal', while child-care *burdens* are 'social'. The Court hastily acknowledges the inequity of these social costs, which are disproportionately borne by women. However, under the rhetoric of choice bolstered by the public/private divide, these costs originate in society, not in law. The Court can exercise its power only in the realm of the legal; inequities in the social realm, however abhorrent, cannot be resolved by the courts. Symes, Iacobucci concludes, has only shown the existence of a social burden. The Court can do nothing about this kind of burden. It can see the problem, and grieve, but it cannot act.

These two 'we are powerless to help' arguments show how the rhetoric of choice can be deployed as a means of avoiding decision-making responsibility. Such deployments may reflect not so much a desire to reinforce existing distributions of power as a desire to avoid becoming explicitly embroiled in the conflict. The Court paints a picture of itself as a powerless external observer. The reality is that, in using the rhetoric of choice, the Court actively participates in the construction of gender. It does so by policing a very specific boundary between law and society. This traditional boundary has allocated many forms of gender disadvantage to the realm of the social, a realm where the disempowered have even fewer resources to back up their claims for justice. The Court acknowledges the gendered implications of the boundary, but seems to suggest that it (like Symes herself) is equally constrained by the boundary. Such a suggestion completely obscures the crucial role that the Court plays in constructing the boundary itself (Bourdieu, 1987). The Court determines which dimensions of the child-care burden will be seen as legal and which dimensions will be written off as merely social. My argument here is not that the separation of legislative from judicial powers is unimportant, nor that the concept of public and private realms is completely fraudulent. Rather, the Court's supposedly neutral practice of relying on the 'not my department' branch of the rhetoric of choice is not so neutral. Through its deployment of the rhetoric of choice and its invocation of the public/private divide, the Court directly participates in the social construction of gender.

The majority also deploys the rhetoric of choice in a second way: as a disciplining rhetoric of blame. Recall the majority's conclusion: Symes had failed to produce the right kind of evidence—that married women paid more money for child-care expenses than married men. In his final comments, Mr Justice Iacobucci steps back from the 'we are powerless to help you' stance and suggests that Symes nonetheless had made bad tactical and strategic choices— choices that left her at least in part responsible for her own loss. Her errors, he tells us, had to do with her focus on businesswomen and the inadequacy of evidence she provided in support of her case. Symes, he says, belonged to a particular subgroup of women—married women who were entrepreneurs—and that the evidentiary focus was 'skewed' in this direction (p. 559). In his view, 'her focus upon self-employed women to the exclusion of women employees is a very curious aspect of this case' (p. 560). He goes on to suggest that 'the appellant thought it desirable to distance herself from employees in this case' (p. 560). Iacobucci concludes that an overly narrow focus on married businesswomen was just the wrong choice—a choice that left the Court with no evidence of discrimination. Symes lost because she made bad choices.

According to the Court, she should have structured the case differently, introduced different kinds of evidence. Iacobucci suggests a number of scenarios under which the court's ruling might have been different (p. 560). Symes could have established the circumstances of single mothers. She also could have focused on parents rather than just mothers. Iacobucci chastises Symes, saying that her focus on gender 'effectively ignored the relevance of a parental status distinction' (p. 561). Further, in focusing exclusively on her own situation, Symes had failed to consider the other kinds of hardships worked by s. 63. Not only did she neglect to consider 'parental status', but also 'business people in a loss position' and 'farmers'. He calls her to task for failing to consider 'low-income Canadians'. Further, in the context of his Charter discussion, he describes her arguments as having been presented in 'curious isolation': she had invited the Court to consider the Charter only with respect to self-employed women, suggesting a remedy could be granted without considering 'the position of other women, other parents, or the government's overall response to child care needs' (p. 565). Iacobucci says that her 'instrumental' approach was 'inappropriate' (p. 565). Put most plainly, Symes lost because she was overly focused on her own needs. She did not pay enough attention to the needs of others.

One can't help but agree that it would be good were all members of society to attend to the needs of others. However, in courts of law, attention to the needs of others has rarely been a prerequisite for success, let alone an explanation for failure. As Madame Justice L'Heureux-Dubé comments in dissent (p. 510):

> In *Andrews*, the Court did not look at the respondent and justify the infringement of his rights under s. 15 on the basis that, in all other aspects of his life, as a white male lawyer of British descent, such discrimination on the basis of citizenship was acceptable, since he was likely better off than most other persons in the disadvantaged group of non-Canadian citizens.

As she notes, it has generally been sufficient for applicants to establish the ways in which *they* have been disadvantaged by a law or program. Thus, the comments by the majority might seem unusual. They are less unusual when one foregrounds the codes for female behaviour (Bepko, and Krestan, 1990). One of the codes for women is to 'be unselfish and of service'. That is, women are to care for others before caring for themselves.

The majority spoke of skewed evidence, the exclusion of women employees, inappropriate instrumental approaches, the failure to consider single mothers, wage-earning women, fathers responsible for child care, low-income Canadians, and even farmers. Such language resonates with the pulsing echo of the familiar indictment: selfish. The rhetoric of choice is used not merely as a means of allocating responsibility, but also as a disciplining rhetoric of blame. Using this rhetoric of blame, the Court participates in the construction of gender by policing the boundaries of appropriate female behaviour. The Court condemns Symes for being selfish.

It is of more than passing interest that the 'disciplinary method', if I may call it that, invokes the progressive discourses of disadvantage. That is, in its rhetoric of blame, the Court alludes to the intersection of class privilege and gender disadvantage that had left many feminists feeling ambivalent about the case. On one level, one is tempted to cheer that the majority affirms feminist discussions of intersectionality. The majority seems to see that categories of disadvantage are complexly interrelated and seems to recognize the need for a contextual intersectional analysis. However, such optimism may be misplaced; the Court does not itself engage in such an analysis. It does not conclude, for example, that the current tax system must be revised because it gives business people unfair advantages over their wage-earning counterparts. The attention to feminist discourses of class disadvantage is superficial at best. The Court's language draws on these feminist discourses, but not as a challenge to class-based disadvantage. Rather, the Court invokes 'class' and the rhetoric of 'choice' to police the gendered codes for female selflessness.

In the majority decision, we get a snapshot of law as a gendering practice. The Court does, at least, acknowledge that there *is* an ongoing struggle over the construction of gender. However, it uses the rhetoric of choice to suggest that it is not a participant in these struggles, only a mediator of law. The Court applies the rhetoric to characterize itself as a powerless observer of inequalities existing outside the jurisdiction of the law. Having done so, it turns the blade and uses the rhetoric again as a disciplinary tool. In doing so, it participates in the construction of gender by policing and maintaining the rules of appropriate gender behaviour. In short, while disclaiming the jurisdiction to participate directly in the reconstruction of gender, the Court employs the rhetoric of choice, which is one of the mechanisms through which the battles over the meaning of gender are conducted.

Conclusion

Beliefs about the meaning of gender, work, the family, race, class, and the public/private divide lie in deep and intersecting fault lines, and shifts in these beliefs have enormous implications. The rhetoric of choice is often deployed when there is movement at these fault lines. Where the rhetoric of choice is employed in ways that suggest its neutrality, it tends to turn the focus away from the socially contested nature of meaning and away from the 'political' role of those who participate in the construction of this meaning. Instead, it turns the focus of attention to individual responsibility in specific individual cases. Explicit struggles about the social construction of meaning are reformulated as simple problems of responsibility that can be answered with the near-binary construction of 'choice', 'no choice', or 'not my department'. The role of power in constructing social meaning is left unexplored. To return to the question posed by Mr Justice Major: '. . . to what extent does it matter that the question of having children is a matter of choice?' My answer would be: 'That depends on what question concerns you. Is your concern with the allocation of responsibility, or with Law's participation in the construction of gender?'

Its simplifying tendency may be one of the attractions of the rhetoric: it provides a relatively uncomplicated decision-making model. This model may be tempting. Choice has the advantage of producing resolutions that appear fairly consistent with the past, resolutions that suggest stability and continuity—resolutions that don't require one to venture into the sometimes fearful unexplored darkness of the caves below. But the simplicity of the model provided by the rhetoric of choice can only be a panacea in a world where meaning is constantly under construction. Gender is constantly being (re)produced, and law participates in its production. Law is a gendering practice, and the rhetoric of choice is one moment in this practice.

In this discussion, I have been critical of many deployments of the rhetoric of choice, but I would like to make it clear that I do not think that talk about choice is meaningless. On the contrary. Discussions of choice and agency are of great importance at this period in time (Nedelsky, 1989; Mann, 1994; Keller, 1986). My concern is that all uses of the rhetoric of choice do not really advance these discussions. The rhetoric of choice may fail us to the extent that its use deflects the focus from fundamental struggles over meaning, to simpler and more superficial questions about responsibility and blame. It fails even more when this simplification obscures the racialized, classed, and gendered presumptions that produce differential conditions governing choice.

In the *Symes* case, one can see how this simplifying rhetorical process works. The case was threaded through with complex intersections of privilege and disadvantage. It engaged fundamental questions about the meaning of motherhood, work, class. Feminist controversy surrounding *Symes* reflected the very important ongoing dialogues about the ways that privilege and disadvantage are constructed along intersecting dimensions of class, race, sexuality, and gender. But in the courtroom, the empowering rhetoric of choice was often used as a rhetoric of individualizing responsibility and blame. Important questions about intersectionality and meaning were left unanswered.

Can the language of choice be deployed to advance feminist claims in the legal arena? How should feminists think about the relationship of 'choice' to issues of advantage and disadvantage? Feminists need to consider whether other discourses, such as those based on substantive inequality, might be used to better effect in some contexts. However, though the rhetoric of choice poses a dilemma, I do not argue that the rhetoric be abandoned. The rhetoric of choice is sufficiently important that we should be very careful not to misapply Audre Lorde's powerful assertion that the master's tools will never dismantle the master's house (Lorde, 1984: 112). Damaging deployments of the rhetoric of choice need not bring feminists to conclude that choice is a tool that 'belongs' to the master. Rather, such deployments should serve as reminders that it is critical to be attentive to the ways the rhetoric of choice is *used*: it can be used to obscure the working of power in the construction of gender, and it can be used to focus attention on areas where there is movement along the fault lines of meaning deep in the caves below.

For those interested in the social construction of power, it is important to remain attentive to how the rhetoric of choice functions to shape beliefs about the legitimacy of the reigning social constructions of power. It is possible to accept that individuals make better, worse, and indifferent choices without absolving them from some responsibility for these decisions . . . and at the same time, focus on the ways that inequitable preconditions for choice are created and maintained. A clear focus on potential uses and misuses of the rhetoric may allow people to participate more explicitly in the ongoing social construction of meaning in ways that encourage decision-makers to deal directly with questions of meaning raised by the caves below rather than pointing helplessly to the summit above.

Notes

1. R.S.C. 1952, c. 148 as am. by S.C. 1970–71–2, c. 63.

2. This section reads as follows:
   9.(1) Subject to this Part, a taxpayer's income for a taxation year from a business or property is his profit therefrom for the year.

3. The text of the section says:
   18.(1) In computing the income of a taxpayer from a business or property no deduction shall be made in respect of
   (a) an outlay or expense except to the extent that it was made or incurred by the taxpayer for the purpose of gaining or producing income from the business or property;
   . . .
   (h) personal or living expenses of the taxpayer except travelling expenses (including the entire amount expended for meals and lodging) incurred by the taxpayer while away from home in the course of carrying on his business; . . .

4. The deduction can in theory be claimed by men or women. However, where there are two parents supporting a child, the deduction can be claimed only by the parent earning the lower income. To date, successful claimants have predominantly been female parents. The text of the section reads as follows:

63.(1) Child care expenses.– Subject to subsection (2), there may be deducted in computing the income of a taxpayer for a taxation year the aggregate of all amounts each of which is an amount paid in the year as or on account of child care expenses in respect of an eligible child of the taxpayer for the year.

. . .

(3) . . . (*a*) 'Child care expense'.– 'child care expense' means an expense incurred for the purpose of providing in Canada, for any eligible child of a taxpayer, child care services including baby sitting services, day nursery services or lodging at a boarding school or camp if the services were provided
>   (i) to enable the taxpayer, or the supporting person of the child for the year, who resided with the child at the time the expense was incurred,
>   (A) to perform the duties of an office or employment,
>   (B) to carry on a business either alone or as a partner actively engaged in the business . . . .

5. In 1982, the regulations under s. 63 of the Income Tax Act provided a $1,000 deduction per child. In 1985, this amount was raised to $2,000 per child. Symes's second child was born in 1983. Thus, for the years 1982 to 1985, the Minister of National Revenue would have allowed Symes a deduction of $9,000. The actual amount Symes paid for child care during this period was in excess of $50,000.

6. A number of articles explore many of these issues. See Cassin (1993), who focuses on the non-neutrality of taxation and the need to incorporate the real world into 'neutral' categories like 'business expense'; Cossman (1990), who examines the failure of Symes to account for the needs of non-businesswomen; Eansor and Wydrzynski (1993); Grbich (1990–1); Iyer (1993–4); Macklin (1992); Steele (1991); Woodman (1990a, 1990b); Young (1994a, 1994b).

7. Quoted in Daryl Slade, 'Opinions divided on child-care vote' *Toronto Star*, 17 Dec. 1993, A2.

8. 'Women's group backs rejection of tax claim', *Toronto Star*, 18 Dec. 1993, A16.

9. *Montreal Gazette*, 19 Dec. 1993. Following an article summarizing the case and the majority and dissenting reasons, the *Gazette* asked the question, 'Do you agree that self-employed women should not be allowed to deduct the cost of child care as a business expense?' In other words, do you agree with the majority judgment? Of the 2,006 readers who called to respond, 981 said no and 1,025 said yes. That is, 49 per cent agreed with the dissent and 51 per cent agreed with the majority.

10. Law Society of Upper Canada, *Transitions in the Ontario Legal Profession:*

A *Survey of Lawyers Called to the Bar Between 1975 and 1990* (Toronto, 1991).

11. From the song 'My I.Q.' on the record *Puddle Drive* (Buffalo: Righteous Babe Records, 1994).

Comprehensive Bibliography

Abner, Erika, et al. 1990. 'No More Than Simple Justice: Assessing the Royal Commission Report on Women, Poverty and the Family', *Ottawa Law Review* 22, 3: 573–606.

Adams, Perry. 1995. 'The Other Mother', in Arnup (1995).

Adamson, Nancy, et al. 1988. *Feminist Organizing for Change: The Contemporary Women's Movement in Canada*. Toronto: Oxford University Press.

Adelberg, E., and C. Currie, eds. 1993. *In Conflict with the Law: Women and the Canadian Justice System*. Vancouver: Press Gang Publishers.

—— and the Native Women's Association of Canada. 1993. 'Aboriginal Women and Prison Reform', in Adelberg and Currie (1993: 76–92).

Agnew, Vijay. 1996. *Resisting Discrimination: Women from Asia, Africa, and the Caribbean and the Women's Movement in Canada*. Toronto: University of Toronto Press.

Anderson, B. 1983. *Imagined Communities: Reflections on the Origin and Spread of Nationalism*. New York: Verso.

Anderson, E. 1993. *Value in Ethics and Economics*. Cambridge, Mass.: Harvard University Press.

Anderson, K. 1991. *Vancouver Chinatown: Racial Discourse in Canada, 1875–1980*. Montreal and Kingston: McGill-Queen's University Press.

Arnup, Katherine. 1989. 'Mothers Just Like Others: Lesbians, Divorce and Child Custody in Canada', *Canadian Journal of Women and the Law* 3: 18–32.

——, ed. 1995. *Lesbian Parenting: Living with Pride and Prejudice*. Charlottetown: gynergy books.

—— and Susan B. Boyd. 1995. 'Familial Disputes? Sperm Donors, Lesbian Mothers and Legal Parenthood', in Didi Herman and Carl Stychin, eds, *Legal Inversions: Lesbians, Gay Men and the Politics of Law*. Philadelphia: Temple University Press.

Association du Barreau Canadien. 1993. *Les assises de la réforme: Égalité, diversité et responsabilité*. Un rapport du Groupe de travail de l'Association du Barreau Canadien sur l'égalité des sexes dans la profession juridique. Ottawa: Association du Barreau Canadien.

Baber, Zaheer. 1991. 'Beyond the Structure/Agency Dualism: An Evaluation of Giddens' Theory of Structuration', *Sociological Inquiry* 61, 1: 219–30.

Bacchi, Carol L. 1990. *Same Difference: Feminism and Sexual Difference*. Sydney: Allen & Unwin.

Backhouse, Constance B. 1984a. 'Canadian Prostitution Law 1839–1972', in *Prostitution in Canada*. Ottawa: Canadian Advisory Council on the Status of Women.

——. 1984b. 'Desperate Women and Compassionate Courts: Infanticide in

Nineteenth Century Canada', *University of Toronto Law Journal* 34: 446–78.

Bala, Nicholas, and Susan Miklas. 1993. *Rethinking Decisions About Children: Is the 'Best Interests of the Child' Approach Really in the Best Interests of Children?* Toronto: Policy Research Centre on Children, Youth and Families.

Bannerji, H. 1995. *Thinking Through: Essays on Feminism, Marxism, and Anti-Racism*. Toronto: Women's Press.

Barrett, Michele, and Mary McIntosh. 1982. *The Anti-Social Family*. London: Verso.

Barry, Kathleen. 1979. *Female Sexual Slavery*. New York: New York University Press.

Bauman, R.W. 1991. 'Liberalism and Canadian Corporate Law', in R.F. Devlin, ed., *Canadian Perspectives on Legal Theory*. Toronto: Edmond Montgomery.

Beaman-Hall, Lori. 1996. 'Legal Ethnography: Exploring the Gendered Nature of Legal Method', *Critical Criminology* 7, 1: 53–74.

Beauvoir, Simone de. 1949. *Le deuxième sexe*. Paris: Éditions Gallimard.

———. 1989 [1952]. *The Second Sex*, trans. H.M. Parshley. New York: Knopf.

Belcourt, M., R.J. Burke, and H. Lee-Gosselin. 1991. *The Glass Box: Women Business Owners in Canada*. Ottawa: Canadian Advisory Council on the Status of Women.

Bell, Laurie, ed. 1987. *Good Girls/Bad Girls: Sex Trade Workers and Feminists Face to Face*. Toronto: Women's Press.

Bell, Shannon. 1994. *Reading, Writing, and Rewriting the Prostitute Body*. Bloomington: Indiana University Press.

———. 1995. *Whore Carnival*. Brooklyn, NY: Autonomedia.

———. 1997. 'On ne peut voir l'image [The image cannot be seen]', in Cossman et al. (1997).

Belleau, M.-C. 1993. 'Classicisme et progressisme dans la pensée juridique des États-Unis selon l'analyse historique de Morton J. Horwitz', 34 *Cahiers de droit*, 1235.

———. 1995. 'Les juristes inquiets: Critical Currents of Legal Thought in France at the End of the Nineteenth Century', S.J.D., Harvard University.

———. 1997. 'The "*Juristes Inquiets*": Legal Classicism and Criticism in Early Twentieth Century France', *Utah Law Review*: 379–424.

Benkov, Laura. 1994. *Reinventing the Family: The Emerging Story of Lesbian and Gay Parents*. New York: Crown Trade Paperbacks.

Bepko, C., and J. Krestan. 1990. *Too Good For Her Own Good*. New York: Harper & Row.

Bhaskar, Roy. 1986. *Scientific Realism and Human Emancipation*, 2nd edn. London: Verso.

Bill C–49 An Act to Amend the Criminal Code (Sexual Assault). Ottawa: Government of Canada, 15 June 1992.

Boivin, Michelle. 1992. 'Le féminisme en capsule: un aperçu critique du droit', *Revue femmes et droit*: 357–410.

———. 1995a. '*In memoriam* Marlène Cano', Cahiers de droit 36: 3–4.

——. 1995b. 'Les acquis du féminisme en droit: reconceptualisation de la représentation des femmes et de leur place dans la société canadienne', *Cahiers de droit* 36: 27–59.

Bottomley, Ann, ed. 1996. *Feminist Perspectives on the Foundational Subjects of Law*. London: Cavendish.

Bouchard, Josée. 1995. 'L'indemnisation des victimes de harcèlement sexuel au Québec', *Cahiers de droit* 36: 125–60.

——, Susan B. Boyd, and Elizabeth Sheehy. 1999. 'Canadian Feminist Literature on Law: An Annotated Bibliography', *Canadian Journal of Women and the Law* 11, 1–2.

Bourdieu, Pierre. 1987. 'The Force of Law: Toward a Sociology of the Juridical Field', trans. R. Terdiman, *Hastings Law Journal* 38: 805–53.

—— and Loïc J.D. Wacquant. 1992. *An Invitation to Reflexive Sociology*. Chicago: University of Chicago Press.

Bourque, Dawn M. 1995. '"Reconstructing" the Patriarchal Nuclear Family: Recent Developments in Child Custody and Access in Canada', *Canadian Journal of Law and Society* 10, 1: 1–24.

Boyd, Susan B. 1989a. 'Child Custody, Ideologies and Employment', *Canadian Journal of Women and the Law* 3, 1: 111–33.

——. 1989b. 'From Gender-Specificity to Gender-Neutrality? Ideologies in Canadian Child Custody Law', in Carol Smart and Selma Sevenhuijsen, eds, *Child Custody and the Politics of Gender*. London: Routledge, 126–57.

——. 1990. 'Potentialities and Perils of the Primary Caregiver Presumption', *Canadian Family Law Quarterly* 7, 1: 1–30.

——. 1991. 'Some Postmodern Challenges to Feminist Analyses of Law, Family and State: Ideology and Discourse in Child Custody Law', *Canadian Journal of Family Law* 10: 79–113.

——. 1992. 'What is a "Normal" Family?, C v. C (A Minor) (Custody: Appeal)', *Modern Law Review* 55: 269–78.

——. 1995. 'W(h)ither Feminism? The Department of Justice Public Discussion Paper on Custody and Access', *Canadian Journal of Family Law* 12, 2: 331–65.

——. 1996a. 'Best Friends or Spouses? Privatization and the Recognition of Lesbian Relationships in *M. v. H.*', *Revue Canadienne de Droit Familial* 13: 321–41.

——. 1996b. 'Is There an Ideology of Motherhood in (Post)Modern Child Custody Law?', *Social and Legal Studies* 5, 4: 495–521.

——, ed. 1997. *Challenging the Public/Private Divide: Feminism, Law and Public Policy*. Toronto: University of Toronto Press.

—— and Elizabeth A. Sheehy. 1986. 'Feminist Perspectives on Law: Canadian Theory and Practice', *Canadian Journal of Women and the Law* 2, 1: 1–52.

Boyle, Christine. 1994a. 'Reform Initiatives in Canada', draft copy of a paper to be published in the *South African Law Journal*, circulated in Fall 1994 seminar, 'International Perspectives on Women and the Law', co-sponsored by Simon Fraser University School of Criminology and University of British Columbia

Law School.

————. 1994b. 'The Judicial Construction of Sexual Assault Offences', in Mohr and Roberts (1994).

———— et al. 1985. *A Feminist Review of Criminal Law*. Ottawa: Minister of Supply and Services Canada.

Brandt, Paul. 1963. *Sexual Life in Ancient Greece*. New York: Barnes & Noble.

Brock, Deborah. 1984. 'Feminist Perspectives on Prostitution: Addressing the Canadian Dilemma', MA thesis, Carleton University.

————. 1987. 'The Sex Debates: Toward a Feminist Epistemology and Ontology', *Atlantis* 13, 1: 98–110.

————. 1990. 'Regulating Prostitution/Policing Prostitutes: Some Canadian Examples, 1970–1989'; Department of Education (OISE), University of Toronto.

————. 1998. *Making Work, Making Trouble: Prostitution as a Social Problem*. Toronto: University of Toronto Press.

Brockman, Joan. 1992. 'Bias in the Legal Profession: Perceptions and Experiences', *Alberta Law Review* 30: 747–808.

Brodsky, Gwen, and Shelagh Day. 1989. *Canadian Charter Equality Rights for Women: One Step Forward or Two Steps Back?* Ottawa: Canadian Advisory Council on the Status of Women.

Brophy, Julia, and Carol Smart, eds. 1985. *Women-in-Law*. London: Routledge & Kegan Paul.

Brown, Wendy. 1995. *States of Injury: Power and Freedom in Late Modernity*. Princeton, NJ: Princeton University Press.

Brownmiller, Susan. 1975. *Against Our Will: Men, Women and Rape*. New York: Simon and Schuster.

Budgen, Mark. 1984. 'Angry Vancouver mayor calls pornography committee a sham', *Globe and Mail*, 10 Jan., 5.

Bunting, Annie. 1992. 'Feminism, Foucault, and Law as Power/Knowledge', *Alberta Law Review* 30: 829–42.

Busby, Karen. n.d. 'LEAF and Pornography: Litigating on Equality and Sexual Representations', unpublished paper.

Butler, Judith. 1990. *Gender Trouble: Feminism and the Subversion of Identity*. New York: Routledge.

————. 1993a. 'Imitation and Gender Subordination', in H. Abelove, M.A. Barale, and D. Halperin, eds, *Lesbian and Gay Studies Reader*. New York: Routledge, 307–20.

————. 1993b. *Bodies That Matter: On the Discursive Limits of Sex*. New York: Routledge.

————. 1994. 'Gender as Performance: An Interview with Judith Butler', *Radical Philosophy* 67: 32–9.

Cain, Maureen. 1994. 'The Symbol Traders', in Cain and Christine B. Harrington, eds, *Lawyers in a Postmodern World: Translation and Transgression*. New York: New York University Press.

Cameron, Deborah, and Elizabeth Frazer. 1987. *The Lust to Kill*. Oxford: Polity

Press.

Canadian Broadcasting Corporation (CBC). 1995. 'The Trials of London'. Four CBC radio documentaries on the program, *Ideas*.

Caputo, John D. 1993. *Against Ethics: Contributions to a Poetics of Obligation with Constant Reference to Deconstruction*. Bloomington: Indiana University Press.

Carlyle, Nathalie. 1995. *Canadian Directorship Practices: Compensation of Board of Directors*. Ottawa: Conference Board of Canada.

Cassin, A.M. 1993. 'Equitable and Fair: Widening the Circle', in Maslove (1993: 104–34).

Cheffins, B.R. 1997. *Company Law: Theory, Structure and Operation*. Oxford: Oxford University Press.

Chesler, Phyllis. 1973. *Women and Madness*. New York: Doubleday.

Chunn, Dorothy E. 1999. 'Feminism, Law and "the Family": Assessing the Reform Legacy', in E. Comack, ed., *Locating Law: Essays on the Race/Class/Gender Connections*. Halifax: Fernwood.

———— and Shelley A.M. Gavigan. 1988. 'Social Control: Analytical Tool or Analytical Quagmire', *Contemporary Crises* 12: 107–24.

———— and R. Menzies. 1996. 'Canadian Criminology and the Woman Question', in N.H. Rafter and F. Heidensohn, eds, *International Feminist Perspectives in Criminology*. Milton Keynes: Open University Press, 139–66.

Cipriani, Lucille. 1995. 'La justice matrimoniale à l'heure du féminisme: analyse critique de la jurisprudence québécoise sur la prestation compensatoire, 1983–1991', *Cahiers de droit* 36: 208–43.

Clark, Lorenne, and Debra Lewis. 1977. *Rape: The Price of Coercive Sexuality*. Toronto: Women's Press.

———— and ————. 1991. 'Women, Property and Rape', in Jane Banfield, ed., *Readings in Law and Society*, 4th edn. North York, Ont.: Captus Press, 291–7.

Cole, Susan. 1987. 'Sexual Politics: Contradictions and Explosions', in Bell (1987).

Collins, Patricia Hill. 1990. *Black Feminist Thought: Knowledge, Consciousness, and the Politics of Empowerment*. London: HarperCollins Academic.

Comaroff, J. 1994. 'Foreword', in Lazarus-Black and Hirch (1994: ix–xiii).

Concerned Residents of the West End. 1982. 'A Submission to the House of Commons Standing Committee on Justice and Legal Affairs: Respecting Soliciting for the Purpose of Prostitution', Issue 83 (Ottawa, May).

Connell, R.W. 1995. *Masculinities*. Berkeley: University of California Press.

Coombe, Rosemary. 1989. 'Room for Manoeuver: Toward a Theory of Practice in Critical Legal Studies', *Law and Social Inquiry* 14: 69–121.

Cornell, Drucilla. 1991. *Beyond Accommodation: Ethical Feminism, Deconstruction, and the Law*. New York: Routledge.

————. 1993. *Transformations: Recollective Imagination and Sexual Difference*. New York: Routledge.

Corrigan, Philip. 1987. 'On Moral Regulation: Some Preliminary Remarks', *Sociological Review* 29, 2: 313–37.

Cossman, Brenda. 1990. 'Dancing in the Dark: A Review of Gwen Brodsky and

Shelagh Day's *Canadian Charter Equality Rights for Women: One Step Forward or Two Steps Back?'*, *Windsor Yearbook of Access to Justice* 10: 223–36.

———. 1997. 'Family Inside/Out', in Meg Luxton, ed., *Feminism and Families: Critical Policies and Changing Practices*. Halifax: Fernwood.

———, Shannon Bell, Lise Gotell, and Becki Ross. 1997. *Bad Attitude/s on Trial: Pornography, Feminism and the Butler Decision*. Toronto: University of Toronto Press.

——— and Carol Rogerson. 1997. 'Case Study in the Provision of Legal Aid: Family Law', in *A Blueprint for Publicly Funded Legal Services: Report of the Ontario Legal Aid Review*, vol. 3. Toronto: Queen's Printer.

Couture, Joseph. 1994. 'The Story keeps changing', *Xtra* no. 260, 14 Oct.

———. 1995a. 'London kiddie porn cops overzealous?', *Xtra* no. 276, 26 May.

———. 1995b. 'London's Trials', *The Guide: Gay Entertainment, Politics and Sex* (July).

Crenshaw, Kimberle. 1989. 'Demarginalizing the Intersection of Race and Sex: A Black Feminist Critique of Antidiscrimination Doctrine, Feminist Theory and Antiracist Politics', *University of Chicago Legal Forum*: 139–67.

———. 1991. 'Mapping the Margins: Intersectionality, Identity Politics, and Violence Against Women of Colour', *Stanford Law Review* 43: 1241–99.

———. 1992. 'Whose Story Is It, Anyway: Feminist and Antiracist Appropriations of Anita Hill', in Toni Morrison, ed., *Race-ing Justice, En-gendering Power: Essays on Anita Hill, Clarence Thomas, and the Construction of Social Reality*. New York: Pantheon Books, 402–40.

———. 1994. 'Mapping the Margins: Intersectionality, Identity Politics, and Violence Against Women of Color', in Martha Albertson Fineman and Roxanne Mykitiuk, eds, *The Public Nature of Private Violence: The Discovery of Domestic Abuse*. New York: Routledge, 93–118.

Criminal Law Amendment Act, Statutes of Canada, 21 Elizabeth II (Ottawa, 19 May 1972).

Culhane, Dara. 1995. 'Justice and Healing: Aboriginal Peoples in Canada', Journal of Human Justice 6, 2: 140–60.

Currie, Dawn H. 1992. 'Feminist Encounters with Postmodernism: Exploring the Impasse of Debates on Patriarchy and Law', *Canadian Journal of Women and Law* 5: 63–86.

——— and Marlee Kline. 1991. 'Challenging Privilege: Women, Knowledge, and Feminist Struggles', *Journal of Human Justice* 2, 2: 1–36.

Czyscon, Janice. 1995. 'On Being a Family', in Arnup (1995).

Davidoff, L., and C. Hall. 1987. *Family Fortunes: Men and Women of the English Middle Class, 1780–1850*. London: Hutchinson.

Davis, Angela. 1981. *Women, Race and Class*. New York: Random House.

Debates, House of Commons, Canada, Fourth Session, Twenty-Eighth Parliament, vol. 2 (Ottawa, 20 Mar.–5 May 1972).

Delacoste, Frederique, and Priscilla Alexander, eds. 1987. *Sex Work: Writings by Women in the Sex Industry*. Pittsburgh: Cleis Press.

Delorey, Anne Marie. 1989–90. 'Rape Trauma Syndrome: An Evidentiary Tool', *Canadian Journal of Women and the Law* 3, 2: 531–51.

Derrida, Jacques. 1975. *Of Grammatology*, trans. G. Spivak. Baltimore: Johns Hopkins University Press.

———. 1992. 'Force of Law: The "Mystical Foundation of Authority"', in Drucilla Cornell, Michel Rosenfeld, and David Gray Carlson, eds, *Deconstruction and the Possibility of Justice*. New York: Routledge.

De Sève, Micheline. 1992. 'The Perspectives of Québec Feminists', in Constance Backhouse and David H. Flaherty, eds, *Challenging Times: The Women's Movement in Canada and the United States*. Montreal and Kingston: McGill-Queen's University Press.

Des Rosiers, Nathalie. 1995. 'La responsabilité de la mère pour le préjudice causé par son enfant', *Cahiers de droit* 36: 61–98.

Dhavernas, Odile. 1978. *Droits des femmes, pouvoirs des hommes*. Paris: Éditions du Seuil.

DiMatteo, Enzo. 1996. 'The Fall of Burly Wilson', *Now Magazine* 14–20 Nov.

Dodds Streeton, J., and R. Langford. 1994. *Aspects of Real Property and Insolvency Law*. Adelaide Law Review Research Paper.

Downtown Eastside Residents Association. 1987. *Expo '86: Its Legacy to Vancouver's Downtown Eastside*. Vancouver: DERA.

Drakich, Janice. 1989. 'In Search of the Better Parent: The Social Construction of Ideologies of Fatherhood', *Canadian Journal of Women and the Law* 3, 1: 69–87.

Duffy, A., N. Mandell, and N. Pupo. 1989. *Few Choices: Women, Work and Family*. Toronto: Garamond Press.

Dumont, Hélène, ed. 1993. *Femmes et Droit: 50 ans de vie commune . . . et tout un avenir*. Montréal: Thémis.

Dworkin, Andrea. 1987. *Intercourse*. New York: Free Press.

Eansor, D.M., and C. Wydrzynski. 1993. '"Troubled Waters": Deductibility of Business Expenses Under the Income Tax Act, Child Care Expenses and Symes', *Canadian Journal of Family Law* 11: 249–85.

Easterbrook, F.H., and D.R. Fischel. 1991. *The Economic Structure of Corporate Law*. Cambridge, Mass.: Harvard University Press.

Eaton, Mary. 1990. 'Lesbians and the Law', in Sharon Stone, ed., *Lesbians in Canada*. Toronto: Between the Lines.

Edwards, Susan. 1981. *Female Sexuality and the Law*. Oxford: Martin Robertson.

Eichler, Margrit. 1988. *Canadian Families Today*, 2nd edn. Toronto: Gage Educational Publishing.

Elliot, Robin. 1992. University of British Columbia Faculty of Law, Selection of Clinic Themes (motion submitted by Chair of Clinic Review Implementation Committee), cited in Taylor (1996: 192).

Elliot, Susan J., and Leslie T. Foster. 1995. 'Mind-Body-Place: A Geography of Aboriginal Health in British Columbia', in Peter H. Stephenson, ed., *A Persistent Spirit: Towards Understanding Aboriginal Health in British Columbia*.

Victoria, BC: Department of Geography, University of Victoria, 95–128.

Elshtain, J.B. 1981. *Public Man, Private Woman: Women in Social and Political Thought*. Princeton, NJ: Princeton University Press.

Elson, D. 1994. 'Micro, Meso, Macro: Gender and Economic Analysis in the Context of Policy Reform', in I. Bakker, ed., *The Strategic Silence*. London: North-South Institute.

England, P. 1993. 'The Separative Self: Androcentric Bias in Neoclassical Assumptions', in Ferber and Nelson (1993).

Estroff, S. 1981. *Making it Crazy: An Ethnography of Psychiatric Clients in an American Community*. Berkeley: University of California Press.

Faith, Karlene. 1996. 'Aboriginal Women's Healing Lodge: Challenge to Penal Correctionalism?', in Jackson and Banks (1996: 174–212).

Fallick, Arthur L., ed. 1987. *A Place To Call Home: A Conference on Homelessness in British Columbia, May 15–16*. Vancouver: University of British Columbia.

Fehlberg, B. 1994. 'The Husband, the Bank, the Wife and her Signature', *Modern Law Review* 57: 467–75.

———. 1997. 'Women in Family Businesses: English and Australian Experiences', paper presented to the Corporate Law Teachers' Conference, Jan.

Ferber, M.A., and J.A. Nelson, eds. 1993. *Beyond Economic Man: Feminist Theory and Economics*. Chicago: University of Chicago Press.

Ferguson, E. 1984. *The Feminist Case Against Bureaucracy*. Philadelphia: Temple University Press.

Fine, Sean. 1995a. 'Court widens rights of custodial parents', *Globe and Mail*, 5 Apr., A1.

———. 1995b. 'Abella sees judges as partners in family lawmaking', *Globe and Mail*, 7 Apr., A5.

Fineman, Martha A. 1992. 'The Neutered Mother', *University of Miami Law Review* 46: 653–69.

———. 1995. *The Neutered Mother, the Sexual Family and Other Twentieth Century Tragedies*. New York: Routledge.

Fiske, Jo-Anne. 1994. 'The Supreme Law and the Grand Law: Changing Significance of Customary Law for Aboriginal Women of British Columbia', *B.C. Studies* 105 & 106 (Spring/Summer): 183–99.

———. 1995. 'Political Status of Native Indian Women: Contradictory Implications of Canadian State Policy', *American Indian Culture and Research Journal* 19, 2: 1–30.

Fleming, Louise. 1995. 'The "Second Mother"', in Arnup (1995).

Folbre, N., and H. Hartmann. 1988. 'The Rhetoric of Self-Interest: Ideology and Gender in Economic Theory', in A. Klamer et al., *The Consequences of Economic Rhetoric*. Cambridge: Cambridge University Press.

Foucault, Michel. 1977. *Discipline and Punish: The Birth of the Prison*. New York: Pantheon Books.

———. 1978. *The History of Sexuality, Volume 1: An Introduction*, trans. R. Hurley. New York: Pantheon Books.

————. 1988. 'Sexual Morality and the Law', transcript of the television program *Dialogues* broadcast by France-Culture, 4 Apr. 1978, in Lawrence D. Kritzman, ed., *Politics, Philosophy, Culture: Interviews and Other Writings 1977–1984*. New York: Routledge.

————. 1989. *Foucault Live: Interviews, 1961–1984*. New York: Semiotexte.

Freedman J. 1994. 'Small Businesses and the Corporate Form: Burden or Privilege?', *Modern Law Review* 57, 4: 555–84.

Frideres, James. 1994. *Native People in Canada: Contemporary Conflicts*. Toronto: Prentice-Hall.

'From the Floor', in Bell (1987).

Frug, Mary Joe. 1992. *Postmodern Legal Feminism*. New York: Routledge.

Fudge, Judy. 1989. 'The Effects of Entrenching a Bill of Rights upon Political Discourse: Feminist Demands and Sexual Violence in Canada', *International Journal of the Sociology of Law* 17: 445–63.

————. 1991. 'What Do We Mean by Law and Social Transformation?', *Canadian Journal of Law and Society* 5: 47–69.

———— and Harry Glasbeek. 1992. 'The Politics of Rights: A Politics with Little Class', *Social and Legal Studies* 1: 45–70.

Furstenberg, Frank, and Andrew J. Cherlin. 1991. *Divided Families: What Happens to Children When Parents Part*. Cambridge, Mass.: Harvard University Press.

Gabaldon, T.A. 1992. 'The Lemonade Stand: Feminist and Other Reflections on the Limited Liability of Corporate Shareholders', *Vanderbilt Law Review* 45, 6: 1387–1456.

Gauntlet. 1994. Special issue in defence of prostitution, vol. 7.

Gaventa, J. 1980. *Power and Powerlessness: Quiescence and Rebellion in an Appalachian Valley*. Oxford: Clarendon Press.

Gavigan, Shelley A.M. 1984. 'The Criminal Sanction as it Relates to Reproduction: The Genesis of the Statutory Prohibition of Abortion', *Journal of Legal History* 5: 20–43.

————. 1986. 'Women, Law and Patriarchal Relations: Perspectives within the Sociology of Law', in N. Boyd, ed., *The Social Dimensions of Law*. Scarborough, Ont.: Prentice-Hall Canada.

————. 1988. 'Law, Gender and Ideology', in Anne Bayefsky, ed., *Legal Theory Meets Legal Practice*. Edmonton: Academic.

————. 1989–90. 'Petit Treason in Eighteenth Century England: Women's Inequality Before the Law', *Canadian Journal of Women and the Law* 3: 335–74.

————. 1992. 'Beyond Morgentaler', in Janine Brodie, Shelley A.M. Gavigan, and Jane Jenson, eds, *The Politics of Abortion*. Toronto: Oxford University Press.

————. 1993. 'Paradise Lost, Paradox Revisited: The Implications of Feminist, Lesbian and Gay Engagement to Law', *Osgoode Hall Law Journal* 31: 589–624.

————. 1995a. 'A Parent(ly) Knot: Can Heather Have Two Mommies?', in Didi Herman and Carl Stychin, eds, *Legal Inversions: Lesbians, Gay Men and the Politics of Law*. Philadelphia: Temple University Press.

———. 1995b. 'Yikes! It's Dykes with Tikes: The Legal Challenges of Lesbians Who Parent', paper presented at the annual meeting of the Canadian Sociology and Anthropology Association, Brock University, June.

———. 1997. 'Feminism, Family Law and Familial Ideology: A Perilous Ménage à Trois', in Meg Luxton, ed., *Feminism and Families: Critical Policies and Changing Practices*. Halifax: Fernwood.

Gavison, R. 1992. 'Feminism and the Public/Private Distinction', *Stanford Law Review* 45: 1–45.

Gény, François. 1919. *Méthode d'interprétation et sources en droit privé positif: essai critique*, 2nd edn. Paris: Pichon & Durand-Auzias.

Giddens, Anthony. 1979. *Central Problems in Social Theory: Action, Structure and Contradiction in Social Analysis*. Berkeley: University of California Press.

Girdner, Linda K. 1986. 'Child Custody Determination: Ideological Dimensions of a Social Problem', in Ed Seidman and Julian Rappaport, eds, *Redefining Social Problems*. New York: Plenum Press, 165–83.

Glasbeek, Harry. 1989. 'Some Strategies for an Unlikely Task: The Progressive Use of Law', *Ottawa Law Review* 21: 387–418.

Globe and Mail. 1997. 'New York fixes its broken windows', 1 Feb., D4.

Goode, Erich, and Nachman Ben-Yehuda. 1994. *Moral Panics: The Social Construction of Deviance*. Cambridge: Basil Blackwell.

Goose, Richard, James Youngblood Henderson, and Roger Carter, eds. 1994. *Continuing Poundmaker and Riel's Quest: Presentations Made at a Conference on Aboriginal Peoples and Justice*. Saskatoon: Purich Publishers.

Gordon, Linda. 1976. *Woman's Body, Woman's Right: Birth Control in America*. New York: Penguin Books.

———. 1988. *Heroes of Their Own Lives: The Politics and History of Family Violence*. New York: Penguin Books.

———. 1991. 'On "Difference"', *Genders* no. 10: 91–111.

Gramsci, A. 1971. *Selections from the Prison Notebooks*, ed. Q. Hoare and G. Smith. London: International Publishers.

Grbich, J. 1987. 'The Position of Women in Family Dealing: the Australian Case', *International Journal of the Sociology of Law* 15: 309–32.

———. 1990-1. 'The Tax Unit Debate Revisited: Notes on the Critical Resources of a Feminist Revenue Law Scholarship', *Canadian Journal of Women and the Law* 4: 512–38.

Green, Jim, et al. 1989. *Downtown Eastside Housing and Residents Survey, 1987–88*. Vancouver: DERA/Canadian Mortgage and Housing Corporation.

Green, Joyce. 1985. 'Sexual Equality and Indian Government: An Analysis of Bill C-31 Amendments to the Indian Act', *Native Studies Review* 1, 2: 81–95.

Greenspan, Edward, and Marc Rosenberg, annotators. 1997. *Martin's Annual Criminal Code*. Aurora, Ont.: Canada Law Book.

Greenwood, Victoria, and Jock Young. 1976. *Abortion in Demand*. London: Pluto.

Hall, E.T. 1961. *The Silent Language*. New York: Greenwood Press.

Hall, K.H. 1995. 'Starting from Silence: The Future of Feminist Analysis of

Corporate Law', *Corporate and Business Law Journal* 7, 2: 149–80.

Hall, Stuart, et al. 1978. *Policing the Crisis: Mugging, the State, and Law and Order*. London: Macmillan.

HALO (Homophile Association of London, Ontario). 1996. 'On Guard: A Critique of Project Guardian'.

Hamilton, A.C., and C.M. Sinclair. 1991. 'Chapter 13: Aboriginal Women', in *Report of the Aboriginal Justice Inquiry of Manitoba*. Winnipeg: Province of Manitoba, 475–506.

Hannon, Gerald. 1995. 'The Kiddie-Porn Ring That Wasn't', *Globe and Mail*, 11 Mar.

———. 1997. 'Metro Sex Academy', *Now Magazine*, 27 Mar.–2 Apr., 18–20.

Harding, Jim. 1994. 'The Urban Social Crisis', in Goose, Henderson, and Carter (1994: 363–83).

Hay, Douglas. 1975. 'Property, Authority and Criminal Law', in Hay et al. eds, *Albion's Fatal Tree: Crime and Society in Eighteenth-Century England*. London: Pantheon.

Health and Welfare Canada. 1987. *National Strategy on Child Care*. Ottawa.

Henry, F., C. Tator, W. Mattis, and T. Rees. 1995. *The Color of Democracy: Racism in Canadian Society*. Toronto: Harcourt Brace.

Herbert, John. 1993. 'Child porn bust in London may be largest in Ontario', *London Free Press*, 11 Nov.

———. 1994. 'London constable demoted for sexual misconduct', *London Free Press*, 2 July.

Herman, Didi. 1994. *Rights of Passage*. Toronto: University of Toronto Press.

Herzlich, C., and J. Pierret. 1984. *Illness and Self in Society*, trans. E. Forster. Baltimore: Johns Hopkins University Press.

Highcrest, Alexandra. 1997. *At Home on the Stroll: My Twenty Years as a Prostitute in Canada*. Toronto: Alfred A. Knopf Canada.

Hodgson, Ellen. 1992. 'Equal Pay for Work of Equal Value in Ontario and Great Britain: A Comparison', *Alberta Law Review* 30: 926–87.

Hoegg, Lois. 1983. 'Summary of Case Law on Soliciting', *National Association of Women and the Law Newsletter* 5, 2: 39–42.

hooks, bell. 1981. *Ain't I a Woman: Black Women and Feminism*. Boston: South End Books.

———. 1984. *Feminist Theory: From Margin to Center*. Boston: South End Books.

Horwitz, Morton. 1992. *The Transformation of American Law, 1870–1960: The Crisis of Legal Orthodoxy*. New York: Oxford University Press.

Hovius, Berend. 1993. 'The Changing Role of the Access Parent', *Canadian Family Law Quarterly* 10, 1: 123–85.

Hunt, Alan. 1993. *Explorations in Law and Society: Towards a Constitutive Theory of Law*. New York: Routledge.

Ingstad, B., and S.R. Whyte, eds. 1995. *Disability and Culture*. Berkeley: University of California Press.

Ireland, P., I. Grigg-Spall, and D. Kelly. 1987. 'The Conceptual Foundations of

Modern Company Law', in P. Fitzpatrick and A. Hunt, eds, *Critical Legal Studies*. Oxford: Basil Blackwell.

Iyer, N. 1993–4. 'Categorical Denials: Equality Rights and the Shaping of Social Identity', *Queen's Law Journal* 19: 179–207.

Jackson, Margaret. 1994. 'Aboriginal Women and Self-Government', in John Hylton, ed., *Aboriginal Self-Government in Canada: Current Trends and Issues*. Saskatoon: Puritch Publishing, 180–98.

——— and N. Kathleen Sam Banks, eds. 1996. *Ten Years Later: The Charter and Equality for Women: A Symposium Assessing the Impact of the Equality Provisions on Women in Canada*. Burnaby, BC: Simon Fraser University.

Jaggar, Alison. 1983. *Feminist Politics and Human Nature*. Totowa, NJ: Rowman & Littlefield.

Jenness, Valerie. 1993. *Making It Work: The Prostitutes' Rights Movement in Perspective*. Vancouver: Aldine De Gruyter.

Jhappan, Radha. 1996. 'Post-Modern Race and Gender Essentialism or a Post-Mortem of Scholarship', *Studies in Political Economy* 51: 15–63.

———. 1998. 'The Equality Pit or the Rehabilitation of Justice', *Canadian Journal of Women and the Law* 10, 1: 60–107.

Johnson, Holly, and Karen Rodgers. 1993. 'A Statistical Overview of Women and Crime in Canada', in Adelberg and Currie (1993: 95–115).

Keller, C. 1986. *From a Broken Web: Separation, Sexism, and Self*. Boston: Beacon Press.

Kennedy, Duncan. 1997. *A Critique of Adjudication: {fin de siècle}*. Cambridge, Mass.: Harvard University Press.

King, Valerie. 1994. 'Variation in the Consequences of Non-Resident Father Involvement for Child's Well-being', *Journal of Marriage and the Family* 56: 963–72.

Kline, Marlee. 1989. 'Race, Racism, and Feminist Legal Theory', *Harvard Women's Law Journal* 12: 115–50.

———. 1993. 'Complicating the Ideology of Motherhood: Child Welfare Law and First Nation Women', *Queen's Law Journal* 18: 306–42.

Kobly, Peggy. 1992. 'Rape Shield Legislation: Relevance, Prejudice and Judicial Discretion', *Alberta Law Review* 30: 988–1017.

Krosenbrink-Gelissen, Lilianne E. 1991. *Sexual Equality as an Aboriginal Right: The Native Women's Association of Canada and the Constitutional Process on Aboriginal Matters, 1982–1987*. Saarbrucken, Germany: Verlag Breitenbach Publishers.

Kruk, Edward. 1993. *Divorce and Disengagement: Patterns of Fatherhood Within and Beyond Marriage*. Halifax: Fernwood.

———. 1997. 'Recognizing the Needs of Children', *Globe and Mail*, 14 May, A29.

Lacombe, Dany. 1988. *Ideology and Public Policy: The Case Against Pornography*. Toronto: University of Toronto Press.

———. 1994. *Blue Politics: Pornography and the Law in the Age of Feminism*. Toronto: University of Toronto Press.

——. 1998. 'Does Law Outlaw Women?', in K.D. Bonnycastle and G.S. Rigakos, eds, *Unsettling Truths: Battered Women, Policy, Politics, and Contemporary Research in Canada*. Vancouver: Collective Press.

Laframboise, Donna. 1997. 'Oh Dad, poor Dad', *Globe and Mail*, 12 Apr., D1.

Lahey, Kathleen. 1985. '. . . until women themselves have told us all there is to tell . . .', *Osgoode Hall Law Journal* 23: 519–41

—— and S. Salter. 1985. 'Corporate Law in Legal Theory and Legal Scholarship: From Classicism to Feminism', *Osgoode Hall Law Journal* 23: 543–72.

Langevin, Louise. 1995a. 'Avant-propos', *Cahiers de droit* 36: 5–8.

——. 1995b. 'Responsabilité extracontractuelle et harcèlement sexuel: le modèle d'évaluation peut-il être neutre?', *Cahiers de droit* 36: 99–123.

LaPrairie, Carol. 1993. 'Aboriginal Women and Crime in Canada: Identifying the Issues', in Adelberg and Currie (1993: 235–47).

Lazarus-Black, M., and S.F. Hirch, eds. 1994. *Contested States: Law, Hegemony and Resistance*. New York: Routledge.

LEAF (Women's Legal Education and Action Fund). 1996. *Equality and the Charter: Ten Years of Feminist Advocacy Before the Supreme Court of Canada*. Toronto.

Lippel, Katherine, and Claudyne Bienvenu. 1995. 'Les dommages fantômes: l'indemnisation des victimes de lésions professionnelles pour l'incapacité d'effectuer le travail domestique', *Cahiers de droit* 36: 161–208.

Loi modifiant le Code civil du Québec et d'autres dispositions législatives afin de favoriser l'égalité économique des époux, L.Q. 1989, c. 55, modified by L.Q. 1990, c. 5.

London Family Court Clinic. 1994. Victim Impact Statement, D.K., 7 Feb., London, Ont.

Lorde, A. 1984. *Sister/Outsider*. Trumansburg, NY: Crossing Press.

Los, Maria. 1990. 'Feminism and Rape Law Reform', in L. Gelsthorpe and A. Morris, eds, *Feminist Perspectives in Criminology*. Philadelphia: Open University Press, 160–72.

Lubiano, Wahneema. 1992. 'Black Ladies, Welfare Queens, and State Minstrels: Ideological War By Narrative Means', in Toni Morrison, ed., *Race-ing Justice, En-gendering Power: Essays On Anita Hill, Clarence Thomas, and the Construction of Social Reality*. New York: Pantheon Books, 323–61.

McCaffery, E.J. 1993. 'Taxation and the Family: A Fresh Look at Behavioral Gender Biases in the Code', *U.C.L.A. Law Review* 40: 983–1060.

McCluskey, M. 1996. 'Economic Illusions in Social Welfare Cuts: Disguising Politics and Values as Efficiency Principles', paper presented to Feminist and Legal Theory Workshop, Columbia Law School.

MacDonald, Lois G. 1992. 'The Violation of Women—Towards a Clearer Consciousness', *Alberta Law Review* 30: 900–25.

McIntyre, Sheila. 1994. 'Redefining Reformism: The Consultations That Shaped Bill C–49', in Mohr and J. Roberts (1994: 293–314).

—— and Mary O'Brien. 1987. 'Patriarchal Hegemony and Legal Education',

Canadian Journal of Women and the Law 2, 1: 69–94.

McIvor, Sharon D. 1996. 'Self-Government and Aboriginal Women', in Jackson and Banks (1996: 77–90).

MacKinnon, Catharine. 1979. *Sexual Harassment of Working Women: A Case of Sex Discrimination*. New Haven: Yale University Press.

———. 1982. 'Feminism, Marxism, Method, and the State: An Agenda for Theory', *Signs: Journal of Women in Culture and Society* 7: 515–43.

———. 1983a. 'Feminism, Marxism, Method, and the State: Towards a Feminist Jurisprudence', *Signs: Journal of Women in Culture and Society* 8: 635–58.

———. 1983b. 'The Male Ideology of Privacy: A Feminist Perspective on the Right to Abortion', *Radical America* 17, 4: 23–45.

———. 1985. 'Feminist Discourse, Moral Values, and the Law—A Conversation', *Buffalo Law Review* 34: 11–87.

———. 1987. *Feminism Unmodified: Discourses on Life and Law*. Cambridge, Mass.: Harvard University Press.

———. 1989. *Toward a Feminist Theory of the State*. Cambridge, Mass.: Harvard University Press.

———. 1991. 'Reflections on Sex Equality Under Law', *Yale Law Journal* 100: 1281–1328.

Macklin, A. 1992. '*Symes v. M.N.R.*: Where Sex Meets Class', *Canadian Journal of Women and the Law* 5: 498–517.

McLaren, John. 1986a. 'Chasing the Social Evil: Moral Fervour and the Evolution of Canada's Prostitution Laws, 1867–1917', *Canadian Journal of Law and Society* 1: 125–65.

———. 1986b. 'The Fraser Committee: The Politics and Process of a Special Committee', in *Regulating Sex: An Anthology of Commentaries on the Findings and Recommendations of the Badgley and Fraser Reports*. Vancouver: School of Criminology, Simon Fraser University.

McLeod, James G. 1991. 'Annotation: Carter v. Brooks', *Reports of Family Law* (3d) 30: 53–66.

Mann, P.S. 1994. *Micro-Politics: Agency in a Postfeminist Era*. Minneapolis: University of Minneapolis Press.

Marcus, Sharon. 1992. 'Fighting Bodies, Fighting Words: A Theory and Politics of Rape Prevention', in J. Butler and J. Scott, eds, *Feminists Theorize the Political*. New York: Routledge, 385–403.

Martin, Biddy. 1988. 'Feminism, Criticism and Foucault', in Irene Diamond and Lee Quinby, eds, *Feminism and Foucault*. Boston: Northeastern University Press.

Martin, Sheilah L. 1992. 'Women as Lawmakers', *Alberta Law Review* 30: 737–46.

——— and Kathleen Mahoney, eds. 1987. *Equality and Judicial Neutrality*. Toronto: Carswell.

Maslove, A.M., ed. 1993. *Fairness in Taxation: Exploring the Principles*. Toronto: University of Toronto Press in co-operation with the Fair Tax Commission of the Government of Ontario.

Mathers, Gabrielle. 1990. 'Achieving Health For All? Geography, Development and the Epp Report', MA extended essay, Department of Geography, Simon Fraser University.

Messerschmidt, James W. 1993. *Masculinities and Crime: Critique and Reconceptualization of Theory*. Lanham, Md: Rowman & Littlefield.

Miles, Angela. 1982. 'Introduction', in Miles and G. Finn, eds, *Feminism in Canada: From Pressure to Politics*. Montreal: Black Rose Books.

————. 1985. 'Feminism, Equality and Liberation', *Canadian Journal of Women and the Law* 1, 1: 42–68.

Miller, Jody. 1996. 'Crime and Oppression: Structure and Agency in the Inner City', *Critical Criminology: An International Journal* 7, 2: 123–8.

Millett, Kate. 1969. *Sexual Politics*. New York: Doubleday.

————. 1971. 'Prostitution: A Quartet for Female Voices', in Vivian Gornick and Barbara Moran, eds, *Woman in Sexist Society: Studies in Power and Powerlessness*. New York: New American Library.

Milovanovic, Dragon. 1991. 'Critical Criminology and the Challenge of Postmodernism', in B. MacLean and D. Milovanovic, eds, *New Directions in Critical Criminology*. Vancouver: Collective Press, 87–94.

Minister of Justice, 'Bill C–49, An Act to Amend the Criminal Code (prostitution)', First reading (Ottawa, 2 May 1985).

Mohammed, Juanita, and Alexandra Juhasz. 1996. 'Knowing Each Other Through AIDS Video: A Dialogue between AIDS Activist Videomakers', in George Marcus, ed., *Connected: Engagements with Media*. Chicago: University of Chicago Press, 195–220.

Mohr, Renate, and Julian Roberts. 1994. 'Sexual Assault in Canada: Recent Developments', in Mohr and Roberts (1994: 3–19).

———— and ————, eds. 1994. *Confronting Sexual Assault: A Decade of Legal and Social Change*. Toronto: University of Toronto Press.

Monture-Okanee, P. 1993. 'Reclaiming Justice: Aboriginal Women and Justice Initiatives in the 1990s', in *Royal Commission on Aboriginal Peoples: Aboriginal Peoples and the Justice System*. Ottawa: Minister of Supply and Services, 105–32.

———— and M.E. Turpel. 1992. 'Aboriginal peoples and Canadian criminal law: Rethinking justice', *University of British Columbia Law Review* (special issue): 239–77.

Moore, Elizabeth. 1991. 'Aboriginal Women in Canada', Statistics Canada, Catalogue no. 89–503E, 147–62.

Moore, S.F. 1978. 'Old Age in a Life-term Arena: Some Chagga of Kilimanjaro in 1974', in B. Myerhoff and A. Simic, eds, *Life's Career-Aging: Cultural Variations on Growing Old*. Beverly Hills, Calif.: Sage Publications, 23–76.

Mosoff, Judith. 1997. '"A Jury Dressed in Medical White and Judicial Black": Mothers With Mental Health Histories', in Boyd (1997: 227–52).

Mossman, M.J. 1986. 'Feminism and Legal Method: The Difference It Makes', *Australian Journal of Law and Society* 3: 30–52.

Munro, Karen M. 1992. 'The Inapplicability of Rights Analysis in Post-Divorce Child Custody Decision Making', *Alberta Law Review* 30: 852–99.

Nahanee, Teressa. 1994. 'Sexual Assault of Inuit Females: A Comment on "Cultural Bias"', in Mohr and Roberts (1994).

———. 1996. 'Aboriginal Women and Self-Government', in Jackson and Banks (1996: 27–38).

Neave, Marcia. 1994. 'Resolving the Dilemma of Difference: A Critique of "The Role of Private Ordering in Family Law"', *University of Toronto Law Journal* 44: 90–131.

Nedelsky, J. 1989. 'Reconceiving Autonomy: Sources, Thoughts and Possibilities', *Yale Journal of Law and Feminism* 1: 7–36.

Neely, Richard. 1984. 'The Primary Caretaker Parent Rule: Child Custody and the Dynamics of Greed', *Yale Law and Policy Review* 3: 168–86.

Nelson, Fiona. 1996. *Lesbian Motherhood: An Exploration of Canadian Lesbian Families*. Toronto: University of Toronto Press.

Nelson, J.A. 1996. *Feminism, Objectivity and Economics*. London: Routledge.

Néron, Josée. 1995. 'Foucault, l'histoire de la sexualité et la condition des femmes dans l'antiquité', *Cahiers de droit* 36: 245–91.

Nestle, Joan. 1983. 'My Mother Liked to Fuck', in Snitow, Stansell, and Thompson (1983).

———. 1987. 'Lesbians and Prostitutes: A Historical Sisterhood', in Bell (1987).

Noonan, Sheila. 1992. 'Theorizing Connection', *Alberta Law Review* 30: 719–37.

———. 1993. 'Strategies of Survival: Moving Beyond the Battered Woman Syndrome', in Adelberg and Currie (1993: 247–70).

Okin, S.M. 1987. *Justice, Gender and the Family*. New York: Basic Books.

Olsen, Frances. 1983. 'The Family and the Market: A Study of Ideology and Legal Reform', *Harvard Law Review* 96: 1497–1578.

Ortner, S. 1994. 'Theory in Anthropology since the Sixties', in N. Dirks et al., eds, *Culture/Power/History: A Reader in Contemporary Social Theory*. Princeton, NJ: Princeton University Press, 373–411.

Overall, Christine. 1994. 'Evaluating Sex Work', *Signs* 17, 4: 705–24.

Palmer, Bryan. 1990. *Descent Into Discourse: The Reification of Language and the Writing of Social History*. Philadelphia: Temple University Press.

Parent, France, and Geneviève Postolec. 1995. 'Quand Thémis rencontre Clio: les femmes et le droit en Nouvelle France', *Cahiers de droit* 36: 293–318.

Pask, E. Diane., and M.L. (Marnie) McCall. 1991. 'K.(M.M.) v. K.(U.) and the Primary Care Giver', *Reports of Family Law* 33(3d): 418–29.

Pavlich, G. 1996. *Justice Fragmented: Mediating Community Disputes under Postmodern Conditions*. New York: Routledge.

Persky, Stan. 1995. *Then We Take Berlin*. Toronto: Random House.

Pheterson, Gail, ed. 1989a. *A Vindication of the Rights of Whores*. Seattle: Seal Press.

———. 1989b. 'Not Repeating History', in Pheterson (1989a).

Phizacklea, A. 1988. 'Entrepreneurship, Ethnicity, and Gender', in S. Westwood and P. Bhachu, eds, *Enterprising Women: Ethnicity, Economy and Gender Relations*. New York: Routledge.

Plummer, Ken. 1995. *Telling Sexual Stories: Power, Change and Social Worlds*. New York: Routledge.

Poirier, Donald, and Michelle Boudreau. 1992. 'Formal versus Real Equality in Separation Agreements in New Brunswick', *Canadian Journal of Family Law* 10: 239–56.

Polan, Diane. 1982. 'Toward a Theory of Law and Patriarchy', in David Kairys, ed., *The Politics of Law*. New York: Pantheon.

Pratt, Minnie Bruce. 1991. *Rebellion: Essays 1980–1991*. Ithaca, NY: Firebrand Books.

Pulkingham, Jane. 1994. 'Private Troubles, Private Solution: Poverty Among Divorced Women and the Politics of Support Enforcement and Child Custody Determination', *Canadian Journal of Law and Society* 9, 2: 73–97.

Raheja, G., and A.G. Gold. 1994. *Listen to the Heron's Words: Reimagining Gender and Kinship in North India*. Berkeley: University of California Press.

Razack, Sherene. 1991. *Canadian Feminism and the Law: The Women's Legal Education and Action Fund and the Pursuit of Equality*. Toronto: Second Story Press.

———. 1998. *Looking White People in the Eye*. Toronto: University of Toronto Press.

Reaume, Denise. 1996. 'What's Distinctive About Feminist Analysis of Law? A Conceptual Analysis of Women's Exclusion From Law', *Legal Theory* 2: 265–99.

Report of the Committee on Homosexual Offences and Prostitution. 1963. New York.

Roberts, Nickie. 1992. *Whores in History*. London: HarperCollins.

Robson, Ruthann. 1992. *Lesbian (Out)Law: Survival Under the Rule of Law*. Ithaca, NY: Firebrand Books.

———. 1998. *Sappho Goes To Law School*. New York: Columbia University Press.

Ross, June, Donna Shelley, Linda Richardson, Jean Coutts, Marie Gordon, Elizabeth MacInnis, Doris Wilson, and Elizabeth Johnson. 1992. 'Women in the Class of 1979: Thirteen Years Later', *Alberta Law Review* 30: 843–51.

Rounthwaite, Jane, and Kathleen Wynne. 1995. 'Legal Aliens: An Alternative Family', in Arnup (1995).

Royal Commission on Aboriginal Peoples. 1993. *Aboriginal Peoples and the Justice System*. Ottawa: Minister of Supply and Services.

Royal Commission on the Status of Women in Canada. 1970. *Report*. Ottawa: Information Canada.

Royal Commission on Taxation. 1967. *Report*. Ottawa.

Rubin, Gayle. 1975. 'The Traffic in Women: Notes on the "Political Economy" of Sex', in Rayna Reiter, ed., *Toward an Anthropology of Women*. New York: Monthly Review Press.

———. 1984. 'Thinking Sex: Note for a Radical Theory of the Politics of

Sexuality', in Vance (1984).

Russell, Linda M., Wendy Dennis, and Joan Rock. 1997. 'The horrendous toll of divorce', *Globe and Mail*, 19 Apr.

Said, E. 1978. *Orientalism*. New York: Pantheon.

Scassa, Teresa. 1992. 'Violence Against Women in Law Schools', *Alberta Law Review* 30: 808–28.

Schmitz, Cristin. 1995. 'Custodial parents have right to move away, says Ont. C.A.', *The Lawyers Weekly*, 21 Apr., 1–3.

Scott, J.C. 1985. *Weapons of the Weak: Everyday Forms of Peasant Resistance*. New Haven: Yale University Press.

Scott, Valerie. 1986. 'What's Happening on the Streets?' A public forum sponsored by the Elizabeth Fry Society (Toronto, 15 Oct.).

Segal, Lynn. 1990. *Slow Motion: Changing Masculinities, Changing Men*. New Brunswick, NJ: Rutgers University Press.

Shaver, Frances. 1994. 'The Regulation of Prostitution: Avoiding the Morality Traps', *Canadian Journal of Law and Society* 9, 1: 123–45.

Silvera, M. 1989. *Silenced: Talks with working class West Indian Women about their lives as domestic workers in Canada*, 2nd edn. Toronto: Sister Vision Press.

Simpson, Jeffrey. 1996. 'How we are supposed to understand the best interests of a child', *Globe and Mail*, 7 May, A22.

Singh, Supriya. 1995. *For Love Not Money: Women, Information and the Family Business*. Melbourne: Consumer Advocacy and Financial Counselling Association of Victoria.

Smart, Carol. 1981. 'Law and the Control of Female Sexuality: The Case of the 1950s', in Bridget Hutter, ed., *Controlling Women: The Normal and the Deviant*. London: Croom Helm.

———. 1982. 'Regulating Families or Legitimating Patriarchy?', *International Journal of the Sociology of Law* 10, 2: 129–47.

———. 1984. *The Ties That Bind*. London: Routledge & Kegan Paul.

———. 1986. 'Feminism and Law: Some Problems of Analysis and Strategy', *International Journal of the Sociology of Law* 14: 109–23.

———. 1989. *Feminism and the Power of Law*. London: Routledge.

———. 1991. 'The Legal and Moral Ordering of Child Custody', *Journal of Law and Society* 18, 4: 485–500.

———. 1992. 'The Woman of Legal Discourse', *Social and Legal Studies* 1: 29–41.

———. 1995. *Law, Crime, and Sexuality: Essays in Feminism*. New York: Routledge.

——— and Bren Neale. 1997. 'Arguments Against Virtue—Must Contact Be Enforced?', *Family Law* 27: 332–6.

Smith, Dorothy. 1989. 'Feminist Reflections on Political Economy', *Studies in Political Economy* 30 (Autumn): 37–59.

———. 1990. *The Conceptual Practices of Power: A Feminist Sociology of Knowledge*. Toronto: University of Toronto Press.

Smith, Lynn, et al., eds. 1985. *Righting the Balance: Canada's New Equality Rights*. Ottawa: Canadian Advisory Council on the Status of Women.

Snider, Laureen. 1994. 'Feminism, Punishment and the Potential of Empowerment', *Canadian Journal of Law and Society* 9, 1: 75–105.

Snitow, Ann, Christine Stansell, and Sharon Thompson, eds. 1983. *Powers of Desire*. New York: Monthly Review Press.

Social Text. 1993. Special issue on the sex trade, ed. Anne McClintock, vol. 37 (Winter).

Stackhouse, John. 1997. 'Calcutta's prostitutes fight for rights', *Globe and Mail*, 13 Jan., A12.

'Statement on Prostitution and Feminism', in Pheterson (1989a).

Strange, Carolyn. 1995. *Toronto's Girl Problem: The Perils and Pleasures of the City, 1880–1930*. Toronto: University of Toronto Press.

Statistics Canada. 1991a. Population by Aboriginal Origin, Showing Single and Multiple Responses, Indian Registration and Indian Band Membership, for Canada, Provinces and Territories and Census Subdivision, 1991 Census—20% Sample Data, Aboriginal Data. Catalogue no. 94–326, Table 1.

———. 1991b. Population by Selected Aboriginal Origin, On and Off Indian Reserves and Settlements for Canada, Provinces and Territories, 1991—20% Sample Data. Catalogue no. 94–327, Table 4.

———. 1995. *Women in Canada: A Statistical Report*, 3rd edn. Catalogue no. 89–503E. Ottawa.

———. 1996. *Divorces*, 1994. Catalogue no. 84–213–XMB. Ottawa.

Status of Women in Canada. 1986. *Report of the Task Force on Child Care*. Ottawa.

Steele, D.A. 1991. 'The Deductibility of Childcare Expenses Re-examined: Symes v. R.', *Canadian Family Law Quarterly* 7: 315–41.

Stoddart, Jennifer. 1995. 'Des lois et des droits: Considérations à propos d'un cheminement distinct', *Cahiers de droit* 36: 9–26.

Stone, D. 1984. *The Disabled State*. Philadelphia: Temple University Press.

Stychin, Carl F. 1997. 'Queer Nations: Nationalism, sexuality and the discourse of rights in Québec', *Feminist Legal Studies* 3.

Sugar, Fran, and Lana Fox. 1990. *Survey of Federally Sentenced Aboriginal Women in the Community*. Ottawa: Native Women's Association of Canada.

Supreme Court of Canada, In the Matter of the Constitutional Questions Act, Being Chapter C–180, C.C.S.M. (Ottawa, 31 May 1990).

Taylor, Barbara. 1981. 'Female Vice and Feminist Virtue', *New Statesman* 23: 17–18.

Taylor, Renee. 1996. 'All My Relationships', *New Mexico Law Review* 26, 2: 191–200.

Terdiman, R. 1985. *Discourse/Counter-Discourse: The Theory and Practice of Symbolic Resistance in Nineteenth Century France*. Ithaca, NY: Cornell University Press.

Thane, Pat. 1978. 'Women and the Poor Law in Victorian and Edwardian England', *History Workshop Journal* 6: 29–51.

Thompson, E.P. 1975. *Whigs and Hunters: The Origin of the Black Act.* Harmondsworth: Penguin.

Tolmie, J. 1992. 'Corporate Social Responsibility', *University of New South Wales Law Journal* 15, 1: 268–96.

Toronto Star. 1992. Top court endorses war against pimps', 22 May, A15.

Trainor, Catherine, Josee Normand,and Lisa Verdon. 1991. 'Women and the Criminal Justice System', Statistics Canada Catalogue no. 89–503E, 101–16.

Trebilcock, M.J. 1991. 'Economic Analysis of Law', in R.F. Devlin, ed., *Canadian Perspectives on Legal Theory.* Toronto: Edmond Montgomery.

Tremeerar's Criminal Annotations, 1971–1982. Toronto, 1982.

Turpel, Mary Ellen. 1991a. 'Patriarchy and Paternalism: The Legacy of the Canadian State for First Nations Women', *Canadian Journal of Women and the Law* 6: 174–92.

——. 1991b. 'Aboriginal Peoples and the Canadian Charter: Interpretive Monopolies, Cultural Differences', in Richard Devlin, ed., *First Nations Issues.* Toronto: Edmond Montgomery.

——. 1994. 'Reflections on Thinking Concretely About Criminal Justice Reform', in Goose, Henderson, and Carter (1994: 206–21).

Ursel, Susan. 1995. 'Bill 167 and Full Human Rights', in Arnup (1995).

Valverde, Mariana. 1985. *Sex, Power and Pleasure.* Toronto: Women's Press.

——. 1991. *The Age of Light, Soap, and Water: Moral Reform in English Canada, 1885–1925.*Toronto: McClelland & Stewart.

——. 1994. 'Moral Capital', *Canadian Journal of Law and Society* 9, 1: 213–32.

—— and Lorna Weir. 1988. 'The Struggle of the Immoral: Preliminary Remarks on Moral Regulation', *Resources for Feminist Research* 17, 3: 31–4.

Vance, Carol S., ed. 1984. *Pleasure and Danger: Exploring Female Sexuality.* London: Routledge & Kegan Paul.

Vickers, Jill, ed. 1984. *Taking Sex into Account.* Ottawa: Carleton University Press.

Vincent, J. 1994. 'On Law and Hegemonic Moments: Looking Behind the Law in Early Modern Uganda', in Lazarus-Black and Hirch (1994: 118–37).

Visano, Livy. 1987. *This Idle Trade.* Concord, Ont.: VitaSana Books.

Visweswaran, K. 1994. *Fictions of Feminist Ethnography.* Minneapolis: University of Minnesota Press.

Waddams, S.M., ed. 1993. Special Issue on the Corporate Stakeholder Debate: The Classical Theory and its Critics, *University of Toronto Law Journal* 43, 3.

Walkowitz, Judith. 1980. *Prostitution and Victorian Society: Women, Class, and the State.* Cambridge: Cambridge University Press.

——. 1983. 'Male Vice and Female Virtue: Feminism and the Politics of Prostitution in Nineteenth Century Britain', in Snitow, Stansell, and Thompson (1983).

Waring, M. 1990. *If Women Counted: A New Feminist Economics.* San Francisco: Harper & Row.

Weedon, C. 1987. *Feminist Practice and Poststructuralist Theory.* Oxford: Oxford University Press.

Weeks, Jeffrey. 1981. *Sex, Politics and Society: The Regulation of Sexuality Since 1800*. London: Longman.

Wendell, Susan. 1996. *The Rejected Body: Feminist Philosophical Reflections on Disability*. New York: Routledge.

West, Candace, and Don H. Zimmerman. 1987. 'Doing Gender', *Gender and Society* 1, 2: 125–51.

Wexler, Joan G. 1985. 'Rethinking the Modification of Child Custody Decrees', *Yale Law Journal* 94, 4: 757–82.

Williams, J. 1991. 'Gender Wars: Selfless Women in the Republic of Choice', *New York University Law Review* 66: 1559–1634.

Williams, Karen. 1995. 'A Good Mother', in Arnup (1995).

Williams, Patricia. 1991. *The Alchemy of Race and Rights*. Cambridge, Mass.: Harvard University Press.

Williams, R. 1977. *Marxism and Literature*. Oxford: Oxford University Press.

Williams, Toni. 1990. 'Re-forming "Women's Truth": A Critique of the Report of the Royal Commission on the Status of Women in Canada', *Ottawa Law Review* 22, 3: 725–59.

———. 1991. 'Of Scientism and Storytelling: Perspectives on the Economic Analysis of Remedies for Breach of Contract', in R.F. Devlin, ed., *Canadian Perspectives on Legal Theory*. Toronto: Edmond Montgomery.

'World Charter for Prostitute Rights', in Pheterson (1989a).

Young Offenders Act R.S.C., 1985, c. Y–1 in Greenspan and Rosenberg (1997).

Zeitlin, M. 1989. *The Large Corporation and Contemporary Classes*. Oxford: Polity Press.

Index

intergenerational sex, fuels moral panic, 47

International Whores Congress, 93

intersections between feminism and nat/cult in Québec, 19–37; 'strategic intersectionality' explained, 22–3

interventions to assert humanness, 139, 145, 147–9, 152, 154

intra-gender differences, 2–3

inversion of hierarchies, 51, 52

Jhappan, Radha, 62

'john school', 97n19

Johnson, Kelvin, 199

Johnson, Rebecca, 15, 199–222

justice: for Aboriginals, 124–34; for the disabled or disadvantaged, 140, 155–6

kinship group for Aboriginals, 131

Korniakov v. Korniakov, 110

Lacombe, Dany, 88–9

landlord-tenant matters for Aboriginals, 133–4

Langevin, Louise, 23–4, 27

language of consent, 73–4

Lapointe v. Lapointe, 161, 162, 164

law: as an instrument, 2, 3–7; constraining and enabling practice, 13–16; as a discourse. *see* legal/medical discourse; gendering effects, 7–8, 14, 16, 17–18, 67–72, 76–8. *see also images of women in legal system*; as a hegemonic process, 2, 10, 12, 18; intent differing from practical effects, 11–12, 60–78; and justice. *see* justice; role in women's liberation, 2–18

law schools, feminism in (Québec), 24, 25, 26

lawyers, as litigators, 107

Lazarus-Black, M., 146

legal discourse. *see* discourse, law as

Legal Education and Action Fund (LEAF), 8–9, 12, 94, 203; in *Gordon v. Goertz*, 158, 163, 164, 167–70, 176, 178n13, 179nn16, 19

Legal Services Society of British Columbia, 123

legislation/adjudication divide, 19, 29, 32–4

lesbian and gay people, 87, 88, 194

lesbian parents, 100–118; adoptions, 114–16, 118n11; birth parents and social parents, 103, 111–12; cases, 15–16; custody after leaving straight relationships, 106, 107–11; inside or outside the law?, 101–2; just like other mothers?, 103; social parents and others, 112–14

Levesque v. Lapointe, 162

liberal feminism, 3–5; contributions, 6; convergence with radical feminism, 7–8; 'first wave' and 'second wave', 4; problems with, 6–7, 9; view of the state and law, 9

limited liability, 186–8

London Free Press, 42, 43, 45, 46

London moral panic. *see* moral panic in London

Los, Maria, 62, 64

Lubiano, Wahneema, 67

Luhmann, Niklas, 65

MacEachern, R. v., 57–8, 59n3

McGowan, R. v., 48

McGuffin v. Overton & Porter, 113

MacGyver v. Richards, 161, 162, 163, 164, 167

McIntyre, Sheila, 60, 62

MacKinnon, Catharine, 5–6, 9, 27, 64

'mainstreaming', 4

male domination: law and state policy, 4, 5–6, 9, 59, 66–8, 92, 139, 214–18. *see also* hegemonic masculinity

male prostitution, 50–1, 59, 84–5

Marcus, Sharon, 72, 74, 76, 77

Marx, Karl, 71–2

media: challenges to moral panic. *see* CBC *Ideas* series; fuel for moral panic, 42, 43–4, 45, 46, 58

medical/legal discourse, 145, 146, 150, 154, 155

Messerschmidt, James, 68, 73, 76

Miller, Peggy, 93

Millett, Kate, 89, 90

Milovanovic, Dragan, 70

modern approach to law, 2

Moore, Folk, 153

moral panic in London: categories in crisis, 46–51; deconstructive reading of